The Big M

Ted Mahovlich

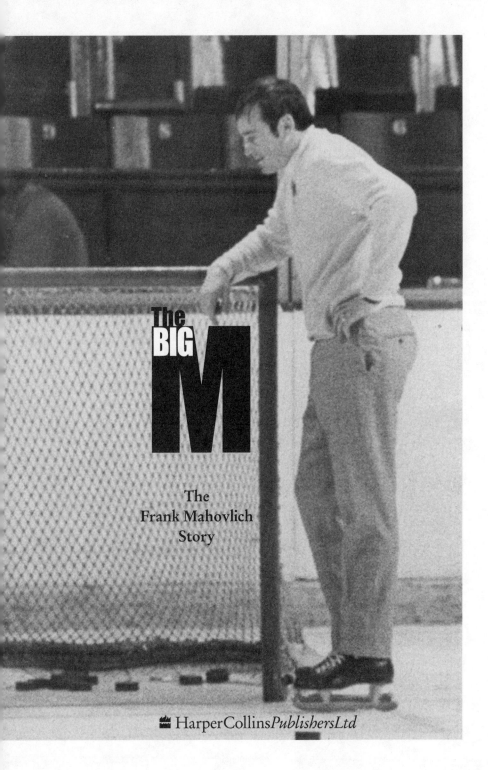

The BIG M

The
Frank Mahovlich
Story

HarperCollins*Publishers*Ltd

http://www.harpercanada.com

HarperCollins books may be purchased for educational, business,
or sales promotional use. For information please write:
Special Markets Department, HarperCollins Canada,
55 Avenue Road, Suite 2900, Toronto,
Ontario, Canada M5R 3L2.

All photographs are reprinted courtesy of
the Mahovlich family except where noted.

First HarperCollins hardcover ed. ISBN 0-00-200010-5
First HarperCollins trade paper ed. ISBN 0-00-638647-4

Canadian Cataloguing in Publication Data

Mahovlich, Ted, 1968–
The Big M: the Frank Mahovlich story

ISBN 0-00-200010-5

1. Mahovlich, Frank.
2. Hockey players – Biography.
I. Title.

GV848.5.M34M33 1999   796.962'0929   C99-930442-9

99 00 01 02 03 04 HC 6 5 4 3 2 1

Printed and bound in the United States

To my family

Foreword

On most nights, he would skate out of his own end with those powerful, giant strides . . . beyond one man, then another . . . and by now, there was no longer a roar in the arena, but a noise engulfing it. Frank Mahovlich, the Big M, was in full flight, and there was no finer sight anywhere in hockey.

I was there to watch him from the start of his Original Six years whenever the Canadiens traveled to the Gardens in Toronto or the Maple Leafs visited the Forum in Montreal. I didn't see him quite as often during the 198 regular-season games he played with the Detroit Red Wings, but then there he was, wearing the Canadiens sweater for three full seasons and part of a fourth, and playing on top of his game, as Canadiens management hoped and expected he would.

The Mahovlich NHL legend was born and grew in Toronto, where he enjoyed his greatest years and overcame terrible adversity, but he was apprecated in Montreal long before he was acquired by that organization from the Red Wings. "I'd love to get that Mahovlich," Canadiens general manager Sam Pollock told me on several occasions. "Those people in Toronto are always complaining about him, but I know I can do something with him."

Some of those people—starting with Maple Leafs coach Punch Imlach—would tell you that Frank Mahovlich could have done better than the Hockey Hall of Fame numbers he eventually put on the board. Imlach often suggested there wasn't enough fire in his belly. He would tell me: "I'd give a hundred bucks to anyone who can wake him up."

The record books show that the six-foot, 205-pound Frank Mahovlich I knew, admired and enjoyed on and off the ice hardly ever could be described as a sleeping giant. Eighteen NHL seasons; four Stanley Cups with the Maple Leafs and two with the Canadiens; 533 goals and 570 assists in 1,181 games represent eye-snapping productivity for someone who spent most of his NHL years in a six-team league. He was not the best player I have ever seen—Bobby Orr was—but he surely was among the best.

He was special. He was one of a kind. He still is.

Bobby Hull once said: "Frank Mahovlich was likely the greatest junior player I ever saw. I was always so amazed at the kind of maturity he had at such a young age. On a given night, Frank Mahovlich was the greatest player that ever played. He was like that in junior, and he was like that in pro."

Is there a better labor of love than a son writing about his father, as Ted Mahovlich has done? I don't think so. He has been able to capture his great moments, listen to the marvelous stories only hockey players can spin during a once-in-a-lifetime opportunity to play with his father in old-timers' games across Canada, and describe the demons he overcame. It is a story of pride, of family, of caring and of accomplishment.

One of my favorite stories about Senator Mahovlich goes back to the 1973–74 season. He had scored 31 goals and 49 assists that year, but there were recurring reports that he had decided to join the upstart World Hockey Association. "What's this about you going to the Toronto Toros next season?" I asked him on the charter carrying the Canadiens to one of their few remaining playoff games.

"Aw, gee," said Frank, "I don't want to talk about anything like that. Right now, my focus is on the playoffs. I'll promise you one thing, though—I'll keep you informed.

Mahovlich was as good as his word.

The telephone rang in my home on a Saturday morning several days after the Canadiens had been eliminated from the playoffs.

"It's Frank, Red."

"Yeah, Frank, what's up?"

"Remember I told you I'd keep you informed once the season was over?"

"So?"

"I just want to tell you I'm going out to play some tennis!"

Click!

Chapter One

The tub is running and I'm recuperating in a room at the comfortable Calgary Ramada. Never having been to Calgary, I thought heading out a week early before joining the tour would be a good thing. Well, my week of fun has left me feeling feverish at the worst possible time. I've decided to take a hot bath to rid myself of the chills.

This afternoon I met up with my father—Frank Mahovlich. Now, as I write the first pages of my journal, he is napping on the bed next to mine. The scene is one I grew up with. On the afternoon prior to a Saturday night game, Dad would be watching pro golf with the volume low, occasionally nodding off. Perhaps he is a little more awake now. I believe my own preparation has caused him to be concerned—after all, this is going to be one of the more significant nights of my life. But he may simply be amused.

It all began some time last summer. Dad and I had discussed my writing a book about him, and with his blessing I had set the wheels in motion. Shortly thereafter I met with him for weekly interviews that would provide me with a basic text for the book. Then in the autumn I got a phone call from my mother.

"How would you like to go on the road with Dad?"

Immediately I knew what Mom had in mind. It was a once-in-a-lifetime opportunity. Every year Dad spends two or three weeks with a team of NHL alumni that tours across Canada

1

and the United States. While the Greatest Hockey Legends tour runs coast-to-coast throughout the hockey season, the players rotate on and off the team according to their personal schedules. Through this arrangement Dad gets to play hockey and catch up with his old pals. For myself, needless to say, this would be the ultimate scenario for gathering stories, interviewing teammates, and generally getting a taste of the life that was my father's for nearly forty-five years.

Naturally, I did what any fan would do, even if he or she were not writing a book about hockey: in a split second I instructed my mother to sign me up.

After the necessary arrangements were made, Dad called me back and gave me the real news—the reason I'm regretting the need for the hot bath, and why tonight is more significant than any other in my life to date. I am to have the amazing and undeserved fortune of playing on the Greatest Hockey Legends team.

Day 2—Morning

Let me begin my journal's second entry by saying that yesterday was a day that will stay with me as long as I live. As soon as I boarded the team bus Dad introduced me to all the fellows. "Rocket, this is my son Ted." "Ted, I'd like you to meet Bobby Hull." The introductions continued until I was so giddy with the thought of stepping on the ice with these guys that I just wanted to laugh out loud. I savored every moment, studied all the players, and while focusing on their pre-game banter I heard the tour's promoter enthusiastically announce that our game at the Calgary Saddledome, the home of the Calgary Flames, was sold out. This news pleased everyone, as the games are for charity, and the bigger the crowd, the better the atmosphere for the match.

The team arrived at the rink, which the bus drove into— one of the many firsts of my hockey career that took place on this exhilarating occasion—and we each grabbed a bag and took it to our dressing room. The stalls in the visiting team's dressing room became occupied quickly and I settled for the one next to the door. I made a point of not sitting beside Dad, although I made sure he was in earshot. I was as nervous as a kid on the first day of school. In walked Gilbert Perreault singing Elvis Presley; he said hello and sat down next to me. Conversations were flying in every direction. Next through the door came Eddie Shack. Due to my fever I was trying to retain my body heat by wearing a watchman's cap while getting changed. This regrettable decision inspired Shack's opening remarks, "Hey Teddy, what's with the hat? I could see using it for a shield in a shitfight, but c'mon." On cue I ditched the cap.

Over in the corner Morris Lukowich was stretching next to Dad and Red Storey. Lukowich was telling them about his bad back courtesy of the Mike Milbury cross-check. Red said something to console him and added that many tall players have had back trouble and cited Mario Lemieux. With a look that questioned Red's comparison of five-foot-seven Morris Lukowich to the towering Mario Lemieux, Dad pointed out, "Red, Morris isn't a very tall guy." Red paused, looked around the room and replied, "He is for a midget."

The jokes and jabs continued until the team's leader, Jean-Guy Talbot, gave a pep talk and announced the starting line-up. After his briefing Jean-Guy walked over to me and asked, "Ted, will you play right wing?" I nodded. "Fine, you'll be playing with Gilbert Perreault and Guy Lafleur." Thinking this was another joke, I braced myself for shield-in-a-shitfight, part two, when I realized he was serious. Then it began to sink in. I was playing on a line with two of the most prolific goal scorers the world has ever seen—Lord have mercy.

The call came for show time and the team made its way to the ice. The opposition, as for most games on the tour, was a team made up of the local police force aided by a few retired hockey pros—for this game, ones who resided in the Calgary area. I noticed Jim Peplinski in the warm-up and wondered how long it had been since he had played with the Flames.

Amazingly, the size of the crowd didn't bother me as I thought it would. So many feelings were rushing over me that the only thing I noticed being self-conscious about was my ear-to-ear grin from sheer happiness, which made me feel slightly foolish despite the fact that most of the players were laughing and having fun in the pre-game skate. My mind went back to a Peewee tournament in Quebec City—the last time I had ever played in front of a real audience and, sadly, the peak of my hockey career.

The game began and before long I was oblivious to the crowd. Lafleur and Perreault might have lost a stride or two since the seventies, but they were moving like the wind in my world. Three shifts into the game I took a pass at our blue line and saw Lafleur move to open ice up the left wing. I fed him the puck and skated as hard as I could to the left wing while he cut to center. Our paths crossed and Guy left a drop pass that I took wide by the first defender. I was now on a two-on-one with the Flower in a sold-out Calgary Saddledome—19,000-plus spectators whom I became acutely aware of as they rose to see the game's first good scoring opportunity. The lone defenseman was trying to force me to shoot. I threaded a pass under the defender's stick at the point when Guy turned on the jets. The pass was on the tape and immediately Lafleur rifled a shot. In close, Guy's shot rose quickly over the goalie's shoulder on the glove side and continued over the crossbar. The puck rattled off the glass and the play turned back up-ice. Our line headed off for a change. On the bench while catching my breath Guy turned to me in acknowledgment of my play and said, "Sorry, I should have had that one." Although I knew I really didn't belong there, or even had a right to be on that ice, at that moment I felt like a welcome guest.

Now the team is on the bus headed for Red Deer, Alberta. Although Dad and I did not get to play a shift together last night, I'm certain we will. That is something I truly look forward to. It's amazing to think that we have played hockey all our lives but, until I joined this Legends team, never played a game together.

I am struck by the camaraderie among this bunch. No wonder Dad keeps on playing. I'm also looking forward to seeing this part of Canada for the first time, a part of touring that Dad always enjoys. Exploring this part of the country is actually where the Mahovlich family story begins.

———————

Peter Mahovlich Sr. was stocky—strong as an ox, with bear-paw hands. Mother Cecilia was no frail thing either. They grew up together in a small Croatian farming community called Gornji Ośtrc. Her family name was Buchar, and she, like everybody else in the village, worked the land. The Mahovlichs were slightly better off than most because they owned some land. When Peter's father passed away and Peter announced his plans to marry Cecilia—a girl from a poor family—he met with disapproval from his uncles. They made it clear that marrying Cecilia was both foolish and irresponsible and that such action would force them to protect their own best interests. True to their word, Peter's uncles denied him his rightful inheritance of the land his father had left him. Still, undeterred by their protest, Peter Mahovlich remained true to his own word and married Cecilia Buchar on January 1, 1928.

On the threshold of their life together, the newlyweds contemplated their future and what lay in store. The thought of staying in their hometown was less than enticing, as Gornji Ośtrc had little to offer. To stay and work the land would be to accept a life of sweat, soil, and poverty. Having higher aspirations, the couple, like thousands of other Europeans, determined to move on. The destination they decided upon was Canada.

First, Peter went on his own, so that he could get established prior to his wife's arrival. He began his search for a new home on the Canadian west coast. British Columbia, so rich with natural resources, was an awesome sight to the newly landed immigrant; Peter was certain he'd found the Promised Land. Eager to earn the fare for Cecilia's journey, he looked for work immediately. Both logging and mining jobs were abundant—Peter chose the latter in Nanaimo. Although he was ready and willing for hard labor, life on the farm in Gornji Ośtrc was like a stroll in the park compared to working underground. The conditions were damp and filthy, with little regard for job safety. In other words, an ideal place for immigrants. All the challenges that Peter hoped to find in Canada he got in spades—and then some.

Nevertheless, filled with determination, Peter worked his way across Canada at various jobs but mainly as a miner. While searching for a place to put down permanent roots he heard of a small mining town where many Croatians had settled, a place called Timmins in northern Ontario. He moved east to see what the town had to offer. What he had heard about Timmins proved true, and to Peter's delight he was able to get reacquainted with several friends from back home, all of whom were gainfully employed. With work and familiar faces at hand, Peter decided Timmins would be the place to raise his family. Shortly after securing a job there, he wrote to Cecilia about their new home. He gave his wife instructions to sail to Montreal, then take a train to North Bay, Ontario, where he would meet her. Cecilia made the journey with a friend whose husband would also be waiting with Peter. So it was that in North Bay, after being apart for nearly three years, Peter and Cecilia were reunited.

Hard work began to pay off and the Mahovlichs found themselves living in a modest fourplex apartment. Their first of three children arrived on April 22, 1935, a girl they named Anne. Peter continued working in the mines hoping to save enough to build a house for his growing family. Their second child was born in the same fourplex on January 10, 1938, a boy they named Francis William—soon to be known as Frank.

Over the next couple of years Peter saved enough for their first home. On Cedar Street North they built a small house that they moved to when Frank was three years old. The small wood-framed structure had two bedrooms, each with a bed and a dresser. The only bedroom decoration to speak of was the crochet work Cecilia added to all the white linen and the delicate window valances. The front door led into the kitchen, where Cecilia would iron shirts and press linen while preparing the next meal. The kitchen also doubled as the living room, where the family gathered at the end of the day. Coming in from the cold, family and friends found warmth next to the large potbellied stove. With no modern conveniences, the house was spartan in character, but it was kept immaculate by Cecilia.

It didn't take long for newcomers to learn that hockey was the pastime for youngsters in northern Ontario. The long, cold winters assured easy-to-maintain outdoor venues; all a boy needed was a puck, a stick, and a pair of skates and he was ready to go. Not surprisingly, Frank's first childhood memories are of the hockey rink beside their house on Cedar Street North. Cecilia would carefully bundle up her son so he could go outside and play hockey while he waited for his older friends to come home from school. Alone, he would crunch his way down the path of hard-packed snow to his favorite place. "There was a little pond and my Mom gave me some ribbons—red and blue—and a kettle of hot water. I melted them into the ice to make the blue lines and the red line."

As for ice skates, the family could not afford such luxuries; his father had saved enough to build the house, but there wasn't a great deal of money left over. Fortunately, friends in the community were glad to help out where they could. "The skates I got were from my godmother's son and they were a size eleven. I had to put on three or four pairs of socks to make them fit. That was my first time on skates, on that little pond on Cedar Street North."

One day, worn down by Frank's insistence, Cecilia took him to the hardware store to get a hockey stick. A gush of cold winter air followed them into the store, and after they had kicked the slush off their feet, Frank trooped down the narrow aisles to the back.

At the display rack he was immediately attracted to the goalie sticks, which were unique—longer, wider, stronger, and three times the price of a regular stick. Instantly, owning one became the most important thing in the world. He explained to his mother that none of his friends had such a stick and they needed one to play a real game. But of course, between Frank and his object of desire was the exorbitant price of five dollars, which was a great deal of money for the family in such lean times; Cecilia really couldn't justify spending that amount. Frank would not be denied, however, and he pleaded with his mother, looking up at her desperately. So, after a hard-fought battle, Cecilia gave in, warning that he had better take special care of the stick.

You guessed it. By the end of the day the stick was broken. All his mother said was, "No more goalie sticks!"

Several years of mining had Peter Mahovlich longing for a better life—every day he went underground felt like a march into battle. The first thing to assault the senses was the stench of the drying room. Coveralls that had been hung to dry remained damp, soaked with sweat and black with dirt from the previous day's labor. Overworked muscles still ached, serving as a morning reminder that it was just the beginning of another hard day. Once the gear was on one's body, it was into the lift and down the shaft. The lift was like a roller coaster—steel wheels clattered along their course, while a cold breeze ran across the face, down in a free fall that seemed to last forever. Suddenly the ride ended and it was back to work in a bustling underground city in near-total darkness, amid the roar of machinery and screaming drills. At the end of the day, the ride up was like a diver's swim to the surface after running out of oxygen. Above ground, a slight pressure in the chest and an anxious energy was released in a long-awaited breath of fresh air.

An opportunity Peter heard about from a friend got him thinking about a change of scene. A dairy farm, which included a large stone farmhouse, had come up for sale just west of town. Although they could not afford the farm on their own, a close friend of the family liked the idea and went in as a partner. Working day after day in the wide-open country, smelling the hay and manure, feeling the sun and the wind, and just being with the family was a welcome change for Peter. The two families worked together, sharing the chores. Once the cows had been milked, Peter loaded the containers into his red Ford pickup truck and drove to the local dairy to sell their product. Economically, the family was no better off than when Peter was in the mines, but milking a cow was considerably less dangerous than milking the earth.

Unfortunately, the dynamics of two bosses caused the partnership to fail and after eight months the farm had to be sold. The Mahovlichs then settled in Schumacher, a small town on the outskirts of Timmins (and now part of the city of Timmins), and Peter went back to work in the mines.

Once again comfort was found in the familiar faces of the large Croatian community that lived there. At the Croatian hall Frank and Anne took music lessons, playing mandolin-like instruments called *tamburitzas*. There was also regular choir practice, which Frank particularly enjoyed. However, celebrating the Croatian culture was more of a recreational activity than requisite learning for the Mahovlich kids. Cecilia was an appreciative immigrant who wanted her family to embrace the Canadian way of life rather than cling to the past.

Anne remembers that not all English-speaking Canadians welcomed immigrants when she was a young girl. Many mornings her father would walk out the front door to find their neatly stacked woodpile toppled over. Cecilia would feel discouraged, but her husband calmly rebuilt the woodpile, knowing that in time they would be accepted like everyone else, and he offered words of reassurance to his concerned wife. "Don't worry, Mother, things will settle down," he'd call across the yard. In time, the prediction proved accurate.

Peter and Cecilia were so grateful to be in Canada that they rarely talked about Croatia to their children. Anne used to ask about her parents' homeland, wanting to know what it was like and why they had left, and spoke of visiting Gornji Ośtrc. Cecilia adamantly replied, "There is nothing there for you."

Despite these feelings, Cecilia remained very loyal to her family who had stayed in Croatia. Whenever there was a little extra money she faithfully sent parcels containing clothes and shoes back home. After dinner she would gather all the items on the kitchen table and prepare the parcel for mailing. Frank watched as his mother wrapped the goods in canvas and then carefully sewed the package shut to discourage postal thieves from browsing through the contents. This was a strong concern of hers, and by the time she was finished with her needle and thread, it would have been easier to open a football than one of her special deliveries. Cecilia would rest assured only when, a few weeks later, a letter would arrive with thanks for the clothes.

Years later, in 1972, Frank would feel a new appreciation for his mother's efforts when he visited the village of Gornji Ośtrc. Anne recalled, "Mother wasn't going to tell them [he was coming]. She was afraid they'd whitewash the whole town if they knew." So Frank arrived unannounced, and was amazed at what he saw.

A dirt road winding through a rugged countryside led him to his parents' old home. When he reached the crest of the road, he saw a woman kneeling by a stream with her back to him. Meaning to ask about the whereabouts of his relatives, Frank continued walking toward her. The woman, who was gathering clothes that she had been washing in the stream, sensed his presence and turned around. She appeared to be startled, and for a moment Frank was concerned that he may have frightened her. But then the woman set her basket of clothes on the ground and broke into tears. To his amazement, this stranger knew exactly who he was: "My brother's son, my brother's son!" she exclaimed.

In a short while Frank was in the company of all his relatives, being treated like royalty in this most humble of surroundings. The conversation was slow, for Frank had to struggle in the Croatian language, which he had last spoken in his childhood. But the tears and laughter that came from his aunts and uncles suggested he was doing an adequate job translating stories of Cecilia, Peter, and the rest of the family. Frank was very surprised at how well-informed his relatives were thanks to his mother's letters home.

Frank recalled the visit with wonder in his voice. "They were fifty years behind the times. They had nothing but the necessities—a floor of hardened earth and a red-tiled roof. A chicken would come through the living room and go right into the barn—and later we had it for dinner." Of all the unfamiliar sensations overwhelming him, what shocked Frank most was to see that the only decorations in his relatives' home were two pictures hung in the kitchen, one of his sister Anne and the other of the brothers Frank and Peter in their hockey uniforms.

For a young and healthy kid, there was no better place to be raised than Schumacher—provided you weren't bothered by long, cold winters. The town was named after Frederick W. Schumacher, a wealthy entrepreneur from Columbus, Ohio, who had made a fortune selling cough syrup. What set his product apart from the competition was the fact that it contained enough alcohol to soothe a broken leg. The cool, damp conditions in the northern Ontario mines caused the men underground to be bothered by the occasional scratchy throat. Needless to say, Schumacher's wonder syrup, with a twenty-seven-percent alcohol content, was the best remedy in town (it also sold extremely well during Prohibition). With numerous investments in property, the "king of cough syrup" increased his fortune through gold mining.

Although he was a sharp businessman, Schumacher was equally well known for his generosity. At Christmas time, every youngster in town would get a gift. In late December, Schumacher would visit the public school and distribute the presents. Children would fill the gymnasium, sit on the floor with their friends, and anxiously wait their turn. For the kids from less fortunate homes it would be the biggest gift they'd receive. The tradition remains one of Frank's favorite childhood memories. "It was very considerate of Mr. Schumacher to come up. He would do the shopping himself for all the gifts. He'd go to Eaton's, purchase the sleighs, the hockey sticks, and the sweaters, and ship them up. It was great."

Saturday evening was "Hockey Night in Schumacher" and the Toronto Maple Leafs were the team to cheer for. While it was freezing cold outside, the Mahovlich family gathered in their warm kitchen. Cecilia would be busy making donuts for any guests who might drop by on Sunday. The radio was tuned to the voice of Foster Hewitt and everyone listened intently while they enjoyed fresh donuts and milk. On occasion, Cecilia's brother, Mike Buchar, who was stationed at the Camp Borden, would come up for a weekend visit. Stories of the great "Kid Line"—Charlie Conacher, Joe Primeau, and Busher Jackson—were invariably told, and young Frank absorbed every word. Discussions of the current Leafs would follow—Syl Apps, Teeder Kennedy, and Max Bentley.

One year, the young Leafs fan dropped his support in favor of the Detroit Red Wings. Mr. Schumacher had given several hockey uniforms as Christmas gifts that year; when Frank opened his present to find the Detroit jersey, he felt like he had joined the team.

Rarely is a bad word spoken by the Mahovlichs about growing up in Schumacher. All in all, the family did quite well; with their simple tastes, they enjoyed all the pleasures life offered them. Even the stories of hardship, which Frank has related to his family over the years, have mellowed into comic anecdotes.

Many parents tell hardship stories when their kids seem ungrateful about something, and Frank Mahovlich, the father, was no exception. When a suitable situation arose, his children would be regaled with the grim aspects of living up north. A favorite story was about how Anne and Frank had to walk eight miles to school in the winter, when the wind would cut like a blade on a deathly cold day. The tale served its purpose, but eventually the truth came out that the eight-mile walk had been far from a daily routine. Usually their father Peter picked them up after school in his truck, but he was late on two occasions. And when the family lived on the dairy farm the two siblings had trekked a portion of that distance. Once they moved to Schumacher, school was directly across the street from their house.

People also tend to forget incidents that aren't particularly flattering. Once again, Frank Mahovlich is no exception to this rule. This is illustrated by a story only recently passed on by his sister. Eager to hone his hockey skills at a young age, Frank practiced his shot daily. Anyone who has ever played hockey knows that the game is infinitely more fun when there is a goalie to shoot at. Knowing this, Frank would shamelessly convince his sister Anne to play net. Being a good sport far beyond the call of duty, she would strap old Eaton's catalogues to her legs in place of the goalie pads that the family could not afford, and brave the cold night and frozen pucks.

When the story surfaced some fifty years later in a family conversation, Anne's husband waved his fist in the air and cried, "Can you believe that sonofabitch shot pucks at my wife!"

The first organized hockey Mahovlich played was for the Schumacher Public School junior team. Most of the junior-team players were in grades five or six, while the intermediate and senior teams were made up of seventh- and eighth-graders. Frank was in the third grade when the junior team coach asked him to try out. For his age, he had the jump in size, and the hours spent on the pond had made him a good skater. The coach watched as the eight-year-old displayed a natural ability unlike anything he had ever seen. After the first practice Frank had made such an impression that he was welcomed to the team.

Prior to joining the squad, the new recruit had to sign a standard consent form that protected the school from liability in the event of injury during a game. This formality was the most trying task the third grader would face in his young career. "I was so young I wasn't writing yet, so I printed my name. They said 'No, you have to write your name,' and I said, 'I don't know how to write.'" The coach made an exception and by the end of grade four Frank was playing on the senior team—and writing his name.

Having excelled in hockey at Schumacher Public School, Frank was soon recognized for his ability in and around the community. The first case of outside interest came from the Timmins Central School team, which had entered a tournament in North Bay. Each team was allowed to bring two players who attended another school in the surrounding area, so, logically enough, the Timmins coach had hunted down the two players who had done the most damage against his own team, one of whom was the rising star of Schumacher. When the invitation was put to Frank, the thought of joining the opposition factored little in his decision. Filled with the excitement of getting to travel, he gladly accepted the offer of a free trip to North Bay.

What made the tournament weekend a special memory wasn't the fact that the Timmins team won; nor was it Frank's standout performance. It was the destination. Frank recalled, "I had never been that far south."

Raising Frank was relatively easy for Cecilia, as he inherited his mother's polite manners. If anything, what frustrated his family was Frank's tendency to be painfully shy—a trait that hindered him in his duties as a *Toronto Daily Star* delivery boy. "I used to go down to the train station and the train would come in with the papers," Mahovlich explained. "I'd pick up the bundle, snap the wire with a pair of pliers, and deliver them. There must have been thirty customers, but they were all over town, so I had to go on my bike." The dilemma arose when Frank had to go collecting, a chore he dreaded. The thought of disturbing people after work and asking them to hand over their cash was not his idea of fun. Sitting at the kitchen table, he would try to muster up courage while Cecilia chimed in first with encouragement, then with pleading. "But Frankie, they owe you money," she would say. Frank remembers with a cringe, "Some of the people would hide—God, it was awful. Maybe they never had the money. You learned a lot about people though, and it gave me responsibility as a young boy." Recently confronted with the fact that on several occasions his sister had to go collecting with him, Frank conceded "that might have been true."

As parents, both Cecilia and Peter supported their kids in all their endeavors—but when it came time to ask permission for something, they would run to their father. Cecilia was more of a disciplinarian and that simply wasn't in Peter's nature. On occasion, memories of Peter Sr. come back to Frank and he thinks aloud about his father. Peter had a real understanding of life's big picture, believing that those who live honestly and take care of the less fortunate live a better life.

This is not to say he was a pacifist. One day Frank had come home with the stains of tears on his cheeks. Noticing that his son was visibly upset, Peter asked him what was wrong. An older kid in the neighborhood had beaten up Frank in the school playground across the street from their house. After hearing the story, Peter put his hand on his son's shoulder, looked him straight in the eye and said, "You go and hit him back, and he won't bother you again." On the way to meet his rival, Frank's adrenaline ran high. Knowing that failure was not an option, he looked for an advantage and picked up a sizable rock, hefty enough for the challenge. All shyness disappeared, fear turned into rage, and visions of the confrontation and the bully's moment of enlightenment raced through his mind. As it turned out, Frank only needed to show he wasn't afraid. When the older kid saw the determined boy with a rock clenched in his fist, he quickly fled the schoolyard, never to be a problem again.

The academic side of school was not as interesting to Frank as sports. Even the subjects he was good at got little of his attention in the classroom. Baffled by her son's indifference to school, Cecilia would sit him down and ask arithmetic questions in hopes of discovering where the problem lay. Frank would answer with relative ease. Frustrated, she would say, "Now do the same at school." It was no use, though; the boy's mind wandered incessantly to sports—baseball, football, track, swimming, and especially hockey.

Outside, with a stick in his hands, Frank was in his element. Whether it was winter on the ice or summer shooting a tennis ball against the wall, his determination was absolute. Time would slip away while his mind fell into a groove of repetition; often, he played through the dinner hour. He could be found on the rink on the coldest night, sometimes as late as 11 p.m., shooting pucks. Eventually, a neighbor would yell out a window, "Go home, Frankie. It's freezing out there and we're trying to sleep!" For years, Cecilia shook her head and said, "The poor boy is sick," until she realized that her son did not merely have an affinity for sports—it was his calling.

The same understanding was not as easy to come by for Anne, who would have to take up the slack on the chores when her brother was hard at play. For example, every summer, Peter had a load of manure delivered to the house to fertilize Cecilia's impressive vegetable garden. When the sun beat down on the delivery, it didn't take long for the pile to get noticeably ripe. Anne remembered moving the load without the help of her brother. "We had a garden up in the bush and the manure truck would just dump it in the driveway. We'd have to move it because of the smell. I'd say to Dad, 'Why do I have to carry the manure on my back, up to the garden?' Dad would reply, 'Oh, that's good for you.' And I would say, 'But Frank is in the schoolyard playing ball!' 'That's okay— that's his future. He might be a baseball player.' And I had to carry the manure on my back!"

On October 10, 1946, Peter Jr. was born. Arriving nine years after Frank, the newborn boy became the joy of the family and a constant source of amusement for Anne and Frank. Because of the age gap between them, little Peter saw Frank as a second father, and so, in many ways, their childhood experiences were very different.

Whatever effect this may have had, what is certain is that, all their lives, the Mahovlich brothers have been known to be like night and day. Frank has always been the quiet and sensitive one, at times intensely focused, preferring to avoid the spotlight rather than attract it. Peter, on the other hand, has an outgoing personality, a wicked appetite for fun, and a general disregard for popular opinion. Teammate and friend Guy Lafleur recalled, "Frank was mature and Peter was like a kid, always joking around. We used to say they came from different families, that it wasn't the same mother and father. They were completely different. But they made a nice pair together."

Although as youngsters they grew in many different directions, they were led down the same career path. From the moment they donned their first pairs of skates, they fell in love with the game of hockey.

At the tender age of thirteen, Frank began his first of two years in Juvenile (eighteen and under) for the Schumacher Lions. The team was made up of students and a few young men who had already started working in the mines. Surrounding areas provided the competition from towns such as nearby South Porcupine and Timmins. It was during his first year of Juvenile that Frank was discovered by the NHL.

At that time, the NHL had yet to implement the draft—the system in present-day hockey whereby teams take turns selecting amateur players and thus share the wealth of talent throughout the league. Back when Frank was playing Juvenile, the NHL used the scout system. Teams employed scouts who traveled across the country, watched hundreds of kids play hockey, tried to sniff out those with potential, and reported to management. When a club was interested in a player, the scout had to sell the potential recruit, and more importantly his family, on the team he represented. The process of recruiting a player might involve months of visiting his family while monitoring his progress on the ice. If a player committed, the NHL club would send him to a farm team, likely an affiliated junior team, until he was ready for the big leagues. Once a player signed with a team, he was the property of that organization to use as it saw fit.

The first team to approach Frank was the Detroit Red Wings. The Chicago Blackhawks, the New York Rangers, and the Montreal Canadiens all followed suit and had representatives pay the family a visit.

Another team hoping to win the Mahovlichs over was the St. Catharines Teepees, a Junior A club. The team had yet to be affiliated with the Chicago Blackhawks, but with Junior A hockey being a big draw in those days, St. Catharines was as much a contender as the NHL teams. Rudy Pilous, the coach and general manager of the Teepees, knew that if he could sign the promising Frank Mahovlich to a four-year commitment, he would fill his rink with paying customers. With keen business acumen, Pilous offered a farm in St. Catharines to Peter Sr. as a signing bonus.

But although the dangled carrot was very tempting, Peter was more concerned about his son's future. He had met with several people in the community he respected for advice on the matter, all of whom had said the same thing—make sure Frank gets an education.

———————

Bob Davidson walked into the McIntyre Arena and stationed himself in the top row of the stands where he liked to watch the game. A crowd of family and friends supporting the two teams occupied the seats in front of him. Cheers rang out as the teams took to the ice. Both the Schumacher Lions and the Timmins Lions called the rink home, as it was the sole arena in the area. The scene was identical to that of any of the hundreds of games Davidson had attended across the country—a hot coffee from the snack bar, a cold rink, and a small town that loved hockey. What set this game apart, though, was a player on the Schumacher Lions whose ability and size were astonishing for a fourteen-year-old. This adolescent skated like a pro, weaving in and out of the opposition like they were pylons in a skating drill. Carrying the puck, he exploded past the defense with such ease that he was impossible not to notice.

Bob Davidson was a scout for the Toronto Maple Leafs. He reported that the kid in Schumacher was someone the team should seriously consider and recommended the Leafs act fast. Davidson knew he wasn't the first to see young Frank Mahovlich play.

One evening after a hockey game, Frank was making his way through a steaming plate of spaghetti when there was a knock at the door. Frank paused, made sure his last mouthful was down, got up from the table, and answered the door. A well-dressed man sporting a homburg and white gloves asked if he could speak with the boy's parents. The gentleman politely introduced himself as Johnny Mitchell and explained that he was visiting on behalf of the Detroit Red Wings. Peter and Cecilia invited their guest to come in and listened intently as he spoke about professional hockey, the Red Wings organization, and the future of their son. In the next few weeks there were representatives from the other teams, who all gave an identical spiel, hoping to get a commitment from Frank.

By the time Bob Davidson of the Toronto Maple Leafs dropped in, Peter Sr. was familiar with the drill. But to his credit, Davidson listened as much as he talked. He probed for Peter's thoughts on his son's future and the conversation revealed the parents' insistence upon a good education. With the knowledge of their Catholic background, Davidson knew his next course of action.

At this time Bob Davidson reported to the owner of the Toronto Maple Leafs, Conn Smythe. Smythe had wisely affiliated his NHL team with St. Michael's College School. With teams in both Junior A and Junior B, the school became a second farm system for the Maple Leafs organization who were already drawing from the wealth of talent on the Toronto Marlboros. As a reputable boarding school, St. Mike's provided an attractive option for families who wanted to make sure their sons got a solid education while playing junior hockey. Smythe encouraged his scouts to exploit the advantages of St. Mike's, emphasizing features related to the school that other clubs could not offer. Helping the Leafs to secure desired players was Father Ted Flanagan, the director of athletics for St. Mike's, who was happy to oblige when called upon.

The key selling feature in this case, of course, was that St. Mike's was a Catholic school. Bob was confident that the Mahovlich family, who were Catholic, would not be hard to convince. Davidson recalled the visit on which he brought Father Flanagan: "I did a lot of work for St. Mike's recommending players and got to know Father Flanagan quite well; he was an excellent man. I took him up to a game in Schumacher on a Saturday night to watch Frank. We had a great time and went back and had dinner with the Mahovlichs after the game."

Cecilia prepared a feast for the visitors and afterwards the Toronto representatives began their sales pitch detailing the benefits of St. Michael's. One of the toughest challenges for a Junior A player was keeping up with the workload at school, and the traveling time for road games made it even harder. The fact that St. Mike's was centrally located benefited players because they spent less time on the road and therefore had more time for their studies. The strict boarding school environment facilitated the monitoring of academic progress and time spent in study. At one point Father Flanagan brought out a school yearbook that depicted a healthy and disciplined student life.

Peter and Cecilia nodded in approval (while Frank listened to a game plan that, as far as he was concerned, sounded like detention). After further discussion, Bob Davidson put forth the Maple Leafs' offer of tuition, room, and board at the school, and a small weekly allowance in exchange for Frank's commitment.

Peter and Cecilia liked everything they were hearing about St. Michael's, and when the Schumacher Lions went to play St. Catharines in the all-Ontario finals, arrangements were made for Frank's father to watch the games and visit the school. It proved to be an exhausting week for Davidson, who found it difficult to keep up with Peter Mahovlich. "I'd pick up Mr. Mahovlich and we would go over to St. Catharines and watch Frank play. Then I'd go back to the hotel and shoot the breeze over a couple of drinks. We'd talk hockey until two in the morning and then I'd go home. I was doing that for four or five games and always went to work the next morning at [Maple Leaf] Gardens. Mr. Smythe told me I had better give it up." Though exhausted, Davidson told Smythe he had gone too far to let up on Mahovlich and was determined to watch the sunrise with Peter, if that's what it took.

Davidson's perseverance finally paid off that summer, when he returned to Schumacher to watch Frank sign the Junior B certificate. "I took it down to Mr. Smythe and he couldn't believe it."

Peter had decided that the Catholic education his son would get at St. Michael's would be the best choice. The family never regretted the decision, although the reality of St. Michael's was somewhat different from the sales pitch they had been given. The school lured hockey players to the Maple Leafs organization by pushing the educational benefits; however, there was a good reason why there weren't many schools with Junior A teams (in fact, St. Mike's was the only one). High school education and Junior A hockey mixed like oil and water. The time commitment for Junior A was demanding for any student. Even if a hockey player passed his courses, his marks were usually below what they should have been. For several years the school looked the other way so that they, in partnership with the Maple Leafs, could reap handsome profits from the arrangement.

In fairness to St. Mike's, they did offer a better chance at an education than most other scenarios. However, the bottom line was, Frank Mahovlich's scholarship was awarded so he could play hockey. The Basilian Fathers at St. Mike's understood their end of the bargain, and those who didn't like it had no say in the matter. If Frank, or any other player on scholarship, could benefit from the education being offered, all the better. But hockey always came first. Eventually, the conscience of the Basilian Fathers, under the leadership of Father Matthew Sheedy, put an end to their affiliation with the Maple Leafs, and their glory days as a cradle for future hockey stars came to an end.

Chapter Two

Day 2—Evening

Today's game was an afternoon affair in Red Deer, Alberta, in which I played defense. I was mildly concerned because defense is a position that I haven't spent a great deal of time at. Our goalie Gilles Gilbert is a great guy. He called me over in the warm-up and told me to just play the puck to him if I ever had two guys on me and I was the last man back. To my relief the Red Deer team didn't give us any trouble. The most difficult aspect of the game was the arduous waiting in wet equipment between periods while a charity auction took place.

While waiting to play the last period, some of the fellows were nearly dozing off. I was having a conversation with defenseman Don Awrey when, suddenly, what sounded like a bolt of lightning splitting an oak tree sent the entire dressing room into cardiac arrest. Screams and curses were directed at Guy Lafleur who stood next to the equipment table he had just whacked his stick over. The Flower moved toward the door wearing a satisfied grin after catching the team off-guard in a ritual he's well known for. I had read about Guy inspiring his team in this manner and was thrilled to have been a victim. Awrey commented, "I hate it when he does that—scares the shit out of everyone."

Afterwards, the players joked around as usual while they showered and prepared for the reception that follows a Legends game. Gilles Gilbert told me that when he started his career he had to supplement his income by working summers "lifting dead buddies." Still in the cautious mode of not wanting to bite at what sounded like a joke at my expense, I refrained from asking the obvious questions. Shortly thereafter I discovered that "dead buddies" was really "dead bodies" as pronounced in Gilles' French accent.

The story took a morbidly comedic direction when Gilbert mentioned the time he and his partner had had to move a massive pine box containing a midget. In transport the corpse had slid back and forth with a loud thud at every turn. My reaction was equal parts amazement and disgust. Don Awrey was listening in. Apparently Awrey has some knowledge of bodies and their capabilities, and knowing Gilbert well enough to egg him on, he exploited the opportunity. Awrey winked and turned to Gilbert, asking "Don't dead people shit themselves?" This sent Gilbert into a fit of laughter while the rest of the guys in earshot started to howl. "Oh, you have to be careful and pick them up by the ankles," Gilbert got in between gasps, "or they'll shit and piss all over you."

However nasty I thought my worst summer job was, I've been silenced forever by Gilles Gilbert.

Day 3—Morning

This morning we hit the road to Edmonton, Alberta. The coach the team travels in is equipped with a television set and VCR, and today the team watched the movie *Slap Shot*. The moment was not wasted on me. A few of the players in the film had been, at one time or another, teammates of people on our bus. Stories started going around about real incidents that paralleled scenes in the film. Jim Dorey, who had played on the Toronto Toros of the World Hockey Association with Dad, said to him, "Hey Frank, remember Goldie?" Dorey leaned forward to relate a story about Bill "Goldie" Goldthorpe, who had the same blond Afro and demeanor as *Slap Shot*'s Oggie Ogilthorpe. "Teddy, one night we were playing against Goldie

Goldthorpe—I'll never forget it. He jumped on your dad's back and Frank skated the entire length of the ice wearing the goon—twice! Literally, he piggybacked him down the rink and turned and skated the entire length back again." Dad laughed at what must have been an exaggerated tale, but having heard enough stories about the WHA I could imagine it wasn't far from the truth.

The film ended and I began to quiz Eddie Shack on the days prior to his tenure, alongside my father, with the Toronto Maple Leafs. On the bus Eddie is among friends and is a quiet version of the hockey persona the rest of the world knows. At any given moment this could change but during our conversation he was laid back and offered a blunt recollection of playing against Dad in Junior. "You were always concerned about him making you look like a complete jerk." Shack played for the Guelph Biltmores while Dad played for St. Michael's Majors. Even from those days, stories about Frank Mahovlich foreshadowed his dominating presence on the ice in the NHL.

———

For the fifteen-year-old Frank Mahovlich, the city of Toronto was a world away from Schumacher, Ontario. In the fall of 1953, Frank made the journey to the big city and his new home at the corner of St. Clair Avenue and Bathurst Street, St. Michael's College School. Peter Buchmann, a fellow Timmins' native, rode the train with Frank and the two discussed hockey and what life was going to be like at their new school. The long journey ended when the train pulled into Union Station and the conductor announced the arrival. Immediately the two restless passengers began jockeying for position, trying to make their way toward the end of the car. After collecting their luggage, Buchmann and Mahovlich boarded the northbound Bay streetcar in front of the impressive Royal York Hotel. Frank was beaming with excitement while the streetcar toured through downtown Toronto and continued north to their destination.

In Schumacher one could walk anywhere in five minutes. By comparison, the time spent on the streetcar seemed like an eternity to Frank. After what felt like a long while, he grew concerned that they might have missed their stop. To ease his mind he walked to the front of the streetcar and asked the driver, "Have we passed St. Michael's yet?" Without taking his eyes off the traffic in front of him, the driver replied that they had a ways to go. People got on and off the car as it continued to make its way uptown. So much time passed that Frank and Peter were certain they had missed their stop. Once again Frank approached the driver and asked, "Did we pass St. Michael's?" The driver spoke in a stern voice that offered the same response as his last.

To a small-town boy on his way to a new school in Canada's largest city, every passing minute on the streetcar seemed like ten. More time passed and Frank became intent on getting a more reassuring answer from the driver. "Are you sure we haven't missed St. Michael's?" The driver spun around and barked, "Sit down, shut up, and I will tell you when we reach St. Mike's!" Their stop finally came—and with it, an overwhelming sense of relief. Frank sheepishly thanked the driver and disembarked with hopes of finding more amiable people at his new home.

Grade-nine boarders at St. Mike's lived in a residence adjacent to the school's football field. Frank's room was on the third floor of a building called Tweedsmuir House. The students in boarding came from locations all over Ontario and Frank found himself in the company of strangers. Being as shy as he was, he felt alone and homesick for the first couple of weeks, knowing only Peter Buchmann, who lived in another residence. Eventually his roommate, Pat Hannigan, who was two weeks late for school, arrived, bringing a change of spirit for Frank. Hannigan was another hockey player from Schumacher—one of Frank's pals from back home. A personable and lively sort, Pat's company enabled his roommate to feel at ease in his new surroundings. If Frank was reserved and shy, that was easily compensated for with the arrival of Hannigan. In no time both roommates got into the routine and began enjoying their new way of life.

The daily proceedings of a boarding school were quite different from anything the Schumacher boys were accustomed to. In the morning, a loud bell woke the students, which was akin to being woken by a starter's pistol at a track meet. After a quick shower the boarders dressed in their school uniforms and raced across the football field to the cafeteria, where they would wolf down breakfast prior to their first class. Sleeping in was not an option.

After morning classes, the lunch crowd was packed into the cafeteria, where boarders and day students dined, each screaming to the guy next to him so he could be heard over the din. The fare at lunch was a short rotation of school cafeteria classics—hot roast beef sandwiches (the highlight of the week), chicken legs, waterlogged pasta, slightly burnt grilled cheese, and extra greasy fish and chips on Friday. If the food was mediocre, you wouldn't know it by how much of it they moved.

Dinner was at 5:30 p.m. and then there was a study period from 7 to 9 p.m. One half-hour of television was permitted in the common room after study, and lights went out at 10 p.m. Needless to say, in such a structured day there wasn't a great deal of time to goof off—which was the whole idea. As a result, the first year at St. Mike's showed a significant improvement in Frank's academic performance.

The fall of 1953 in Toronto marked the beginning of two very important relationships in Frank's life. First, he had begun his fifteen-year affiliation with the Toronto Maple Leafs. Most long-term relationships have their ups and downs and, as we shall see, this was certainly the case with Mahovlich and the Maple Leafs. The second important tie that marked the new era was his relationship with lifelong friend Billy Kyle. The two made each other's acquaintance while living on the third floor of Tweedsmuir House. A mutual love of sports and poker was the ground on which the friendship grew.

Kyle, thinking back to grade nine and the time he got to know Frank, begins to laugh at the image that comes to mind. Frank wasn't the well-proportioned athlete he developed into years later, according to Kyle. "He had a big ass! Everybody used to kid him, but he could sure run. In grade nine he was chubby, but you could tell he had a lot of growing to do. You knew he was going to be a big man."

Despite his awkward proportions, Frank thrived on the sports that gave St. Mike's a great reputation. The constant emphasis on team sports kept school morale high and got everyone involved. The one sport all students played was baseball. Every year there was a fastball tournament for the boarders that all parties took very seriously. The teams were made up of the residence floors, which were divided by grade. In their first year Mahovlich, Kyle, and the rest of the grade-nine team won the tournament, beating out the grade-thirteen team in the finals. The heated battle left the older students shocked by their defeat. On the grade-thirteen team was another soon-to-be-Maple-Leaf and close friend of Frank's, Dickie Duff.

At the high school level, St. Mike's was competitive in all sports, but the focus was clearly on hockey. In his first year, Frank was to play Junior B for the St. Michael's Buzzers, who, prior to the beginning of the season, had their training camp with the Junior A team at Maple Leaf Gardens. So, for the first time, Frank would skate at the legendary venue, whose vast ice surface he had envisioned skating patterns on as a youngster playing shinny in Schumacher. The daydreams would become reality.

The streetcar dropped him off at the hockey temple he knew through the voice of Foster Hewitt. Walls of yellow brick encased the memories and ghosts of Canadian legends. With his gear slung over his shoulder he confidently made his way to the dressing room. Once inside the Gardens, Frank was surprised to find that it wasn't really that spectacular. In fact, it was like any other rink, same unmistakable dressing-room aroma, same sound when the puck hit the boards, and the red line ran across center ice between two blue lines. The Gardens just had a few more seats. With no feeling of awe clouding his thoughts, Frank got down to business.

In addition to practice at the rink, the team did dry-land training at the school to get in shape. In charge of conditioning for both the Junior A and B teams was Ace Percival, one of the old guard who favored old-school methods of training. The star for the Junior A team that year was Jack Caffery, a great athlete who was 185 pounds of solid muscle. In one of Percival's favorite drills he paired off players to carry each other the length of the football field on their backs. The names where called out and Caffery was matched with the hefty grade-nine kid Mahovlich. Frank rolled his eyes at the prospect of lugging the well-built Junior A star, who took the initiative of hopping up on his partner's back. What proved to be a struggle at first resulted in the chubby ninth grader getting into excellent shape in the pre-season. Caffery, who was fit from day one, had no trouble hauling Frank the length of the field.

Once the hockey season got under way there was a noticeable difference in playing hockey for the Buzzers, something that Frank had never experienced before. When they played against Protestant schools, games that started out physical would grow violent and often turn into brawls. Frank found it odd, for in Schumacher Catholic and Protestant kids played together and religion was never an issue. This, however, was apparently not the case in Toronto.

One evening when St. Mike's was the visiting team for a game in Unionville, just north of Toronto, a fight started that saw both teams spill onto the ice. Sticks and gloves scattered while players grabbed the closest opponent, trying to land a clean punch in a swirling melee. The referees watched, unable to control the situation. In a noble effort to stop the fighting, someone thought of playing the national anthem. With no sign of true patriot love ending the battle, the wives and girl-friends of the home team leaped onto the ice and jumped on the backs of the St. Mike's players. Finally, all the lights in the arena were turned off, and the chaos finally ended. But the lights-out solution resulted in Frank falling on a blade that sliced through his pants and carved a gash on his backside. After the incident, Father Flanagan, director of athletics and coach, laid down the law: No more fighting.

But fighting wasn't the only example of anti-Protestant behavior surrounding the team. During practice, Father Flanagan sometimes ran a drill in which five players formed a circle and passed the puck to each other while a sixth player chased the puck trying to intercept. Mahovlich distinctly remembers the team laughing to themselves, because it was always Frank's hometown friend Peter Buchmann whom Father Flanagan instructed to be the sixth man. If the choice was unbiased it was some coincidence, since Buchmann was the only Protestant on the team.

Starting with the Buzzers in his first year at St. Mike's was a calculated move. Although it was felt Mahovlich could have played Junior A that year, the school wanted to give him a year of seasoning in Junior B prior to making the jump. Frank believed the decision was wise despite the monetary sacrifice involved. When a Junior B player moved to the next level, there was a significant raise in pay that made the transition attractive. "In 1953 I was playing Junior B hockey," Mahovlich recalled, "and getting eighty dollars a week, plus room and board—which was pretty good. I was licking my chops because the Junior A players were making one hundred thirty dollars a week, and there were a lot of rumors saying they were going to get three hundred dollars the next year."

However—and this was lesson number one in Mahovlich's hockey education—he soon felt the effects of management's uncontested control of the purse. "The Junior A management got together and said, 'Hey, we've got to put a ceiling on this.' They decided to lower the salary to sixty dollars a week. So I went from Junior B making eighty dollars a week, to playing Junior A, where I had to take a twenty-dollar cut in pay!"

Mahovlich gets steamed when he looks back on the injustice. The Sunday afternoon Junior A games used to pack Maple Leaf Gardens, often drawing 15,000 people. Conn Smythe made a fortune off Mahovlich and the other school kids performing at a professional level, but because they were students he got away with paying them next to nothing. Smythe was also notorious for hyping the religious rivalry between his own two teams, the Toronto Marlboros and St. Mike's. It was good for business.

After successfully completing grade nine, Frank went home to Schumacher for the summer. From now on, his father would have a job waiting for him every year upon his return. This first time, he became caretaker of the local swimming pool at $30 a week. On the day of his arrival back home, he found himself painting the pool, a job that had to be done immediately. For the rest of the summer it was basic maintenance—cleaning the washrooms being his least favorite chore. Despite latrine duty, the use of a swimming pool and being able to work outdoors made it an ideal job. Frank took advantage of the facility to stay in shape, adding swimming to his repertoire of competitive sports. Over the next three summers he became an excellent swimmer and competed in regional swim meets. To his surprise he won the 100-yard, open freestyle award of northern Ontario. "I never thought I would beat everyone at the meet—but I did."

Baseball, too, was popular in Schumacher, and both Cecilia and Peter would go to watch their son play. Frank's team would pile into his father's red Ford pickup to get to the park. A genuine sense of community pervaded as families came out to mingle with friends. "My dad used to enjoy razzing the other team and would really jaw with their fans. Gosh, it was funny." As in all the sports he played, Frank's natural competitive spirit raised his game. Next to hockey, Frank loved baseball the most, and even considered a career at first base. When he traded in his skates and stick for a bat and glove the results were similarly impressive.

Although no serious offers came from the major leagues, there was some interest. Prior to signing his hockey contract with the Leafs, Frank was scouted by the American League's Boston Red Sox. But the day the scout showed up, the regular pitcher on Frank's team was unable to play and the only other team member who could sort of pitch was Frank.

As the substitute hurler, his only aspiration was to get the ball over the plate and not totally embarrass himself. When Frank took to the mound his stomach was in knots. All eyes were on him. Deep in concentration, he repeated to himself, *Just get it over the plate.* "Batter up!" came the familiar call from the umpire.

Sure enough, the opposing hitters lit him up like a Las Vegas casino. The slaughter went on for what seemed like an eternity, with no relief from the bullpen, because Frank *was* the bullpen. One could say that his filling in on the mound that afternoon gave Frank's hockey career a sense of urgency.

After the game, the Boston scout approached the pitcher on the opposing team. And that was the closest Frank Mahovlich ever came to having Ted Williams for a teammate.

At summer's end, Frank returned for his second year at St. Michael's. It was understood that he'd be playing for the Majors, St. Mike's Junior A team. Circumstances then led to Frank meeting the man he feels had the greatest influence on him as a hockey player. "The Toronto Maple Leafs wanted to make sure I had good coaching, so Conn Smythe asked Joe Primeau to help out. The coach of the Majors, Father Crowley, was primarily a basketball coach who didn't really know the game of hockey. The job was more or less assigned to him because they didn't have anyone else."

With Father Crowley behind the bench, the assistance of Joe Primeau was a top priority for the struggling Maple Leafs. The team lacked a star forward, and management put all their eggs in one basket—the superstar to be, Frank Mahovlich.

Primeau had stepped down from coaching the Maple Leafs and was running his own business when Smythe approached him. The arrangement was that Joe would run the practices at his alma mater and work with the Leafs' top prospect. His credentials as a coach were impeccable. Primeau won the Memorial Cup coaching Junior A, the Allan Cup in Senior A, and the Stanley Cup as the Leafs' skipper. To this day Mahovlich stands by Joe Primeau. "'Gentleman Joe' was the best coach I ever had. He commanded respect without losing his cool, but when you made a mistake, you knew not to do it again. I learned more from him than any coach in the NHL."

The downside to this positive experience was that any coach who followed him couldn't measure up. "I had a very difficult time because no one knew as much about hockey as Joe Primeau." Later on, when the coaches for the Toronto Maple Leafs failed to meet the benchmark set by Primeau, conflicts arose that made Frank's time with the Leafs his most challenging in the NHL. The differences between Mahovlich and Leaf coach Punch Imlach would reach legendary proportions. Today, Frank is polite in his descriptions of his deceased boss when questioned by the media. But, inside, a fire burns, one few people ever see. Mahovlich recently offered a previously off-the-record portrait of Imlach. "Punch Imlach, the Big I. What a crock of shit that guy was."

In consecutive seasons with the Majors, Mahovlich suffered serious knee injuries, but although that kept him off skates, it didn't keep him off the ice. After dinner he would go to the outdoor shinny rink and line up the pucks. With a pair of shoes on the ice, and a cast that put him off balance, Frank blasted away without the help of leverage. At the time his friend Billy Kyle was the equipment manager for the Majors. Kyle was amused and amazed by Mahovlich's dedication to practice and his constant hounding for assistance. One day, due to Frank's temporary handicap, Kyle gave in to his friend. "Frank wanted somebody to get in goal. I said, 'I'll get in goal, but you've got to shoot from center ice.'

"He was halfway down the other end of the rink so I thought, hell—no problem. And he had a cast on his leg for his knee. He could hobble but he couldn't walk. I had pads and gloves on but no other equipment—and no mask. Well, Jesus, I got in the goal and it was getting dark outside—it was about 6:30 at night. First shot, I'm sitting in there, and BOOM. What the hell was that! It was a puck that missed the net and hit the boards. BOOM, again. I thought, 'Christ, I never even saw the damn thing. Coming from center ice and I never even saw it!' I said, 'I'm getting the hell outta here.' I lasted for two shots. I thought I'd get killed."

As soon as Mahovlich was back on skates the results were incredible. Kyle was at the first game when Mahovlich returned from what the doctor had diagnosed as torn cartilage. It was at Ted Reeve Arena. The face-off, center ice. "I remember watching it. He was on left wing. The puck came over to him and he just went slap. It was only five seconds into the period and the puck was in the net. He took one step and wingo!"

The second knee injury Mahovlich suffered with St. Mike's caused him to miss several games. To accommodate his incapacitated status, the school moved him to the preferred residence called St. Clair House. Since the place was located next to the school's main building, the burden of crossing the field in mid-winter on crutches was eliminated.

It was at St. Clair House that Frank became a roommate of Billy Kyle. In the next two years Kyle watched his friend develop into the number-one player in Junior A. As equipment manager for the Majors, he also witnessed the dressing-room scenes in which coach Crowley delivered the game plan. In those days, Mahovlich went by his childhood nickname, Gutch. "All Crowley would do is say, 'Give the puck to Gutchie.'" Kyle paused with a smile as he remembered the reactions of the team. "It used to tick some of the other guys off, but he could take the puck from end to end and that's what they wanted him to do." But no one on the team questioned Frank because no one was more serious about hockey.

When the boarders weren't playing sports in their free time, they could be found crammed around a cot playing poker. Because Frank and Kyle were especially avid card players, the games always took place in their room. The accommodations were designed for three people who shared one dresser and hung their shirts on a hot water pipe that ran just below the ceiling. When six guys gathered for a poker game, the scene was rather cozy. Despite the limited space, their games would often run straight through the weekend from Friday evening until dinner on Sunday.

Living in such cramped quarters was not as irksome as one might suspect. The only time Kyle could remember Gutch losing his temper was with their other roommate, Tom Gorman. The incident was related to the school's strict dress code that included a shirt and tie. On no special occasion, one day in their grade-eleven year, Gorman found himself without a clean shirt. He rummaged through a pile of dirty laundry, and after a brief, fruitless search decided to borrow a shirt from his roommate. Earlier in the day Mahovlich had returned from the cleaners with a parcel of pressed shirts, and assuming good ol' Gutch wouldn't mind, Gorman helped himself.

When Mahovlich, owner of said newly laundered garment, made the scene, he ordered his presumptuous roommate to take off the shirt. Offended, Gorman refused the demand. By now, in his third year at St. Mike's, Frank was no longer chubby; more specifically, he had replaced all that soft weight with solid muscle. He gave Gorman a shove that sent him flying across the room, stopped abruptly by the wall. Off came the shirt while Kyle, a gamer at 150 pounds soaking wet, did his best to restrain the aggressor.

If there were any advantages to being the star of the Majors, Frank felt he did little to exploit them. "I probably could have gotten away with more but I preferred to play by the same rules as the rest of the guys. You could say I kept my nose clean." Outside of the St. Mike's community he didn't know many people. As a result, he stayed around the school and out of trouble. The only cause he had to bend the rules was when he joined a group of guys who would sneak out past curfew to see a late show.

Although Mahovlich favored being treated like everyone else, there was one special privilege he did not refuse. The beds they slept on were of the thin-mattress-on-a-wire-slingshot variety. When Frank began tipping the scales at 200 pounds, his bed stopped making the grade. Knowing full well what the reaction would be from his fellow boarders, he nevertheless arranged to get a second mattress. "All the heavier guys were jealous and gave me a hard time for about a week."

Grade eleven was Frank's second season in Junior A, and already they relied on him to carry the team. Despite injuries that held him to 30 regular-season games, he tallied 24 goals and 26 assists. But though Mahovlich was a dominating force, it was difficult for the team to make a serious run for the Memorial Cup because he had little support. This was due to the fact that St. Mike's had to make up their team entirely from their student body, meaning they had a limited talent pool to choose from—unlike their competition. This is not to say the Majors had no moments of triumph. The team's most successful year of Frank's three seasons with the Majors was 1955–56. In the first round of the playoffs the Majors inflicted an upset on the Guelph Biltmores, the team that featured the young and promising Eddie Shack.

In the next round, the Majors were up against the Barrie Flyers whose coach, Hap Emms, was prepared for the one-dimensional attack of St. Mike's. He ordered a player named Loveday to shadow the Majors' star centerman. This was a well-planned defense, not just the standard order to "cover your man like a glove." If Mahovlich went off for a change, the shadow would literally skate with his man to the bench and wait for him to be off the ice before he would get a change. No matter where he went, Loveday was on him like a wet towel. As soon as Mahovlich hopped the boards, a Barrie player immediately skated to his bench so Loveday could get on. Up until that point, Frank's individual efforts had won games for his team, but against Barrie it wouldn't be enough. The series taught him a valuable lesson that helped him mature as a player. The more attention you get—the more attention you get. Barrie went on to lose in the finals after defeating St. Mike's.

The following season, Frank came back strong and remained injury-free, playing in forty-nine regular-season games. He was watched closely by the Leafs, who liked what they saw in their future star. He had a masterful style of skating that was rare for someone his size. While most rangy youths looked awkward on skates, Mahovlich was spectacular. From behind his own net he'd pick up the puck and begin to gather speed. His powerful legs moved with stunning grace as they propelled him up the ice. Defenders would stand in his path while Mahovlich, who acted with complete disregard, maintained his course. Just before the imminent collision, the streaking centerman would issue a fake and cut to the wing. Without losing stride he'd rocket past the defense and in on goal. A blanket of snow would cover the goalie when he'd slam on the brakes to avoid the poke-check, and with his long reach deposit the puck into the net.

In his final year of Junior A, Mahovlich was unstoppable. His year-end totals vaunted a league-leading 52 goals and an additional 36 assists.

One Sunday afternoon at Maple Leaf Gardens, prior to a Majors game, Frank Mahovlich's name was called over the public address system. A distinguished gentleman in a dark suit proudly walked to center ice to present Frank with the Red Tilson Memorial Trophy for being the best player in Junior A. In his big blue "M" (St. Michael's) jersey, Frank Mahovlich gave his thanks and shook the hand of the presenter. Today, in the Frank Mahovlich trophy den, a black-and-white photograph captures that moment, and when pointing out a few of his best memories the Big M gives says of the picture, "It was a highlight of my career to accept that from Joe Primeau."

The year after he finished grade ten, Frank was promoted to lifeguard at his summer job, but the pay increase was minimal. It frustrated Frank that he did not have as much spending money as most students at St. Mike's. Determined to find a better-paying job the next summer, he considered his options.

In Schumacher there was only one way to earn good money—go underground. Peter Sr. had done just that for the better part of his life. But it was something he chose to do so his children wouldn't have to, as he told his son in no uncertain terms. Working conditions in the mines in the forties and fifties were far from the standards that exist today, and many experienced miners, including Peter Mahovlich, were the victims of crippling accidents. Once, after Peter had fallen down a grade of loose rock, the mine doctor sent him home for three weeks of rest, saying he had lumbago (a sore lower back). Years later, it was discovered in an X-ray that he had broken his hip; it was never reset, and Peter walked with a pronounced limp for the rest of his life. To ensure that his son's fate would not be similar to his own, Peter went to every mine in the area and instructed all the foremen not to hire his son. Knowing better than to disobey his father's wishes, Frank worked out a compromise. In the summer of 1956, Peter got Frank a job working in the lumberyard at the Preston East Dome mine. The pay was good, but more importantly the work did not involve going underground.

In Schumacher, Frank was more social around his old friends than in Toronto. Upon his return he always received an enthusiastic welcome from the community, which was proud to have a Schumacher boy making good on a scholarship. Immediately there would be dozens of friends to catch up with at the numerous parties taking place each summer. Although the disciplined life at St. Mike's hadn't exposed Frank to drinking, summers back home did. Having a few beers with his buddies seemed reasonable enough and that became part of the standard agenda in Schumacher.

Anne was just as keen a partygoer as her brother, and both siblings would meet with their respective friends prior to the summer parties. This presented a minor logistical problem, for Cecilia would not allow her daughter to go out alone. So Frank would tell their mother that he and Anne were going to the movies. Together they would walk down the street until they were out of sight. A rendezvous was established in case they didn't end up at the same party. The idea was that if they contrived to return home together, Cecilia would be none the wiser.

Of course, the ruse required both to return in an inconspicuous state. But on the occasions when they did end up at the same party, their meeting was less celebrated by Anne, for her younger brother had established himself as someone who wasn't cut out for drinking. "Frank would try to drink but he would end up running out the back door and I'd find him throwing up in the laneway. He would be sick for days after and our mother would say, 'Well, the Devil got ya,' and she would scold him." It was inconceivable to Frank how people could enjoy such self-inflicted suffering, but, being young and not so wise, he would try again and again. Looking back, Anne broke out in hysterics. "He used to be so pitiful! Mother used to have him dressed up so nice, in a nice suit with a knitted sweater and a white shirt. And he would make a mess of it."

Aside from keeping him out of trouble, the preoccupation with hockey at St. Mike's prevented Frank from having a steady girl-friend through the season. Prior to his final year, the girls he dated were all from the summers in Schumacher. When it came time for his graduation in the spring of 1957, Frank didn't know any Toronto girls to ask to be his date. Word of his predicament got out, and shortly thereafter a priest at St. Mike's, Father Maurice Whelan, introduced him to Marie Devaney. In order to get to know Marie before the graduation formal, Frank took her out. The memory of that evening caused Marie to get choked up before retelling the story of how she fell in love. A genuine smile crept across her face before she spoke. "He took me to a dance at Casa Loma and we walked from St. Clair Avenue down to Casa Loma and then back up afterwards. We got on the streetcar and went to Swiss Chalet at Yonge and St. Clair. I can remember feeling so concerned; I realized the whole evening had cost him ten dollars. That was a lot of money at that time, and he was a boarder." The date was a great success and Frank made a lasting impression. After taking her out on two other dates, he asked Marie to his graduation formal and she happily agreed. "He was a superb dancer. The best person I have ever danced with."

The spring of 1957 was a busy time for everyone in the Mahovlich family. Anne had just been married on February 16 of that year to Ralph Adams. The wedding was in Schumacher and circumstances in Toronto prevented Frank from attending. Around the time of the wedding the Toronto Maple Leafs informed the hopeful Mahovlich that he would likely be getting a tryout. Because the Leafs were out of the running for a playoff spot at the end of the 1956–57 season, the team could let a rookie step in without negative consequences. St. Mike's instructed Mahovlich that it would be unwise to attend his sister's wedding.

This also suited the school fine, as the Majors were approaching the playoffs and they didn't want their star to miss any games. If there was an ugly side to St. Mike's, it was the complete disregard for family in such circumstances. In previous years, the school had gone so far as to keep Frank from going home at Christmas, ensuring

Frank's attendance at games scheduled around the holiday season. But missing Anne's wedding was the limit. The two had grown up as best friends, and Frank was heartbroken. Characteristically, however, Anne supported her brother in this frustrating predicament, telling him not to worry about the wedding and encouraging him to play well.

After the Majors' first-round elimination by the Guelph Biltmores, it was agreed that Mahovlich would get his tryout. In those days a player was allowed to play three games per season as a nonprofessional. The call was made, and the Leafs brought Frank up to play in their final three games.

The first was against the Montreal Canadiens. In preparation for the game, the Leafs practiced the day before, and the veteran Teeder Kennedy was among them. But the next day, Kennedy was not dressed for the game, signaling the changing of the guard. Mahovlich recounted with sentimental regret, "Teeder Kennedy's last practice was my first." Although Frank was grateful for the opportunity, to this day he wishes he had played in a game with the great Leaf captain.

Nothing about his first game sticks out in his mind except for taking a face-off against Jean Beliveau. Aside from that one image, Mahovlich shrugs off the significance of his first game in the NHL. Having played for St. Mike's at a packed Maple Leaf Gardens, he was used to the crowds. As soon as he got into the play, Frank felt at ease, like he belonged on that ice.

The next two games were against the Detroit Red Wings, the first of which was relatively uneventful for Mahovlich. The second game was memorable for eleven reasons. Mahovlich was breaking out of his zone when he met Johnny Bucyk along the boards. The rookie was battling to get through while Bucyk leveled his stick across Mahovlich's head. The blow cut Mahovlich for ten stitches. Like the majority of opposing players, Mahovlich has long since made friends with his rival. He smiled when he recalled Bucyk apologizing after the incident. "John came up to me and apologized, but I felt it was one of those accidentally on purpose things."

After getting stitched up Frank returned to the ice for the eleventh reason, his first NHL goal. A few years ago Frank was chatting with Glenn Hall, the night "Mr. Goalie" got inducted into the Canadian Sports Hall of Fame. As they reminisced, Mahovlich pointed out, "You know that I scored my first NHL goal against you." The modest Hall winced before offering, "Yes Frank, I know. And I regret that yours is a fairly common distinction."

After graduating from St. Mike's it was time for Frank to address his future in hockey. Because he was the top prospect in Junior A, the consensus was that Mahovlich would be offered a good contract. The Maple Leafs tested him and were undeniably impressed. They responded by offering Junior A's Most Valuable Player what was considered at that time to be a respectable contract. It was the payoff for years of hard work; but still, Frank wasn't about to make a hasty decision. He went to see Father Basil Regan, his principal at St. Mike's, for guidance.

For their meeting, Father Regan had pulled Frank's academic records, and, though he already had a good idea of what was there, he studied them for a moment. Then, in a definitive tone, he advised, "Frank, take that contract and sign it as quick as you can, before they change their minds!"

They both laughed, and Regan extended his sincere blessings and congratulations on a great achievement. The fact was that Frank had gone to St. Mike's so that he could eventually join the Toronto Maple Leafs. With the amount of pressure on him and the number of games he played, his studies had suffered considerably. It was a deliberate tradeoff, a sacrifice he accepted in hopes of a greater good. Hockey was a calling for a select group of people, and to play for the Leafs was every kid's dream. Father Regan knew it, and Frank Mahovlich lived it.

Frank's next meeting was considerably more formal. His father joined him to meet with Conn Smythe for the signing of his first NHL contract. And they knew there wouldn't be any negotiating. Mahovlich recalled the way it was. "At that time all the NHL teams were in cahoots. Every team knew what all the players were making and there was a standard for a rookie. I was one of the better finds in the minors so they gave me $10,000 to sign and $10,000 per year, for two years." This was $3,500 more than Frank's contemporary, Bobby Hull, was signed for in the same year. While commenting on their modest contracts, Hull offered that he hadn't developed into the player Frank was in Junior A. "Frank Mahovlich was likely the greatest Junior player I ever saw. I was always so amazed at the kind of maturity he had at such a young age."

The meeting with Smythe was businesslike and pleasant. Also present at the signing were Billy Reay and Howie Meeker, the coach and general manager respectively. From the start Frank sensed their expectations and knew about the trouble the team was in. "They were all pleased because Toronto wasn't going anywhere and they had something to look forward to. I remember in my last year of Junior, Conn Smythe used to have me come down to the Leaf games to watch and get used to what it was like. He'd have Clancy running from his box down to the bench with orders for the coach. It was a bad situation."

The first thing every hockey player did after signing his first contract was go out and buy a new car. Not wanting to break any long-standing traditions in his first week, Mahovlich decided he should comply. Howie Meeker recommended a dealership owned by a friend of Meeker's in his hometown of Hamburg, Ontario. Frank chose a beautiful 1957 Buick Special, black with a red pinstripe running down the side. It cost him $3,200.

One might assume that, in a small town, special treatment would be accorded a newly signed member of the Toronto Maple Leafs. Mahovlich insisted that such was not the case. The people in Timmins and Schumacher saw him as just another one of their boys making good. "Everybody looked at you—well, you're home, settle down and do your thing. Nobody gawked at you like you were a god or something. You were just doing your job, and they expected that of you in Timmins. We had Bill Barilko and Allan Stanley. They were from the North." The people were proud and had a high standard of excellence. Timmins was and always will be a town steeped in hockey tradition.

Nowhere was the humility Mahovlich spoke of more prevalent than in his own home. "I remember I went home that summer and my sister was having a party, and I arrived with my brand-new car. I drove it home at about thirty miles an hour. I was so careful it took me about eight hours. I got home and I said to my mom, 'Hi Mom,' and I gave her a kiss. 'Are you going to come and look at the new car?' I asked. I thought they'd be so anxious to see me and see my new car. Well, it wasn't so. She said, 'Park it down the street and come join the party. I'll see it tomorrow—it'll be there tomorrow.'" Mahovlich laughs. "In other words, it wasn't a big deal in her mind. So I said, 'Okay.'"

Asked if his mother had purposely reacted that way to keep his feet on the ground, Frank replied, "No—that's just the way she was. If she was doing it, she did it a lot, she put me in my place a lot."

Slinging cases at Doran's Brewery was Frank's last summer job before starting his professional hockey career. The physical labor kept him in great shape and Mahovlich was now filling out his six-foot-one frame. Going into his first training camp, Frank felt confident about his fitness and his ability to play at the next level. It was the lifestyle he had maintained that had brought him to where he was, and so Frank made no special changes to his routine. "I never felt excited or psyched up. It was natural for me, right from when I was a kid. Put on the skates and everything was natural. If it happened, it happened. If it didn't happen, it didn't happen. I always figured God gave me the ability, and go out there and do your best. Sure enough, things happened."

Talent and perseverance weren't the only things that helped Mahovlich become a Toronto Maple Leaf. Frank was acutely aware of the role his family played in his success. Taking care of the people who took care of him became his next priority.

A lifetime as a miner had taken its toll on his father, so with the money Frank received from signing with the Leafs he bought a home for his parents in Toronto. This gesture showed the love and respect that was in Frank Mahovlich's nature from day one. When asked to discuss the purchase, he did so without mention of his own generosity. "We looked for a home for a while and Bob Davidson helped us. He recommended Leaside because he lived there and it was a very nice community. There were a lot of St. Michael's students that I knew that lived there, and it was good for young Peter, who was ten years old at the time."

Cecilia and Peter Sr. were agreeable to the move; many of their friends who had worked in the mines had relocated to Toronto. The Leaside home Frank purchased for his parents was at 192 Bessborough Drive. For the next five years he lived there with his parents and younger brother.

Chapter Three

On the bus en route to the game tonight, Norm Ullman, who grew up in Edmonton, was our tour guide. Norm explained the significance of all the familiar places in his old neighborhood, and when the bus drove by his grade school it created a nice moment that Norm and the rest of the guys really felt.

A minute passed and the attention shifted to Bobby Hull, who had begun reciting Robert Service's poem "The Cremation of Sam McGee." The words evoked fond memories for me and I gave Dad a nudge. He smiled back at me, knowing that I was thinking of the many times he had recited that poem at home when my brother and sister and I were growing up. The guys were thoroughly impressed with Bobby's mastery of the work. As an entertainer Bobby Hull is a natural; every line was delivered with appropriate facial expressions while he waved his index finger, which is slightly crooked at the end, and he delivered a dramatic finish. Ullman, who seems the most reserved of the bunch, was pleased to witness the literary side of Bobby Hull, and piped up, "Did you learn that in school?" "Naw," replied Hull. "I've got a book of poetry that I read on the john."

At the rink several additional players joined the team for a one-off appearance for tonight's game. Jean-Guy Talbot approached me and delivered the news I didn't want to hear. "Ted, we've got a lot of extra players tonight, you'll have to sit this one out." I had that unmistakable sinking feeling in my gut

44

and, although it is somewhat pathetic and I hate to admit it, for a split second I felt rejected. I knew that I should be happy just to be in the dressing room with those guys so I quickly put my desire to play in check. Jean-Guy is a great guy and I assured him that I didn't mind.

As I moved my hockey bag to make room for the others, I shook off my disappointment. Then Lanny McDonald came in and took the seat beside me. (His moustache is unbelievable. It actually seems larger in person.) As it turned out, his greeting to the team got me involved. "Guys, I need gloves— anyone got extras?" I turned to him, smiled, and said, "No problem Lanny." I got my gloves from my hockey bag and placed them on his gear, while Lanny extended his hand in thanks and formal greeting. Dad was sitting across the room and I went over and told him that I wasn't going to dress tonight. Knowing my disappointment, he immediately told me not to worry. "You'll get plenty of ice time on this trip." His reassurance not only made me feel better, it reminded me that he can be a thoughtful guy. I'm pretty lucky. Not everyone has such a good dad.

So tonight I watched the game as a spectator from our bench, where guys were huffing and puffing. Our opponents, drawn from the Edmonton police, were an excellent team, and it was all the Greatest Hockey Legends could do to handle them.

Part of the entertainment, and damn fine entertainment it was, was the refereeing provided by Red Storey, Rocket Richard, and Eddie Shack. They are decidedly respectful of the Legends team. Near the end of the game, when our guys were down a goal, they took it upon themselves to correct the situation. After Red called a bad penalty against the cops, we pulled our goalie and replaced him with two attackers who went unnoticed for the duration of the game. It was seven on four and Wilf Paiement had their goalie pinned on the ice leaving the top half of the net open. At this point both benches and the fans were howling. With seconds remaining and no less than six of our players in the crease, we tied the game. It became clear to me that our guys don't like to lose. I figure we'd have been awarded a penalty shot(s) at the end of the game if we hadn't scored. The cops didn't like getting robbed but the fans ate it up.

Day 4—Morning

As I ran out of steam while writing last night, this morning I'll finish the summary of yesterday. After the game, the Edmonton police had a banquet at their station house, which we attended. Rather than take the bus back to the hotel, I opted to walk with Wilf Paiement—someone I had watched on television who, although was a good player, was never a public figure to the point where I was able to form an opinion of him. Besides, I believe players often adopt a persona for the media and public that allows for privacy in their personal lives. Professional appearances aside, Wilf Paiement is as nice a guy as you could ever hope to meet. This was amusing to me because I really didn't expect to like a player from an era of the Maple Leafs I've been trying to forget.

We talked about hockey, family, being on the road, the dynamics of personalities on hockey teams. He asked about Dad, whom he found interesting. (The man many know only as the Big M is indeed an interesting character—so much so that I'm writing this book.) Whatever précis I offered to Wilf last night, I would add that the many sides of my father are not easily understood. Along with the family man and loving parent I knew first, another person evolved during forty-plus years in the hockey business—perhaps the most critical of which were the early years.

In Mahovlich's rookie season, training camp for the Maple Leafs took place in Sudbury, Ontario. After Frank and the family moved into their new Leaside home, he arranged to get a ride to Sudbury with the Leafs coach, Billy Reay. The summer vacation was over and Mahovlich had his bags packed, ready for whatever the big league could throw at him—or so he thought. What he wasn't prepared for was the requirement described over the phone the day before Reay picked him up. "I got a call from Billy Reay who said, 'Be sure to bring your golf clubs, we have golf tournaments at training camp.' Well, I had never golfed before in my life. I didn't own any clubs and I was scrambling to find a set—but I eventually did. Billy Reay picked me up the following morning. I was so concerned about remembering the golf clubs that I forgot my skates!"

The team stayed at the Nickel Range Hotel. When Mahovlich arrived he was assigned the veteran, Sid Smith, as his roommate. Not seeing a future for himself with the Leafs, Smith left during camp and went on to play that season for the Whitby Dunlops. After Sid's departure, Frank roomed with the lively Tim Horton.

Recalling his earliest impressions of life at training camp, Mahovlich described a routine more serene than one might expect given the company he kept with the likes of Horton. "You're away from your family and all the players were concentrating on playing hockey. You would practice twice a day and then go on the road for exhibition games. I can remember the train rides from North Bay to Ottawa. It was the fall and all the leaves were just changing color. We went down by the Ottawa River and both sides were just loaded with color. That was exciting for me." Being based in Sudbury also allowed Frank to visit his sister Anne when he wasn't at the Idlewild Golf Club. Frank didn't win any of the tournaments but he learned the game and has been frustrated by it ever since.

Changes in the team's roster during training camp made it evident that the Maple Leafs were in a rebuilding phase. Veteran players like Teeder Kennedy and Sid Smith had left, and in the wake of their departure a leadership void was created. Another problem, one that related directly to Mahovlich, was the fact that, offensively, Dickie

Duff had been carrying the team single-handedly. It was no secret that the Maple Leafs brass were looking to their newly signed rookie to help out in that department.

So Mahovlich became the focus of media attention, which the Maple Leafs management happily went along with. "King Clancy called me Moses, because I was going to lead the team out of the wilderness." Although Clancy's biblical nickname made the newspapers it was a reporter who popularized the moniker that became Mahovlich's alias. "You hear stories that it was different people, but I thought it was [*Toronto Star* columnist] Red Burnett that nicknamed me the Big M. Red followed us around and he was at almost every game. I mean you'd sit with him at breakfast, he was there at dinner—he was around you all the time."

In that first season, 1957–58, Mahovlich played on several different lines. Despite the imminent upheaval in the Maple Leafs management, which kept the atmosphere around the team unsettled, and despite the team's growing pains which included missing the playoffs, Mahovlich's offensive production met the expectations of his backers. His impressive regular season performance totaled 20 goals and 16 assists, securing his position with the Maple Leafs at the age of nineteen. This was no small feat at a time when most players had to linger in the Senior A ranks prior to cracking the line-up of an Original Six team.

Up against Mahovlich for top rookie honors was Bobby Hull of the Chicago Blackhawks, who incidentally also had made the transition to the NHL seamlessly. As a long-time rival, Hull spoke with vivid admiration on the subject of the Big M. "He could always skate those big long strides. No one could take the puck and blow past you any better than Frank could. I remember after we turned pro—and I might say that he beat me out for the rookie of the year award in 1957–58, and deservedly so—I tried to stop him one night at Maple Leaf Gardens in Toronto. I was 193 pounds and just as hard as a concrete sidewalk. He went over top of me like I wasn't even there. Just one stride and he blew right over top of me! I watched him go by lying on my back. On a given night, Frank

Mahovlich was the greatest player that ever played. He was like that in Junior, and he was like that in pro."

At the end of the season the Maple Leafs gave a $1,000 bonus to the winner of the Calder Trophy for being the rookie of the year. Although Mahovlich's salary was enough to live off comfortably, he was grateful for the additional income. In those days it was the norm for players to supplement their salaries in one way or another. A common but not so lucrative method was through public appearances organized by the team. Used to promote the club, as well as the game, it was more or less considered part of the job. The downside to an appearance deal was that players had no say in where they went—for example, a day trip to Moncton, New Brunswick was not unheard of. Players had nothing against Moncton; it was just a considerable distance to travel for a fee of ten dollars, which was the amount players were paid regardless of the destination.

On a recent summer evening, while looking through some old hockey books, Mahovlich came across a photo of the Maple Leafs' trainer, Tim Daly. In the days of the Original Six, trainers were not required to have a qualified background in sports medicine—and that's putting it mildly. In Daly's case, he was better skilled at tending bar than giving medical assistance to injured players. Daly's love for the bottle was so extreme that Conn Smythe fired him five times over for his drunken exploits. Each time, he would show up for work the next day as if nothing had happened, and Smythe would forget the incident. By the time Mahovlich joined the Maple Leafs, Daly had ascended to a position as a quasi-mentor. The job entailed looking after the young players, which included taking them to public appearances.

The picture of Daly reminded Mahovlich of his first public appearance, to which the old trainer had accompanied him. The engagement was scheduled for a church in Richmond Hill, a suburb north of Toronto. Frank drove to the church in his cherished Buick Special and picked up his mentor on the way. When they arrived, Daly was fighting a terrific hangover but mustered a short pep talk for his rookie. "Now go up there boy, introduce yourself and sign some autographs." With Daly's encouragement, Frank introduced himself to the priest and the parish. After saying a few words, a group of autograph seekers met the Big M outside. While attending to the young fans, Mahovlich looked over his shoulder to see where Daly had made off to. In horror, he spied his mentor discreetly urinating on the side of his precious Buick Special.

Welcome to the Toronto Maple Leafs, son.

Throughout his rookie year, the hype surrounding Mahovlich had continued, and the young star got used to the pressure. The newspapers would watch a hockey player's every move and monitor his professional and personal progress daily. To minimize the attention he was drawing, Frank focused all his energy on hockey. This meant dating in public was out of the question during his freshman year. Besides, the last thing a rookie needed was the press attributing a bad game to a night on the town gallivanting with a young lady.

Consequently, Frank waited until the end of the season before calling on Marie Devaney. Then, when Bob Pulford and Billy Harris and their dates joined Frank and Marie for an evening of dancing at the Old Mill, and the two men saw Mahovlich arrive in the company of a beautiful girl, they were flabbergasted. Their shy teammate hadn't so much as mentioned a girlfriend, let alone one who appeared delightedly familiar with his company.

The summer of 1958 was spent at Assumption University in Windsor, Ontario, and once again Frank put his interest in Marie on hold. While she studied French at Laval University in Quebec City, Mahovlich hoped to earn a degree by attending university in the off-season. That year he spent six weeks taking two courses with fellow St. Mike's alumni Dickie Duff and Murray Costello. Although he enjoyed school, Frank's most memorable event of the summer was seeing Mickey Mantle hit two homers at Tiger Stadium. During the game, Mahovlich, the old first baseman from Schumacher, made a barehanded catch off a foul ball. The one-handed effort garnered a nod of approval from Yankee shortstop Tony Kubek, who witnessed the grab. When the three weren't at Tiger Stadium, their favorite pastime was golf.

The Maple Leafs' last-place finish in the 1957–58 season indicated that changes had to be made in Toronto. Adding to this time of trouble was the handing over of the reins from Conn Smythe to his son, Stafford. Lacking the hockey knowledge of his father, Stafford would be aided by Punch Imlach, whom Conn hired midway through the season as general manager.

With his sharp eye on the running of the ship, it didn't take long for Imlach to implement significant changes. While monitoring a Billy Reay practice, Imlach questioned the coach's competence in front of the team and a group of onlooking reporters. Shortly thereafter, Imlach fired Reay and made himself head coach. The public manner in which Imlach had let his dissatisfaction be known, which Mahovlich had witnessed, contributed to Frank's belief that Imlach lacked class.

Much later, in conversation with Mahovlich, longtime friend and teammate Dick Duff said of their old boss, "Punch was brash and cocky as hell—but he gave us confidence." This was true, and it was confidence the Maple Leafs were in dire need of. Imlach also gave the team direction, something Mahovlich was grateful for. So, initially, Frank felt that playing for Punch wasn't that bad. "I thought Imlach was good for the first three or four years. He got the most out of everybody and turned things around. As coach and general manager he put his money where his mouth was—after shooting it off. He immediately traded to get Allan Stanley from the Boston Bruins. That was one of his best deals."

Allan Stanley played on the point with Tim Horton and together they were as dependable as water for thirst. Both were popular team men, despite their propensity for stirring up trouble. A favorite Allan Stanley story in the Mahovlich repertoire originated from a scene that followed a game in Boston, after Stanley had joined the Leafs. "After each game, four players would take a cab together back to the hotel. One night after a game in the Boston Garden, Dick Duff and I were waiting for Horton and Stanley. There were these two girls waiting outside the dressing room standing next to Duffy and me. This one girl thought the world of Stanley and said to her friend, 'My, doesn't that Allan Stanley look like a Greek god!' Dickie turned to the girls and said, 'He may be a Greek god to you, but he's just plain Greek to us!" Whatever his appearance, Stanley would play a key role as a leader for the Maple Leafs in their pursuit of the Stanley Cup.

At the end of the 1958–59 season the Maple Leafs were the fourth-place team. By squeaking them into the playoffs, Imlach improved on the previous year's finish and gave the team something to build on. Mahovlich recalled that the team was fortunate to finish with a playoff berth. "We were ten points out of a playoff spot with five games to go. The Rangers had to lose five and we had to win five in order for us to get in. It was kind of a miracle, but it happened." Once again, Dick Duff had led the team in scoring, with 29 goals and 24 assists, followed by Billy Harris and Frank Mahovlich. Harris played center between Gerry Ehman on right wing and Mahovlich on left, a successful trio that was dubbed the "HEM-line."

The Leafs made it through the first round of the playoffs by defeating the Boston Bruins, but fell to the powerhouse Montreal Canadiens in the finals. That was the legendary Habs team that was in the process of winning five consecutive championships. For Mahovlich, the opposition in that playoff was the best he ever faced. "Montreal had Jean Beliveau, Marcel Bonin, and Bernie Geoffrion—Henri Richard, Maurice Richard, and Dickie Moore—then Don Marshall, Phil Goyette, and Claude Provost was their third line. Gosh, they were loaded. They didn't have a weakness. They beat us four games to one."

———————————

After their defeat by the Habs, Frank's attention turned back to Marie Devaney, who was now attending the Ontario College of Art. Frank's courtship of Marie began in the 1958–59 season, his second year as a Maple Leaf. Marie had followed his career in the newspapers and was well aware of the pressure he was under. Knowing Frank's predicament, when her old flame resurfaced after

Family portrait: Frank on his father's knee with sister Anne, mother Cecilia and Uncle Steve.

The Big M as a toddler with his dad, Peter.

Schumacher Public School "Blue and Red" after a winning season. Frank wears the "A".

Schumacher Lion—1951.

The Schumacher Lions. Frank is to the captain's right.

Schumacher High School football team. Frank is number 21. High school buddies number 7, Brian Grant, and number 11, Pat Hannigan.

Frank with sister Anne in Schumacher.

St. Michael's Buzzer in front of Tweedsmuir House. He wore number 9.

Second love—baseball.

A classic move by the captain of the St. Michael's Majors.

Frank receives the Red Tilson Memorial Trophy from "Gentleman Joe" Primeau.

Frank with his
first car—the
black Buick.

Marie Mahovlich
on the ferry to
Nantucket.

Dick Duff
and Frank at
Assumption
University in
Windsor,
Ontario.

Clarence S. Campbell, NHL president, presents the Calder Trophy to
Frank for Rookie of the Year honors, 1957–58. (Courtesy of The Hockey
Hall of Fame)

Peter Mahovlich Sr. with Bob Davidson—two great scouts.

Frank in Boston with Eddie Shack (l.) and Bob Baun (r.) before a game against the Bruins.

Game over! With "Tex" Ehman.

"I wanted a piece of Leo Labine, but George Hayes is in the way."

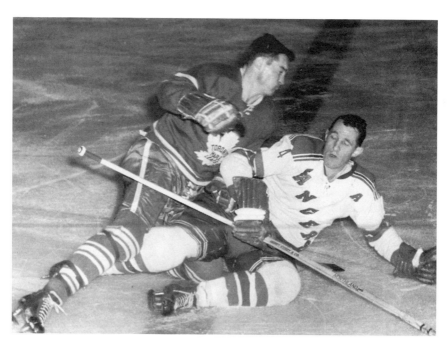

Getting even with Gadsby. Frank received angry letters from fans over this photo when newspapers ran it.

Left: Frank hoists the Stanley Cup—his first. Chicago, 1962.

Below: Frank with linemate and friend Red Kelly.

Gordie Howe playing goal. (Courtesy of The Hockey Hall of Fame)

Gadsby clips The Big M. (Courtesy of The Hockey Hall of Fame)

Going to the backhand. (Courtesy of The Hockey Hall of Fame)

Slam dunk! (Courtesy of The Hockey Hall of Fame)

Playing the man—in this case Blackhawks checker Eric Nesterenko.

Fighting for the puck with Blackhawks Pierre Pilote and Stan Mikita.

a year-long absence, she was understanding. Shortly thereafter the two were going steady. Marie would attend each home game at Maple Leaf Gardens and sit with her mother, Elizabeth, who enjoyed a good game of hockey immensely.

Apart from spending his time with Marie, Frank managed a week off in the summer of 1959 with two of his buddies on the Leafs, Dickie Duff and Carl Brewer. The group decided on the sunny destination of Nassau, an island in the Bahamas. Mahovlich had never been on a real vacation and looked forward to the getaway. "It was my first time ever on an island. One thing I remember about that trip was when we got off in Miami to switch planes. We went to check our bags and the girl behind the counter checked the bags and then said 'Follow me.' She led us out onto the tarmac. On top of carrying the luggage, she's out there on the tarmac waving in the plane. I said, 'What the heck is this?' We had to get on the tiniest little plane to get over to Nassau. With the Leafs we had flown on Viscounts, but this was like a five- or six-seater. We were all scared."

In his recollection of their vacation, Carl Brewer laughed at how innocent they were. "It was a wonderful, wonderful holiday. I always thought it was strange though, because here's three guys and we're all devout Roman Catholics. So we're down in Nassau, three swinging nineteen- and twenty-year-olds. We didn't drink, we didn't smoke, and we didn't talk to girls. I often think back to it, and there it was. Girls weren't coming on to us, but you know, there were plenty of girls around. And it was, 'No chance with us!' We didn't even talk to them!" Despite their aversion to confronting the female gender, the three teammates enjoyed the restful beaches, dining in excellent restaurants, deep-sea fishing, and the requisite round or two of golf.

Upon returning, Frank resumed his pursuit of a degree at the University of Ottawa. "I took courses in history and business administration but it was very difficult at that time because no one would leave you alone." With several personal appearances and other hockey-related obligations, the long-term plan of obtaining a university degree was put off indefinitely. In subsequent years, Frank worked for Montreal Trust in the summer while staying fit playing baseball.

The next season brought more new faces to the Toronto Maple Leafs, showing a steady improvement in the team. One trade in particular would have a profound effect on the career of Frank Mahovlich. Defenseman Marc Reaume was sent to Detroit in exchange for the veteran Leonard "Red" Kelly. The general manager for Detroit, Jack Adams, had tried to make a trade with the New York Rangers but when that fell through, Imlach snatched up Kelly. Now Punch had to work Kelly into the line-up.

In 1959–60, a second-place finish overall showed that the Maple Leafs were well on their way to becoming contenders. Once again, they made it to the finals and had to face the indomitable Montreal Canadiens. In retrospect, Mahovlich puts one other team on a par with the Habs of that year. "The greatest team I ever saw play was Edmonton, the team they had with Gretzky, Messier, and Kurri— and the 1959–60 Montreal Canadiens. That year they beat us four straight." The win over Toronto gave Montreal their fifth consecutive Stanley Cup, a record that still stands. Mahovlich's 18 goals and 21 assists that season indicated he had yet to explode into the offensive threat people expected. Frank also felt he could better his offensive production and resolved to address the issue with his coach. "I went up and had a conversation with Imlach. I was upset that my ice time didn't compare to Bobby Hull, or anybody that was scoring a lot of points." Imlach took the concern under advisement and assigned Frank to the power play.

As it turned out, the 1959–60 season would prove to be the calm before the storm. Enter new linemate, Red Kelly. Open to experimentation, Punch decided to move the veteran defenseman to center on a line with Mahovlich and right winger Bobby Nevin. In doing so, Imlach rejuvenated the career of Kelly and found the missing piece to the Frank Mahovlich puzzle. The chemistry between Frank and Red was immediate. The two played with an unspoken understanding of each other's abilities, and exploited those talents with lethal precision. On the topic of Red Kelly, Mahovlich had nothing but praise for his teammate and friend. "Red had a knack of attracting a player toward him. As soon as that player made an error, he would leave the puck for you. He was a great playmaker. A Lady Byng man, a real gentleman, and a great guy."

With the additional ice time and his new line, the goals came fast and furious. Mahovlich recalled, "In 1960–61, Kelly, Mahovlich, and Nevin were the big line. That may have been the best line formed in Toronto." Frank speaks highly of the trio he so rightly enjoyed playing with, but with that success came more pressure. At the halfway point in the season, it appeared that the 50-goal plateau was within reach for the Big M. In those days, the 50-goal season was an incredible accomplishment and the press began to critique Mahovlich nearly shift by shift. As the media game went on, the journalists covering Frank analyzed and reanalyzed the situation. If a game passed without a goal, Mahovlich was an overrated bum. If the following game's performance produced a goal or two, he would be back on track. The day-to-day focus ignored the big picture. As a line, Kelly, Mahovlich, and Nevin were the top three point leaders on a team that was rapidly earning contender status.

As was to be expected, physical attention from the opposition was more forthcoming than ever. And although the Big M was never interested in fighting, on the rare occasion when an opposing player insisted, Mahovlich was never known to back down. During a game against the New York Rangers, Bill Gadsby swung his stick in a fashion that demanded an appropriate response. "Gadsby tried to take my head off one night at the blue line. I ducked and he caught me on the shoulder. There was a bloody welt left on my shoulder from his stick. As we were going down I was throwing punches. Then the next day, the photo that appeared in the paper made it look like I was the instigator of it all. He was going down and I was firing punches at him. In the mail the following week I got five of these photos, with notes—'You dirty so and so, this is what you do?'" Mahovlich laughs. "I went to visit Gads a few years ago and he had the picture hanging in his recreation room."

Past the halfway mark of the season, Red Kelly got injured and Mahovlich's scoring streak cooled off. At a time when his game could have used a boost, life threw the Big M an unexpected curve. After a road game, Mahovlich was to attend a charity dinner in London, Ontario that turned into a nightmare. At the Hotel London, sports celebrities gathered for the London Sportswriters and Sportscasters' Rotary Club dinner to benefit the Crippled Children's Treatment Centre. With the number of newsmen and professional athletes in the same room the atmosphere was like a gigantic press conference. A reporter approached Mahovlich and inquired about his successful year and the contribution of his injured centerman, Red Kelly. The exchange spawned an article in the next day's *London Free Press* that little resembled Mahovlich's actual thoughts. In the article, a journalist named Harry Eisen set the scene by rattling off a list of the celebrities in attendance. At the top of his roster was "Frank Mahovlich, the Toronto Maple Leafs scoring ace." In response to a question about the forty goals the Big M had netted, the paper quoted the leading Leaf as follows: "No, I don't think Red Kelly had anything to do with it."

The next morning Frank headed back to Toronto and picked up a newspaper to read on the train. As he browsed through the sports page, the bold print caught him like a slap in the face. "Mahovlich Can Get Along Without Kelly, Big 'M' Says." Mahovlich became very agitated when recalling that experience. "The question was whether Red was helping me or not. I said, 'He's got to be helping me, if I'm scoring. I mean, we're all working together, right?' I guess the guy thought I wasn't that excited so he wrote what he wanted. The next morning I woke up and boom! Headlines in the paper— Mahovlich says this about Kelly."

Frank's comments were presented in a headline designed to create controversy. But even the story the paper ran was not as negative as the headline suggested. Mahovlich had explained, "I scored four goals in Chicago when Billy Harris was my centerman and Kelly was back on defense." Because Kelly was injured, Harris filled in his spot, which was no hindrance in Frank's mind. Mahovlich was just as happy to play with Harris as he was with Kelly, or any other teammate for that matter.

The morning of February 1, 1961 at 6:29 a.m., Red Kelly lay fast asleep in his Toronto home. It was the morning after the London charity dinner and at 6:30 a.m. Kelly received a phone call from the same reporter who had cornered Mahovlich. Still half asleep, Red answered the phone. The voice stated, "Last night at a banquet in London, Frank Mahovlich said you had nothing to do with him scoring forty goals." Fully aware that he had just awoken Red, the reporter repeated the charges. Kelly replied, "Frankly, I'm not really interested in hearing this" and hung up. Frank and Red were roommates on the road for the entire time the two were Maple Leafs. On the team no one was closer to Frank than Red, who would be the last person Frank would want to hurt or offend. The story that appeared in the *London Free Press*, which followed in the Toronto news, was a damaging attempt to gain notoriety. The notion that Frank Mahovlich had anything but respect and gratitude for Red Kelly was absurd.

The article made Mahovlich livid. "It wasn't good for the morale of the team and it wasn't good for me." The honesty and respect he extended to people was something he expected in return. Without saying a bad word, Frank was made to look like he'd stabbed his friend in the back. When Red pulled into the parking lot the next day for practice, Frank immediately approached him to apologize. Red felt bad that such an article had come out in print but recognized it for what it was worth. Seeing how upset his teammate was, Red told him to forget about it. Kelly had years of experience in dealing with reporters, which he acknowledged was part of the job. "You'd talk to all of them, but you wouldn't say anything."

Punch Imlach was sitting in his office when Frank arrived to discuss the matter with management. After rehashing the evening in London—which the Leafs had sent him to—Mahovlich asked for the team's support in suing the paper. Punch agreed with Frank's protest but felt that legal action would only draw more attention to the issue. The best they could do was let it blow over. From that point on Mahovlich was wary of reporters. "It was hard on me trying to explain something I never did. Now that there is television, that doesn't happen as much. What you see is what you get. In those days it was all newspapermen interviewing you, your word against his word. Imagine that. That's how tough it was."

As the end of the 1960–61 season approached, Mahovlich needed two more goals to hit 50. Kelly could see that Frank was distracted and wanted to encourage him to focus on scoring. "He only had to get two more goals. I got hurt and couldn't play. I went down to the dressing room to talk to Frank because I didn't think he was really going for it. 'Frank, you've got forty-eight goals, for crying out loud. Only two more goals and you're at fifty!' That was a real milestone in those days." Red's intentions were genuine and appreciated, but despite this encouragement Frank's total remained at 48. Although it would have been nice to make 50, a club record had been set that would last over twenty years. Along with his 36 assists, Frank led the team in scoring, followed by Red, who, as a veteran defenseman turned forward, amassed 20 goals and 50 assists.

The playoffs in 1961 marked the end of the great Montreal Canadiens' reign, which was halted at the hands of the Chicago Blackhawks. The Detroit Red Wings had defeated the Maple Leafs in the first round and went on to lose to Chicago in the Stanley Cup final. Although the Maple Leafs exited the playoffs early, the team had a core of solid players hungry for the Cup. Mahovlich knew that in the following year his team would make their move. "There was a group of us, I would say a nucleus of about five or six players, Dickie Duff, Bobby Pulford, Bob Baun, Carl Brewer, and myself, who had great success in junior. All of a sudden, we started to gel. We were beginning to gain confidence from a number of older players like Allan Stanley, Red Kelly, and George Armstrong, who had been there for a while. And Timmy Horton of course. The mixture of the age with the youth really gelled, and then Johnny Bower came along and helped quite a bit with the goaltending."

In the 1961–62 campaign Mahovlich repeated as point leader with 33 goals and 38 assists. Kelly was third in scoring behind another graduate of St. Michael's, Dave Keon. Playing center between Duff and Armstrong, Keon was likely the best two-way player that ever suited up for the Maple Leafs. Mahovlich had been covered by some of the greatest and knew how tough Keon was. "If you ever wanted to neutralize an opposing line, this guy could do it. He had the best skating legs of any player I knew. It's very difficult to go around someone that is back-checking because you can't deke him, and you couldn't deke Davey." With Pulford, Olmstead, and Shack as the third unit, the Leafs had three strong lines that could give any team a run for their money.

Through the season, Mahovlich's focus on hockey facilitated his clean lifestyle. When players would go out after a game on the road, Frank would join them for one or two beers and then retire to his room to read a book. Aside from the occasional protest of Tim Horton, Frank's quiet behavior was respected by his teammates. Eddie Shack was one of the livelier spirits on the team who enjoyed Mahovlich's personal approach to the game. "Frank was a different individual. He wasn't rah-rah-rah! He kept everything to himself. One time at the Gardens he was standing on his head in the training room. I guess that was supposed to get the blood flowing to your head. But the guys would just laugh like crazy, 'What the hell is he doing now!' If he scored a couple of goals, he'd be doing it all the time." A ritual that Shack didn't question was Mahovlich's regular attendance at church. "Frank used to go to church every Sunday. Even the morning after a long train ride to Boston, when you'd get in at two o'clock on Saturday night. Kelly, Clancy, and Mahovlich would always go to church. I used to go myself, and after going to church you always seemed to get two or three goals. So you'd say, 'Shit, I better get to church!'"

Although Mahovlich's career statistics suggest that he attended Mass more frequently than Shack, Eddie was undeniably one of the most colorful players in the game. When the Leafs needed a boost, Shack was the man who got the crowd behind them. To Mahovlich, the dimension that Eddie brought to the team was a luxury. "He'd stir things up and the people would love it. A lot of teams couldn't have done that. They couldn't afford to do it, but we did. Can you have a player like that and still win? He'd run at Gordie Howe, he'd run at Doug Harvey, he'd take on anybody! Eddie was a good hockey player and could have been a lot better, but he got forced into that role."

The first round of the 1962 playoffs had the Maple Leafs squaring off against the New York Rangers. In a hard-fought series, Toronto proved stronger and advanced to the Stanley Cup final. Chicago had defeated the Habs and were looking for their second straight Cup. The Blackhawks' greatest asset was their gunner, Bobby Hull, and the Maple Leafs were only too familiar with his shot. But down the left wing the Leafs had the Big M, an equal threat whom Chicago planned to contain. Mahovlich explained the benefit of the Blackhawks' strategy. "If Imlach could keep me out there, they would leave their checker, Eric Nesterenko, on. He was all over you, but for us, it was far better having Nesterenko on there than Bobby Hull. If you could control the game, you'd win the Stanley Cup."

In the Maple Leafs dressing room there were mixed feelings toward some of the sketchy characters surrounding the team. During the final series Stafford Smythe's buddy, Harold Ballard, was jumping on the Leafs bandwagon. Although Mahovlich didn't mind Ballard cheering on the team, he could see it didn't sit well with some players. "Harold Ballard came down and I can remember Bert Olmstead being upset at it. You never saw Ballard and all of a sudden you see him right when we're about to win the Stanley Cup. He was coming into the dressing room, patting guys on the back before the game, and Olmstead told him off." On the other hand, for players like Carl Brewer, who knew Ballard through the Toronto Marlboros, his presence was nothing new. Since Ballard's support ran deeper than being the Leafs' number-one cheerleader, whether he was liked or disliked didn't matter. In hindsight, Mahovlich believes that he was plotting his ascent to the top of the organization the whole time. "Stafford had him around as a friend but he was making his move. Ballard was there a long time weaseling in, a long time. He did a very good job of it, too." Whatever changes management was going through, that was business the players couldn't control. The best they could do was set their minds on winning the Cup.

The task at hand was made infinitely more difficult by the physical exhaustion Imlach inflicted on his team. Though he is remembered as a man who never played favorites, and it is true that no one got a free ride with Punch, he had a short list of players to whom he spared no quarter. Eddie Shack remembered how their coach was particularly harsh when it came to the bigger players. "He never practiced Keon very much, or Billy Harris, because they were a little bit lighter and he didn't want to burn them right out. But with Frank or Carl Brewer, he'd just work the Jesus out of them. You were so tired and thirsty, and at that time in hockey there was no water on the bench." Feeling completely drained before a game was par for the course for several players.

Frank knew better than to challenge Imlach's treatment of him, but still he hated it. "If you take a horse and run him the day before a race, he won't be the same. He'll have run the race, before the race. That's why in Toronto I always had a difficult time. I left too many games on the practice ice." Despite the exhaustive regimen Mahovlich and others went through, the team displayed incredible resilience in their bid for the Stanley Cup.

Going into Chicago for game six, the Maple Leafs were leading the series three games to two. The team wanted nothing more than to end it that night. Near the midway point of the third period Bobby Hull put the Blackhawks on the board, giving his side a 1-0 lead. It stayed that way for less than two minutes, when Mahovlich teamed up with Bob Nevin for the equalizer. "I thought I made a real good play in that game. When I watched the replay it happened so darn fast it looked like a fluke. It doesn't happen that fast when you're in the play. I could see Bobby Nevin out of the corner of my eye at center, and I gave him the pass. He fired it into the net and scored the tying goal."

The hero of the game was rough-tough Dick Duff. At 14:14 of the third period, nearly four minutes after Nevin's marker, Dickie scored the winning goal. It gave the Toronto Maple Leafs their first Stanley Cup since Bill Barilko had netted the Cup winner in 1951.

What should have been the most joyous moment of Mahovlich's career was diminished by the physical toll Imlach's practices had exacted. Having won the Stanley Cup, Frank remembered being happy, but in an exhausted way. "It just seemed like it was another game. At that time we practiced so hard that you didn't feel elated nor did you feel let down. It was kinda like, geez, it's over. It's good that it's over."

In the dressing room, a more contented atmosphere enabled Frank to enjoy the victory, if only for a moment. "I remember we won, and after you don't know what to do. The game is over and everything is done. So I went down to the room and they brought the Stanley Cup there. I had never lifted it up, and in those days players just held it beside them. It was so light that I decided to pick it up over my head. While I had it over my head a guy clicked a photo and it made the front page of the paper. I still have the picture at home and it's a great memory."

The victory celebration was abruptly terminated by the sobering words of the Leafs' coach and general manager. "We won the Cup in Chicago," recalled Eddie Shack. "We had a few cocktails and Imlach says, 'If you're not on the bus in five minutes, you won't be on the team next year!' Holy smokes, eh! And I was on the bus— and Frank was too."

Chapter Four

Day 4—Afternoon

This morning we drove from Edmonton to Grand Prairie. Jim Dorey has come to the end of his stay with us and has been replaced by Dave "Tiger" Williams. From what I know about Tiger it won't be long before things get interesting. I remember the last time I saw Tiger Williams play—a charity game between the Toronto Maple Leafs alumni and the Montreal Canadiens alumni at Maple Leafs Gardens. In the spirit of the event Tiger was interviewed during the warm-up alongside the Barenaked Ladies who had made it onto the ice to sing the national anthem. One of the band members made a witty remark that got a rise out of the crowd. Regrettably for him, the joking remark was at Tiger's expense. Whether it was something that had to do with Tiger's role on the Leafs or his rugged good looks I honestly can't remember. What I do remember was Tiger spearing the smug Barenaked Lady guy right between the legs.

We're now in the familiar holding pattern of waiting for the entire team to board the bus before it takes us to the rink. I'm sitting in my usual seat. Dad occupies the pair behind me and Red Storey is behind him. Dad and Red get along famously and usually room together when on tour. Red likes sitting behind Dad on the bus so he can apply the "claw" when Dad's verbal jabs call for retaliation.

They're currently discussing what has been a popular topic on this trip—Alan Eagleson, the former president of the

National Hockey League Players' Association. Dad is telling the guys about a related encounter at a celebrity sports banquet with Bill "Spaceman" Lee, the famous baseball pitcher. Prior to the settling of the NHL pension lawsuit and Alan Eagleson's arrest and conviction for racketeering-related charges, Dad had expressed to Lee his belief that the case would eventually go in the players' favor. Familiar with the case and the excruciatingly long time it was taking to bring Eagleson to justice, Lee summarized, "When you do your laundry, you have to wring it out before you hang it up to dry." The anecdote won a chuckle from the group while Dad added his farewell compliment to Lee, "I told him, 'I don't know why they call you Spaceman; you're down to earth as hell.'"

With the conclusion of the Spaceman story, Tiger Williams arrives and seats himself across from Dad. Happy to see the guys, Tiger offers salutations to all when moments later Morris Lukowich arrives and points out that Tiger has usurped his seat. I've learned that territoriality is very much a reality among hockey players, who find comfort in a seat they can call home, so to speak. Observing the protocol of seat occupation since joining, I have gathered that a player who joins midway through the tour finds an empty pairing and that remains his claim until he leaves the tour. It's sort of an unwritten law the guys respect to ensure that life remains as pleasant as possible in such cozy quarters.

Unfortunately for Lukowich, Tiger, who is the older of the two, feels that the laws of seniority carry more weight—as does he—and defiantly states that it's now his seat. So it's been all of sixty seconds that Tiger has been with us and already he's the focus of an argument. Dad speaks up, backing Morris' claim, and even goes so far as to offer Tiger the seat next to him. Tiger says, "There's no way I'm moving!" Wisely, Lukowich assesses the matter as a headache not worth pursuing and moves to a vacant spot near the front of the bus.

Sitting behind Tiger is Wilf Paiement. Wilf, being a soothing fellow by nature, diverts the attention away from the seat-jacking by asking Tiger what he's been up to lately. Tiger pulls out a container of chewing tobacco and tucks a generous pinch behind his lower lip before telling us that he has just returned from a seminar that he gave on business, teamwork, and marketing. Sporting the baseball cap of the Vancouver Voodoo, his rollerblade hockey team/business venture, Tiger continues with the fundamentals of his marketing sensibilities. "If a guy on my team wants to wear a ball cap he better be wearing one of ours, 'cause if I catch him in a Montreal Canadiens or Philadelphia Phillies cap, he's off my team. I'm paying him so he's not going to market another franchise. We all market ourselves in our appearance. Women wear makeup, they make sure they have the right earrings on, they match their belt with their shoes. Men have to shave and comb their hair. If you don't look presentable, who is going to want to do business with you? Your appearance is how you market yourself." With these words of wisdom Tiger draws a paper cup to his chin and unloads a stream of dark brown drool from his tobacco-stuffed mouth.

The conversation has drifted to a pleasant discussion of vacation destinations the guys have enjoyed with their families. The players talk quite a bit about their families and their wives while on the road. I can see that among friends who have similar lives and who live with the same pressures, a week on the road together can be quite therapeutic. On the subject of couples, I know that within my parents' marriage Dad and Mom are equally difficult and wonderful at the same time. And I'm sure it's the same for most of the characters on this bus and their better halves. From what I've observed of marriage, I can say that it's not always easy and it takes all kinds. And that's probably a fair statement for Mom and Dad.

Marie Mahovlich recalls, "Frank and I had gone out for five years and by then I was twenty-two. We were out on a weeknight, dancing at the Old Mill, and I said to Frank, 'We have gone together for five years now; do you think that we might get married?' He hummed and hawed, then mumbled that he thought so. That night we went home and he asked my mother if it was all right if we got married—my father had died the year before." Marie hated to force the issue, but she felt it was high time Frank made a commitment or let her move on.

The couple decided to keep their plan a secret throughout the 1961–62 season. Knowing Punch Imlach's reputation for ragging players who had something other than hockey on their minds, Frank and Marie strategically announced their wedding only after the season had ended. It meant that all preparations would have to be made in less than six weeks, but Marie was happy to take on the formidable task. Frank was left with one responsibility—to produce the ring.

Several of the Leafs players were married in the early sixties and became friendly with a jeweler in Chicago. He was a hockey fan who was happy to cater to the team. Frank had the fellow design an engagement ring and arranged for him to meet with Marie for approval of the design. After a minor modification the bride-to-be was satisfied and the order was placed. Like every young lady, Marie imagined how Frank might go about presenting her with the ring. Something Frank had said led Marie to believe that he would officially propose to her on March 17, which fell on a Friday. As it turned out, the couple ended up babysitting Frank's two nephews that day, and the big moment was postponed. Confident that her fiancé was waiting for a more romantic opportunity, Marie tried to contain her excitement.

The next evening was the Maple Leafs' Saturday night home game, and all day Frank's mind was on hockey. Before a game Frank maintained a structured routine that he went through without deviation. The team would have a morning skate followed by a meeting in which the game plan would be discussed. Upon his return home his mother prepared him a meal consisting of steak, a baked potato, canned green peas, and vanilla ice cream for dessert would be ready at 1 p.m. After a nap, Frank would relax before driving down to the Gardens with Marie, who would drop him off two hours before game time. Unlike present-day standards, during the fifties and sixties the Maple Leafs management did not deem it necessary to provide a lounge for the wives and girlfriends of the players. Rather than stand in the hallway of the Gardens for an hour and a half, as many spouses and girlfriends would, Marie drove the quick ten minutes home and returned just prior to game time.

On this particular evening Frank sat quietly in the passenger seat while Marie drove him down to the game. Although he was often quiet Frank appeared to be more focused than usual. Without giving his solitude a great deal of thought, Marie attributed his mood to the immense pressure he was under as playoffs drew near. She did not expect what followed when they pulled up to the north side of Maple Leaf Gardens. "I drove him down to Maple Leaf Gardens and he got out of the car on Wood Street. He handed me my tickets for the game in an envelope and said, 'And here's the ring.' I was so upset and mad that I wanted to throw the ring out onto Wood Street, but I knew we'd never find it in the slush. That's what my immediate reaction was. I was very, very disappointed. But Frank was not a person who felt comfortable showing his emotions. He found it very difficult and awkward, so his easiest solution was to simply hand me the ring and get out of the car."

The Toronto Maple Leafs won their first of three consecutive Stanley Cups on April 22, 1962. Following the celebration in Toronto, Marie successfully organized their wedding in record time. The ceremony took place at Holy Rosary Church on June 13, 1962. In attendance were relatives from both sides of the family, a few of the Maple Leafs, and the bridesmaids and ushers who, as Frank recalled, were all friends from high school. "I didn't have any of the Leafs as ushers at my wedding. I think it's because I had lived with the guys in my wedding party and knew them as close friends in those days. With the Maple Leafs, I was never really close to anyone. I chummed with Billy Harris sometimes, Eddie Shack, Dickie Duff, but it wasn't a really close-knit situation. Maybe it was because I was young and lived with my parents at that time. After I left St. Mike's, I kept in touch with Bill Kyle, Tommy Gorman, and Les Kozak. They were my ushers, along with my brother Peter."

The service was conducted by Father Ed Ronan and the St. Michael's Choir School sang. At a social gathering nearly thirty years after their wedding, an easily recognizable face approached Frank and said, "Mr. Mahovlich, I sang at your wedding." Being a devoted patron of the arts, Mahovlich was delighted to meet the celebrated singer and actor Michael Burgess. Frank was doubly pleased to learn that Burgess had been a chorister at his and Marie's wedding.

Immediately after the service, a reception was held at the Roof Garden of the Royal York Hotel. Following the luncheon, the newlyweds rushed to Toronto International Airport to catch a flight to New York.

Now, for the first time in nearly a year the couple were alone without curfew or concern. They checked into a hotel and spent a memorable first night as newlyweds in the Big Apple. Frank laughed when he recalled the reservation they had made. "We were on our way to Barbados and had to spend an evening in New York, at the Barbizon Plaza. The brochure advertised a beautiful view overlooking Central Park. Well, there was no window at all in the darn room. In the washroom there was a little window, about ten inches by ten inches, and that was our beautiful view. We had to take turns looking out the window to appreciate the view of Central Park."

The plan for the honeymoon was nothing but rest and relaxation. The couple spent three or four days in each of Barbados, Martinique, and Antigua. Marie and Frank toured the islands, lounged on the beaches, and did a little snorkeling, and all too soon it was time to return home.

The honeymoon had been just long enough to unwind from the hectic pace set by the playoffs and the hurried wedding. Although the long walks and lying in the sun involved little stress, leaving Antigua was another story. Frank felt their lives were dangerously close to a premature end. "I'll never forget BOAC Airlines. There was something wrong with the plane and it was five hours late getting in. The people getting off the plane arriving in Antigua were all complaining what a terrible flight it was, just horrendous. One fellow said the plane wasn't fit to take off, so the airline grounded the plane and we had to go back to our hotel. We got into a cab and had some kind of a ride. The taxicab driver fell asleep at the wheel and almost drove us over a cliff. We had to shove him to wake him up and we ended up in a barnyard."

Eventually, the honeymooners made it home alive and well. Settling into their new apartment was the first item on their summer agenda. Coincidentally, the location of the newly constructed apartment building was on the site of Frank's first residence at St. Mike's, on Tweedsmuir Avenue. Frank enjoyed apartment living, which suited the professional hockey lifestyle just fine. When the team was on the road there was no maintenance to worry about so they could come and go as they pleased. Marie enjoyed the fact that she was in the neighborhood she grew up in, minutes from downtown Toronto. After they were settled in, the remainder of the summer was spent at the Devaneys' cottage, northeast of Toronto on Lake Simcoe.

In August Frank's thoughts turned to the upcoming training camp. In the fall of 1962 the Maple Leafs trained in Peterborough, Ontario. They had been stationed there each September for the past four years. For approximately three weeks the team would occupy the Empress Hotel. The daily routine began with a 6 a.m. wake-up, breakfast, then practice from 8:00 to 9:30 or 10 a.m. The hotel was about a mile and a half from the rink and the players were supposed to walk it as part of their morning exercise. When Imlach found out his orders to walk to the rink were being undermined, he assigned King Clancy to the case. "A few of us would catch a ride some mornings to the rink," Mahovlich laughs. "Well, King Clancy and Imlach found out, so Imlach gave Clancy orders to spy on us. He planted himself halfway between the hotel and the rink and we called him 'Checkpoint Charlie.' There was King Clancy in his hat and his scarf at seven in the morning, making sure we touched base with him. That was the end of the car rides and everybody had to walk after that."

The walk to the rink was the easy part of the morning schedule. Most practices began with Imlach driving the team through intense conditioning for a solid hour. Drenched from the skating drills, the team continued with a regular practice that left them exhausted. Everyone walked back to the hotel for lunch and a nap before returning to the rink for the afternoon skate. In the evening, dinner was served at 5:00. For the most part, players were tired enough that any burning desire for a night on the town faded by the end of the day. Occasionally the team would take in a movie before turning in, ready to go at it the next day.

At the end of the 1961–62 season, Mahovlich's contract with the Leafs had expired and negotiations to renew were to take place in Peterborough that September. Bargaining with the notoriously cheap Maple Leafs management was not something Frank looked forward to. For management, the process was a real game, and they did everything to ensure that they had the upper hand. There were always a few members of the Leafs brass present to make sure the player felt good and intimidated at these meetings (keep in mind that, at this point in professional hockey, player agents were unheard of).

When Frank scored 48 goals in the 1960–61 season he was supposed to have earned a $1,000 bonus from Conn Smythe that kicked in when he reached 35 goals. That incentive agreement was made when Frank and his father had negotiated his last contract. But with Imlach acting as a member of the Leafs management, Mahovlich got the runaround in full force. "We always dealt with Conn Smythe, so whatever he said was pretty good on a handshake. Previously my dad and I argued for more money and they said, 'Frank's only getting twenty goals a year.' We said, 'What if I get thirty-five goals?' Smythe said, 'We'll give him a $1,000 bonus, and we won't even put it in the contract.' When I went back to get the money, Imlach said, 'Yeah, but it's not in the contract.' My father was with me and he walked out disgusted, saying, 'I don't know why they call him Punch—they should call him Punchy.'" The lesson was learned and the trust was broken between the Leafs and Mahovlich.

Prior to the 1962 season's training camp, Frank met with his father and they discussed what he should be earning. Over the past two campaigns with the Maple Leafs, he scored a team record 81 goals, led the team in total points, and contributed to the first Toronto Stanley Cup victory in eleven years. The Big M had achieved bona fide superstar status. Father and son agreed that a generous raise was in order. "The Leafs management should have taken care of all that business before camp started. My father and I had talked about it and we thought that we'd just see what they'd offer. I had been making $15,000 and was looking for a good raise. I wanted $25,000 or $30,000, which was peanuts, but you couldn't get any more because they'd say, 'Gordie Howe only makes this much' or 'Jean Beliveau is only getting $25,000.' They'd use that against you. All the salaries went to Clarence Campbell [the league president and puppet of the owners], and then all the owners would get together. It was just terrible. Conn Smythe would befriend some of the players, like Ted Kennedy and he would use that. He'd ask Teeder, 'Well, what do you think you're worth?' These guys were such nice guys that they would play for nothing. So, Gordie Howe would say, 'Well, I'll just take a thousand-dollar raise.'"

When the Maple Leafs management was ready to begin contract meetings, they would set up an office in one of the hotel rooms. Midway through the training camp, King Clancy approached Mahovlich after a morning practice and informed him that a meeting had been called between Frank, Punch Imlach, Bob Davidson, and Clancy. Frank immediately recognized the format and knew he was in for a battle. Rather than work out a deal with one boss, he had to take on three.

When he arrived for the meeting, Mahovlich took his seat in the hotel room while Clancy closed the door behind him. Bob Davidson, a fair man, sat quietly as Imlach, the general manager, looked over the figures he was going to present to his star player. As a rookie, Mahovlich could be bullied into a contract. Statistics in junior hockey didn't mean a thing in the NHL. However, the situation was entirely different in 1962. After four seasons, Mahovlich had proven himself and earned the right to a good salary. When Imlach tried to lowball him with an insult for a raise, Mahovlich knew they were simply wasting his time. "When it came time for them to make an offer, their offer was maybe a thousand-dollar raise. It was ridiculous. I just got up and said, 'To hell with you guys!' I didn't even want to argue with them it was so ridiculous. What are we arguing about here? A measly thousand dollars. I said, 'Forget about it. I'm going home if that's the case.' And I walked out on them."

The experience summed up what the players were up against in that era. With all the owners sharing salary information through league president Clarence Campbell, they were able to put ceilings on what they would pay their players. So the men the history books refer to as the builders of the game were also the ones that shamelessly exploited the players who filled their arenas. What made it even worse in Toronto was the fact that the problems ran throughout the Maple Leafs organization. Everywhere you turned you'd find another snake in the grass.

A prime example of this was the man who eventually slithered his way to take over Smythe's operation. Recalling his exit from their contract meeting, Mahovlich spoke in a furious tone. "I remember leaving the hotel room in Peterborough. The three of them started arguing with me and I got pretty upset. So I got up to leave, I opened the door, and who was standing there listening to the whole conversation—Harold Ballard." Whether or not Ballard's exposed eavesdropping influenced his opinion of Mahovlich is debatable. Nevertheless, Ballard would play a key role in the infamous "Million Dollar Deal" that followed Mahovlich's walkout.

As soon as Frank left training camp, in what was an extremely bold move for those days, the news of his defiance hit the papers. The issue was magnified in the press and Frank wanted to resolve the matter quickly but without backing down. Playing hockey for the Maple Leafs had changed his feelings toward the game. Although he still loved hockey, for Mahovlich it had become a job and one that involved a great deal of stress. This reality made him even more determined to secure a good contract. The Leafs management ran a profitable business and worked their employees hard. If they wanted to retain the services of number 27, they were going to have to pay him fairly.

Back in Toronto, Pete Sr. and Cecilia encouraged their son to consider his options. The dishonesty Pete Sr. had experienced in dealing with the Maple Leafs made him concerned for his son. If Frank decided to retire from hockey, the family would be behind him with their full support. In the off-season he had worked at Montreal Trust in financial planning, so he had something to fall back on if worst came to worst.

The situation with Mahovlich was unprecedented in the Maple Leafs organization. While the better players routinely settled for whatever was offered, Mahovlich was willing to hold out, at any cost, for a salary commensurate with those of equal worth throughout the league. For all intents and purposes, Frank Mahovlich had gone on strike, and the newspapers had a field day with the story.

But although the press thought it was big news, from the team's perspective it was just business as usual. When a player asked for a raise, the response from management was like a knee-jerk reaction: no—and if the player didn't like it, tough luck. Eddie Shack related a personal experience that described the realization a player would come to after being denied a raise. "I was asking for a $500 raise. At the time I was making $7,500 and wanted $8,000 for the next year. They said, 'There's no way you're worth that much—go back to Sudbury and be a butcher. So, I went back to Sudbury. When I got home an old friend named Chester Wilcox told me, 'You can come back to Sudbury and be a butcher any time. Whatever they pay you, take it.' It was the opportunity to be someone."

With Mahovlich, the Maple Leafs management played the waiting game for a few days. While "on strike," Frank was spending time with his family, trying not to worry about the whole ordeal. Although he knew the walkout was the right course of action, he was uncertain what the repercussions would be. Eventually, the call came and Frank returned to Peterborough at Imlach's request.

After the aggravating experience of the first meeting, Frank was apprehensive about negotiating his contract with the same group. Then, unexpectedly, Mahovlich's confidence got a boost from a chance meeting with a hockey legend. "They called me back to training camp and our hotel was full, so I had to stay at the McGillis Hotel. And who else was staying there at the same time—Eddie Shore. He was there looking for players for his Springfield team. Imlach would give him four or five fellows that weren't ready for the NHL and Shore would develop them. One morning I'm having breakfast with Donny McGillis and Shore came down. I said, 'Mr. Shore, I'd like you to meet Don McGillis, the owner of the McGillis Hotel.' He said, 'I'm not Mr. Shore.' For a minute I thought, what the hell is this guy talking about. I played bridge with him at an exhibition game in Niagara Falls with Gerry Ehman. I knew it was definitely Mr. Shore, and then he said—'I'm Eddie to you.' Right then and there I felt great."

By the end of training camp nothing had been settled between Mahovlich and the team. Their main concern was to get him back to camp so he wouldn't lose his skating legs. As the beginning of the 1962–63 season approached, neither side was prepared to give in. There was a sense of urgency to resolve the matter, because the Leafs wanted Mahovlich in the line-up for the All-Star game. As Stanley Cup champions, the Toronto Maple Leafs were scheduled to play against the NHL All-Stars in the annual game that, in those days, kicked off the season. "I had to sign a contract or else I couldn't play. They used that to put pressure on me to sign. They were playing a game with me, which I didn't like. It was never like that with the Montreal Canadiens. Sam Pollock [the Canadiens' general manager] always had you sign before training camp started. You went to camp with a clear mind and got ready for the upcoming season."

The night before the All-Star game, there was a banquet held at the Royal York Hotel. Owners and management of the six teams, along with the players participating in the All-Star game, gathered for dinner and the NHL awards ceremony. By the end of the dinner, the stalemate between Mahovlich and the Leafs had still not been addressed. This didn't surprise Frank, and although he wanted to play the following day, he was prepared to miss the game. Later that evening, a series of events transpired that would lead to the biggest financial deal the world of professional sport had ever known.

Throughout the evening at the Royal York, the fact that the Maple Leafs had yet to sign their leading scorer was discussed among management and players alike. Interested in the Mahovlich situation was Chicago owner Jim Norris, and he wasn't the only one. The Blackhawks' All-Star winger Bobby Hull discussed acquiring Mahovlich with his boss the night before the All-Star game. "I said, 'Mr. Norris, get that big sucker—Toronto doesn't know how to use him. We'll put him at center and just let him go! When he comes to the bench we'll tell him he's all right—just stay out there and play." Hull's reference to a big player needing a lot of ice time was something Mahovlich understood and had always battled for. Hull also recognized that the Leafs' restrictive game hampered the Big M's wide-open style, which was not suited to the "up and down the same wing" policy of Imlach. In a pre-season game at training camp, Hull witnessed the Frank Mahovlich he remembered from Junior A. "That year we had an exhibition game in Peterborough against the Leafs. Frank played center ice and went through us like a dose of salts."

After the dinner at the Royal York, a small group consisting of management and team owners continued socializing late into the evening. In a conversation with the Maple Leafs brass, Jim Norris mentioned the fact that they had yet to sign Mahovlich. The discussion came around to what the Leafs' star forward was worth. When the question was put to Norris, he boldly offered one-million dollars to the Maple Leafs for their unsigned winger. Harold Ballard, who had just become a part-owner of the Maple Leafs, was immediately drawn to the proposition. Should Norris' bid be genuine, Ballard saw the opportunity to recoup a large portion of the money he had invested in the Leafs. The circumstances under which the offer was being made—at a social gathering where alcohol flowed freely—provided reason for doubt. Would Norris be so generous in the morning? But despite consuming several drinks, the Chicago owner had been dead serious. With a verbal confirmation from Ballard, Norris confidently pulled out his wallet and produced ten $100 bills as a deposit. An agreement was made that the Blackhawks' general manager, Tommy Ivan, would deliver a cheque for the total sum to Maple Leaf Gardens the following morning.

Peter Mahovlich Sr. was the first in the family to get the news. Sitting at the breakfast table he read the headlines in disbelief. Pete Mahovlich Jr. remembered his father's initial reaction to the outrageous offer. "In his usual no-nonsense way he said, 'Ah, it's bologna!' But it wasn't, and it almost happened." Having the family together in Toronto was very important to Peter Sr. The possibility of Frank being traded was not something he liked to think about. When he read more about the deal, it looked like his son was going to Chicago. The seven-digit figure was hard to believe but the rest of the story was convincing.

Peter looked at the situation rationally and thought, not only had his son been right to leave training camp, but he was more valuable than they had realized. If the Maple Leafs were going to make a staggering million dollars on the sale of Mahovlich, then he was worth a lot more than a mere $25,000 a year. Peter wanted to talk to his son before he signed anything. "My dad phoned me at 7 a.m. and I was still in bed. He said, 'You've been sold to Chicago. Don't sign right away—be careful. Apparently they bought you for a million dollars.' I got up, and the phone rings again. It was the Toronto Maple Leafs and they wanted me down at Maple Leaf Gardens, immediately. I'm wondering what the heck is going on."

Down at Maple Leaf Gardens, a throng of reporters and fans were trying to gain information on the status of Frank Mahovlich. Around 9 a.m., Mahovlich arrived just as bemused as the group crowding the Gardens lobby. Between the phone call requesting a meeting, and the sketchy details in the news, Frank was unsure whether he was still a Maple Leaf or the newest member of the Chicago Blackhawks. The first indication that he was staying in Toronto was the look Frank saw on Tommy Ivan's face when the Chicago general manager passed him on his way out. "I was walking into the office, and Tommy Ivan was walking out with a cheque. The papers wanted to take a picture but he was angry and walked right by."

The office on the second floor of Maple Leaf Gardens was a large area that housed several desks separated by partitions. People were coming and going in frenzy when Mahovlich walked in. Across the room Clancy and Imlach waited impatiently for the arrival of their holdout. "So they said, 'Come on in—here's what you wanted, sign here.' It was all cut and dried. They didn't want to discuss it. They just said, 'Sign here.' I didn't know I was worth a million dollars. I never had a chance to think about it, everything happened so fast. By the time I got to the rink at 9:00, they had me signed. And I thought I won the argument. Well, I didn't win really. When I found out what I was worth, I should have been getting $100,000 instead of $25,000."

The aftermath of the bungled deal with the Chicago Blackhawks was a wave of bad press—mainly directed at the Maple Leafs management. As far as Jim Norris was concerned, the Maple Leafs had reneged on their agreement. Norris made it clear to the press that he was a man of his word, unlike his counterparts in the Toronto organization. The cheque had been delivered the following morning as promised, with approval from the bank. When Ivan was turned away, reporters were left to speculate on what had happened. Did the Leafs really want to sell their leading scorer? Who stopped the deal? What were the motives of the two parties involved? The strongest critic of the "Million Dollar Deal" was sports columnist

Scott Young. In a piece for *The Globe and Mail* (October 12, 1962), Young labeled the event a lame joke turned poker game in which Jim Norris called Toronto's bluff.

As it turned out, the two Leafs directors (Harold Ballard and Jack Amell) who had agreed to Norris' offer were not in any position to do so. When pressed on the issue the Maple Leafs brass had had to fold their hand. "After that," Mahovlich noted, "Ballard didn't like me, because he was embarrassed by the whole situation. He didn't want to back off." The order to renege had come from Conn Smythe, whose direction still carried weight although he had sold his interest in the Maple Leafs (to John Bassett and Harold Ballard). Leafs scout Bob Davidson was out of town when he heard about the deal. When he returned, Smythe expressed his displeasure with Ballard to Davidson who recalled his disbelief over the course of events. "I was working out in the prairies driving to the rinks when it came over the radio. I couldn't believe it. I said, 'They must be crazy!' When I got back to Toronto, Connie Smythe told me that he canceled the deal, and that was that. Harold Ballard didn't know a hell of a lot about hockey. He just thought it was a great thing to be offered a million dollars."

The relationship between Mahovlich and the Toronto Maple Leafs went downhill from that point on. Although he got the raise he was looking for, the backlash would cost him dearly. By making the million-dollar offer, Norris had helped Mahovlich to establish his worth, but at the same time the affair created resentment toward the star winger. Mahovlich had challenged management and come out on top, which was not an example the Leafs wanted set for the rest of their players. And Mahovlich soon found out just how short and bittersweet the taste of victory could be. Once signed to a contract, management could do whatever they wanted with a player. Frank's description of the predicament conveyed just how exasperated he was. "I tried to make money and it hurt me. They'd control my play and say, 'We can't let him score too many goals, or he'll ask for more money.' They tried to keep everybody down. At least, they kept me down. Instead of going to Chicago, I ended up playing for a team that didn't even want me—and yet wouldn't trade me. I would have felt better in Chicago where they would have let me play."

The 1962–63 season was statistically a great year for the Maple Leafs. The team finished in first place overall and won its second consecutive Stanley Cup by beating the Canadiens and the Red Wings, both in five games. Since he had dominated the sports pages leading up to the season, the expectations of Mahovlich reached new heights. Once again Mahovlich responded. For the third year in a row he led the team in scoring, bettering the previous season's totals with 36 goals and 37 assists. Despite his productivity through the season, the playoffs were a bit of a disappointment because he scored only two points. It was a credit to the team that without a major contribution from its leading scorer, the team could whip the Habs four games to one and do the same to Detroit. "When I look back at our team, one guy would lead one night, and another guy would pick up the flag and go the other night. We had five or six great leaders, Red Kelly, Allan Stanley, and so on. But some nights our leaders were different people, and that's what makes a great team."

In hindsight Mahovlich could see that his diminished play at the end of the year was a result of the mental and physical exhaustion he had undergone at the hands of Punch Imlach. Rather than keep his players energized for games, Imlach worked them harder and harder at practice as the year went on. While Frank and others became physically drained, Imlach showed everyone who was boss. In recalling Imlach's approach, the veteran Red Kelly suggested that some players needed to be worked hard, but that wasn't necessarily good for the entire team. "You never agreed 100 percent with any coach you had. Punch did things for, let's say, one individual who wouldn't stay in the best of shape, but it wasn't good for the guys that took care of themselves. We'd all have to suffer because of one guy."

The exhaustive drilling was particularly frustrating for Mahovlich, who was expected to lead the team in scoring. It was a game Imlach played, and in doing so, he caused players who once admired him to hate him. After the 1962–63 season, Mahovlich realized that Imlach was no longer someone he could reason with. "From 1962 on, I had trouble with management. I never really felt comfortable with the team after 1962. It was a real drag on me. My relationship with Imlach had suffered and it never got repaired."

During the years of the Maple Leafs' success in the sixties, Mahovlich's differences with Imlach were well known, but he wasn't the only player suffering such conflicts. Another exceptional talent on the Maple Leafs who didn't march to the beat of Imlach's drum was Carl Brewer. Frank recounted the strengths of his friend and his unique approach to dealing with a tough situation. "Carl was a great skater—ability personified. He could stand still and look great. If anything, he was hindered by some of his antics.

"One time we had an exhibition game in Kitchener. Carl wasn't going to make the trip because he had an injury. Just as we were pulling out from Maple Leaf Gardens, he jumped in front of the team bus hoisting a banner that read 'GO LEAFS GO!'" Brewer used his pranks as a release for the pressure he felt. Like Mahovlich, he couldn't accept the abuse he was subjected to daily. Imlach used Brewer, one of the better skaters on the team, as a benchmark for skating drills. If Carl didn't win a race, the team would continue skating until he did. Then there was the higher standard that came with the arrival of the "China Wall," Johnny Bower.

With only six teams in the NHL, it was difficult for a goalie to secure one of the dozen spots. This left Johnny Bower confined to the minor leagues throughout his twenties and early thirties. When he finally made the NHL as a permanent fixture, he was hungry—a situation that Carl Brewer recalled with some regret. "The greatest competitor I ever saw was Johnny Bower. Johnny was 34 years of age when he made it to the team, and he was desperate, so he would do anything. He had a work ethic that I've never seen in any other human being. Unfortunately, he became the gauge by which Imlach worked the whole team. And it was insane. The games, for me, were a chance to relax and get ready for the next week of practices because that was the only time you could have a letdown. If I was good, and if I was talented, I never had a chance to use it because I never performed in the games—I was too tired."

If Johnny Bower caused hardship for his teammates at practice, the players got their revenge when the pucks came out. Without a face mask, Bower stood his ground with the same intensity that he brought to a game. Mahovlich enjoyed the competitor in Bower and used it to his advantage. Frank felt that if he could score on Johnny during practice, he'd do just fine against the opposition come game time. "When I went in and scored on him, and then teased him— gosh he'd get mad," Mahovlich laughs. "I'd have a hell of a time trying to score again."

After doing two-on-ones, one-on-ones, and breakaways, management drew the line on working Bower. If a player wanted to practice his shot, a board with holes would be set up in front of the net. The other option the Maple Leafs found effective was to hire a practice goalie. One brave soul that accepted the job stood out in Mahovlich's mind. "George Armstrong nicknamed him 'Sockeye' because he smelt like fish from working in a fish plant all day. He was our practice goalie at one time. You could drive the puck at this guy and he would swallow everything! He was so good, Chicago hired him so Hull and Mikita could shoot at him. This guy had more nerve than Dick Tracy. He'd challenge anybody."

In the team hours outside of the rink, after practice or on the road, dealing with Imlach was just as much of a chore for Frank. If the team was dining together at a restaurant, Mahovlich and Imlach felt so uncomfortable that they'd make sure they were sitting at opposite ends of the restaurant. It was a difficult way to get along but Mahovlich had no choice. Veteran players seemed to handle the ill-mannered coach with greater ease. Carl Brewer envied the tact of those older players who didn't let Imlach get to them. "They could accept it because they'd been through a lot of crap. Imlach wasn't a threat to them. They'd just look at him and have another beer."

Mahovlich didn't talk much about the Leafs coach to his family. Most of what bothered him he kept to himself. At home, Marie knew her husband was upset but didn't want to bring it up at the risk of making matters worse. She too had a growing dislike for Imlach. Intentional mispronunciation of Frank's last name (Ma-hal-o-vich) was one of many petty insults that Imlach typically used to get his goat. And he didn't restrict his offensive behavior to the players. Marie became good friends with Marilyn Brewer and recalled an experience Marilyn had with Punch. "Marilyn Brewer gave something to Imlach to give to Carl, after a game. It was something he had forgotten at home—let's say it was his shaving kit. Normally, she wouldn't have bothered but it was something he needed. Imlach went to Carl and said, 'Some girl gave me this, to give to you.' Though he was aware that Imlach knew damn well who it was, Carl protested, 'That wasn't some girl, that was my wife!' But Imlach enjoyed putting people down. It was like that all the time."

In the summer of 1963 Marie and Frank had their first child, Michael Francis. While expecting Michael, Marie had been searching for a house the couple could raise a family in. A suitable home was available in the North Toronto neighborhood at 211 Strathallan Wood. The Mahovlichs moved in that summer and worked on furnishing and decorating their new home. Life had changed considerably for the couple over the past three years. With the new addition to the family and the move to Strathallan Wood, Marie and Frank's personal life was moving in the direction they hoped for.

Unfortunately, the professional side of life was on a different course. Frank had learned that the toughest part of playing hockey had little to do with the game itself. From a simple request for a hockey stick (Mahovlich couldn't use Northland sticks because the Leafs had a deal with another company) to recuperating from an injury, his battles with management were endless.

"We were playing a game in Detroit and Bob Baun hit Bruce MacGregor. MacGregor's skate caught me in the ribs and the heel of the blade went right through my rib cage. I was spitting blood and couldn't breathe. After being X-rayed I was home for a day just trying to catch my breath, and the phone rings. They wanted me to come down, 'just to skate,' so I wouldn't lose my skating legs. They wouldn't leave me alone. Not even for a day. They had to keep me under their thumb—it was unbelievable."

Marie's day-to-day life was a combination of mothering and hockey. Unexpectedly, her outside interests seemed to be consumed by the demands of the hockey lifestyle—albeit with some compensations. The benefits included the pleasure of watching Frank play hockey, summer vacation, and the opportunity to travel, which suited Marie just fine. Next to art, travel was her greatest passion. The only difficult adjustment in Marie's life was learning to cope with the occupational hazards that preyed on Frank. She now shared the burdens her husband brought home, whether they were subjects of conversation or not. Perhaps it would have been different if Frank had felt more comfortable in the spotlight, but such was not the case. In their partnership, Marie would help Frank weather the storm that was on the horizon.

The team that won back-to-back Stanley Cups would welcome several new players during the 1963–64 season. This was a result of players expressing their discontent with the Toronto organization. Too valuable to let go, Mahovlich watched while others were fortunate enough to be traded. "As soon as you started to complain—well, then you'd be gone. And that's what happened. Duff left us, which was a sad point for me because Dick and I joined the team from St. Mike's and were pretty good buddies. He phoned me the morning of the trade, but he was having a tough time with the team the same as I was. It turned out best for Dick. New York traded him to Montreal and he did very well there." The deal saw Dick Duff and Bob Nevin leave Toronto in exchange for Don McKenney and Andy Bathgate of the New York Rangers. As it turned out, Andy Bathgate became a great asset to the Leafs in February of 1964. His leadership and scoring prowess helped the Leafs win their third consecutive Stanley Cup. Assigned to play with Mahovlich and Kelly, Bathgate was a perfect fit.

Like others had done the previous year, Mahovlich took up the flag in the 1964 playoffs and led the team in post-season points with four goals and eleven assists. Dave Keon was the leader in goals, netting seven with his outstanding two-way play. In the first round the Canadiens had stretched the Maple Leafs to seven games in a grueling series. Bruised and battered, several Leafs played through injuries against Detroit in the Stanley Cup final. Once again, they would be pushed to the limit, robbing the Red Wings who at one point were a goal away from winning the Cup. It was Bob Baun's historic overtime goal (while playing with a fractured fibula) in game six that allowed the Leafs to win the deciding game in Toronto, 4-0.

The success of the Maple Leafs was remarkable considering the general decline in team morale. When players continued to voice their grievances with Imlach, again bags started packing. Bathgate, the key player in the trade with New York, was moved to Detroit in 1965. Mahovlich remembered the impetus behind the Bathgate trade. "He wasn't too happy with the way Imlach ran things either. I think he could see it right away and started to complain."

Mahovlich had resigned himself to silence, but Imlach was well aware that Mahovlich disapproved of his manner and methods, and would fine Mahovlich whenever possible. Each fine was preceded by a letter of explanation. Imlach was the judge and jury, and when he said a player was guilty of indifferent play, the player was guilty. Frank would read the offense and see the $100 fine deducted from his next paycheque. "Imlach would put all the money from the players' fines in a pot and use it for a party at the end of the year. So Eddie Shack always kids me about the team parties I threw at the end of the season—paid for with my fines."

Chapter Five

Day 4—Evening

Some of the teams that the Greatest Hockey Legends play are less competitive than others. That was glaringly the case tonight in Grand Prairie. After starting the game on defense I was moved up to forward on a line with Tiger Williams and Morris Lukowich. While some of the more senior players wisely pace themselves on a night when the competition allows, Tiger would insist that the team should score as many goals as we can for the fans. Tiger and Morris, who incidentally have forgotten their tussle, ran up the score and I was grateful to be part of the fun. In two periods our line got no less than 10 goals including my first hat trick of the tour. Not that a hat trick is something to boast about in a 27-6 victory; however, this whole adventure is the hockey equivalent to "Fantasy Island," so I'll say that my contribution was crucial to the win.

Day 5—Morning

This morning we flew to Prince George in a plane that holds the team and not much else. Sitting beside Dad, I commented on the fact that I hadn't been on many flights where I could do a head count without leaving my seat. He confessed that when he joined the NHL it took a while for him to fully adjust to air travel. Immersing himself in a good book was the trick. Our flight was brief and the smell of Prince George's pulp and paper industry greeted us as we disembarked. Due to the intimate venue the team will play two games in Prince George today.

Day 5—Evening

Prior to our double-header this afternoon, Dad and I walked the streets of Prince George and happened by a sports collectibles shop. To his delight Dad found an old hockey card of Pat Hannigan, his buddy from Timmins, which he purchased for its sentimental value. We then surveyed the town for a good lunch spot and got a tip that led us to an all-you-can-eat smorgasbord whose prime rib was tremendous. Just as Dad and I had started in on an equally impressive rice pudding for dessert, the local lunch trade rolled in. At our insistence, Wilf Paiement, who had joined us, got up from the table to procure a rice pudding for himself. Rather than wait in the lengthy queue, Wilf pardoned himself midway through the line and grabbed a cup of pudding. One of the regulars called from the back of the line, "Hey, watch this guy, he's trying to butt in." I guess they're serious about their food in Prince George. Dad and I had a chuckle over that and made our way to the rink.

During the pre-game warm-up, Eddie Shack always does a splendid job of getting a rise out of the crowd. He'll skate around taking the odd slapshot, calling to the fans, "Are you ready to see some old-time hockey" and so on. Part of the act is Eddie's getup, which includes his referee's uniform, the trademark cowboy hat, skates with spurs on them, and a pair of beautiful buckskin snowmobile gloves that have decorative beadwork and tassels.

Once the game is under way, Eddie performs his officiating duties and leaves his stick and gloves on the bench. After the first period of our second game, the team had returned to our dressing room when Eddie realized that his treasured hand-crafted gloves were missing. After he had asked a couple of players if they'd seen them, someone suggested that they were likely underneath the bench. Satisfied with that probability, Shack pulled up a seat and relaxed with the team.

When the second period was over and he had made a thorough search, Shack still couldn't find his gloves and began to panic. Going around the room, Eddie interrogated every player, including Dad, about his prized gloves. I looked at Dad, wondering if this was as serious an issue as it appeared to be.

Then Bobby Hull, who acts as team coach during the game and spends intermissions signing autographs, came in. He looked surprised by the state Shack was in. After Eddie had explained the situation and mentioned that he had left his gloves on the back of the bench, Hull reported that he had noticed three young fellows sitting behind the bench who seemed to be admiring the gloves, and added, "Eddie, I wouldn't trust those guys as far as I could throw 'em!" Well, that was all Shack needed to hear, and with Hull on his heels, he stormed out the dressing room door. Instantly the team fell silent at the thought of the trouble that might ensue. Then to our surprise, before the dressing room door had fully closed, Bobby leapt back into the room, leaving the riled Eddie Shack running to the stands in his skates. With a wicked smile and eyebrows raised, Hull burst out, "*I've got the gloves!*"

Day 6—Afternoon

Today Eddie Shack looked entirely content on the bus with his gloves sitting next to him. A seasoned traveler, Eddie complements his coach seat with an inflatable headrest that he secures around his neck for optimum comfort. At his feet rests a large box of walnuts he has been sharing with the team. With his pocketknife Eddie opens the walnuts and guts the shells with such precision that the walnuts remain intact. Dad loves walnuts and Eddie generously offers him a handful. A few minutes later, Eddie had an equal portion of the shelled nuts for me. Once again I had that feeling of being welcome, and I thanked Eddie kindly. It's a wonderful thing when the simplest gesture can make your day. I looked behind at Dad. In turn Dad nodded to me with a smile that acknowledged Eddie's random act of kindness. Guy Lafleur is another walnut fan and he made his way down the isle from his front seat. "Hey Eddie, walnuts?"

Shack offered the box to Guy, who would be his most frequent customer, and then surrendered his pocketknife.

With Eddie free from walnut duty, I engaged him in a conversation about the old days and the pressure Dad was under as a Leaf. As it was an unpleasant time for Dad and many others, it came as no surprise to me that Shack was somewhat reluctant to discuss the matter. With a mild feeling of guilt I persisted, and Eddie mustered a concise insight into his team-mate and the predicament that ultimately led to his leave of absence. "One of us should have gotten hold of him and said look Frank, you don't have to score fifty goals. Score twenty goals and have some fun. Enjoy yourself and forget the bullshit. For him to have all that dedication. So, he did what he had to do, and I'm fooling around. And he is in the Hockey Hall of Fame and I'm not."

The last three and a half years Mahovlich spent as a Maple Leaf were the most trying years of his life. When he scored 48 goals in the 1960–61 season, Frank created an expectation of himself for all the fans and critics in Toronto. People wanted brilliant results every time he touched the puck. Their rationale was, if Mahovlich could skate through a team once, why couldn't he do it all the time? The fans came to demand that, and nothing less. Unfortunately for Frank, he made it look easy with a natural style that may have appeared effortless, but required the same 110 percent the rest of the players were giving. The tragedy in this was that Mahovlich ended up being the object of public scorn. A pattern developed as early as 1962 that whenever Mahovlich stepped on the ice he was greeted with boos. Imagine going to work and performing as well or better than everyone else in your office and fifteen thousand bosses tell you that you're no good—all day, every day. After games in which Frank was one of the three stars he was booed. On nights that he contributed four and five points, consistently he was subject to rejection. Even when he was introduced at the Stanley Cup parade there was evidence of ill will.

It's hard to fathom how a person could tolerate abuse on that scale, day in and day out, for so long. Carl Brewer remembered the long nights in Maple Leaf Gardens that haunted his friend. "It was hard on Frank, and we knew it. We were glad it wasn't us, but it was hard on Frank. If you think about it, it was a credit to his greatness because the fans wouldn't accept anything less from Frank than what they perceived to be great."

Although many fans in Toronto appreciated Mahovlich, the praise was difficult to hear over his detractors. What made Frank's situation intolerable was the person who became his greatest critic, Punch Imlach. When Frank had a good game, Imlach took the opportunity to insult "Ma-hal-o-vich" by drawing attention to a previous night with less impressive results. On one occasion he insisted Mahovlich continue to practice on his own while offering the rest of the team the afternoon off.

Everyone has a breaking point and eventually Mahovlich arrived at his. In the second week of November 1964, Frank was admitted to Toronto General Hospital, feeling the effects of complete exhaustion.

The physician assigned to Mahovlich, Dr. Allen Walters, diagnosed the worn-out Leaf as suffering from acute depression. Frank remained in the hospital, guarded by tight security at the request of the Maple Leafs management. The secrecy the Leafs brass deemed necessary ultimately drew more attention to the issue—a course of action that frustrated Marie. "The Maple Leafs were devoid of any public relations ability. They could have just issued a statement, and that would have settled things. Of course, when the reporters weren't given any information at all, they just speculated. I can remember there was a radio broadcaster on CKEY, by the name of Joe Morgan. He gave an editorial piece—he seemed to think that Frank had cancer and was about to die. The Leafs let all these rumors swell up. I remember [radio broadcaster] Gordon Sinclair saying, 'No matter what he has, leave the fellow alone—he's a fine person, and he gave us wonderful hockey,' and so on. But the Maple Leafs had no ability to handle things nicely."

At the hospital there were strict orders that no visitors were allowed, with the exception of Marie. In her recollections of that time, Marie cringed at the memory of reporters being so desperate to get the story on Frank that they resorted to going after the wives of other players. "An interviewer from the CBC got hold of Roz Pulford and tried to ask her what Frank was like, or if she could see any signs of anything being wrong. She was very cautious with her answers. When the interview ended, the man from the CBC said, 'We didn't get what we wanted from you.'"

With Mahovlich absent from the Leafs' line-up, the Toronto fans who did care began to show their concern. In a matter of days, Maple Leaf Gardens was inundated with letters for him. If the Big M's fans were silent before, they certainly stepped forward when it was needed the most. Marie was so thankful that she wanted to reply to every single letter. "There was a flood of mail for Frank care of Maple Leaf Gardens, so I went down there and just took it with me. I wanted to personally answer all of it. Harold Ballard wasn't too keen on that because he saw a lot of postage being involved—but I insisted on it. One of the cards was from Bobby Rousseau, who played for the Montreal Canadiens. Now here is a player who played against Frank all the time, and thought so highly of him that he bothered to write a get-well card."

When Frank started to feel better, he began skating at Maple Leaf Gardens to get back into game shape. Off the ice, Dr. Walters worked on getting Frank mentally fit by focusing on things other than hockey. The all-consuming lifestyle was too much for Frank, who would have to learn to relax if he wanted to go on playing. Although he wasn't the only Leaf to be put through Imlach's wringer, he was the only one expected to score 50 goals in the process.

A month off was enough rest for Mahovlich to rejoin the team. When number 27 stepped on the ice for the first time, the crowd at Maple Leaf Gardens erupted in a standing ovation. It was a welcome gesture from the fans who were looking forward to the Big M's return. That season had been a difficult year, not only for Mahovlich but for the Maple Leafs as a whole. The team finished in fourth place and, for the first time in three years, missed the Stanley Cup finals. Even though Frank was absent for a month, he still managed to lead the Leafs in scoring with 23 goals and 28 assists. For the team to be in the running for the Stanley Cup, Mahovlich would have to improve on those numbers the following year.

At the conclusion of the playoffs, Dr. Walters ordered Mahovlich to forget about hockey for a while. Frank and Marie discussed what they might do and agreed that a holiday was in order.

A few years earlier, Marie had visited Europe and she had wanted to return some day with Frank. Up until that time, the idea was never brought up because she thought the Leafs would frown on a long European vacation—for fear Mahovlich would get soft on pastries. When Dr. Walters recommended that such a trip would be great for Frank, Marie was delighted. "We went on one bang-up trip of Europe in June of 1965 for two and a half months. Dr. Walters encouraged us to go—so it was all right with Frank. We sailed from New York City on the *S. S. France*. Frank met all kinds of people throughout Europe, and really came out of his shell. When he returned people said, 'Boy, I've never seen Frank talk so much in all the time I've known him.' The trip really made a big change in him. It was the most wonderful thing that could have happened."

Rejuvenated from the summer, Mahovlich met the press and spoke about his vacation and the upcoming season. All reports were optimistic about Frank's healthy return, and his desire to get back on the ice. His spirits were high and for the time being Imlach had eased off. Mahovlich came back strong in the 1965–66 season and led the team with 32 goals, co-leading in total points with Bob Pulford, who tallied 28 goals and 28 assists.

The improvement in Frank's life was significant, but it didn't change the atmosphere on the team. Despite his return to form, the Maple Leafs were plagued by dissension as several team members were fed up with Imlach. Mahovlich remembered thriving on the workouts in the early part of the year, but eventually it had a negative effect. "When you are younger, you have more zip and more energy. So, Imlach worked me and it was good. The bit was in my mouth and I liked the work. But after thirty-five or forty games, if you're not in shape, you shouldn't be playing hockey. So, he continued that right through the season. Well, you couldn't practice like that every day and still put up with it. If the practice was creative, I didn't mind. But Imlach would take a chair and sit in the middle of the rink, and make us skate around the ice for an hour. It was like a punishment. And he'd just sit there watching us go around and around and around. As a result, the morale on the team was terrible. But because he won the Stanley Cup, the newspapers thought he was doing the right thing. It was a tough situation to live with."

The spring of 1966 saw the Maple Leafs make an early exit from the playoffs. They had become an old team and were beaten handily by the Montreal Canadiens in four games. With time working against them, the future for the team was questionable at best. Players were unhappy with management, Imlach had lost all favor, and any new blood that joined the team was immediately exposed to the negative atmosphere. The Leafs had seen better days. Mahovlich knew it and started counting the ones that remained on his contract. He had other things to consider now, most importantly his family and their future. Marie was expecting their second child while Frank pondered a second career. Although several of his teammates were more than five years older, Mahovlich felt that it might be time to hang up the blades. "I just felt that I didn't want to play on that team anymore. I didn't want to go through what I went through the previous year. Around 1966 I decided that I'd quit playing hockey. A friend of mine, Joe Burns, who was a neighbor, talked about getting into business, so we bought a travel agency—but the Leafs didn't want me to quit."

Nancy Anne Mahovlich was born on July 29, 1966. The birth of Marie and Frank's daughter was a fitting prelude to what became a roller-coaster year for Mahovlich and the Maple Leafs. After some deliberation, Frank's plan to retire from hockey was postponed.

This was due in part to a very persuasive effort on behalf of the Leafs. A manager was hired to run the travel agency and Mahovlich went back to business as usual at Maple Leaf Gardens.

After two disappointing seasons Imlach was feeling the heat. As was indicated by that year's training camp, Punch planned to add some new life to the aging Maple Leafs roster. Brian Conacher, who had just won the Calder Cup with the Rochester Americans, was one of the rookies who hoped to crack the Maple Leafs line-up. "I came to the Leaf camp in the fall of 1966. Brit Selby had been the rookie of the year the year before, and he came to camp about twelve pounds overweight—a very competitive training camp. The Leafs hadn't won the Cup for a couple of years and for the first time Punch was looking at bringing some younger players onto the team. There was Mike Walton, myself, Peter Stemkowski, Brit Selby, Larry Jeffrey, Jimmy Pappin—about a half a dozen of us trying to be the younger guys to make the team. I remember George Armstrong saying, 'If you can survive the training camp, the season will be easy,' because the training camps were really tough. I mean, Imlach really pushed the players hard. Eventually, I made the team that year and Brit Selby didn't."

The 1966–67 Toronto Maple Leafs featured several new additions, but the core of the team was intact. Surviving from the 1962 Stanley Cup team were Armstrong, Baun, Bower, Horton, Kelly, Keon, Mahovlich, Pulford, Shack, and Stanley. The average age of this group was 35, hardly a group of spring chickens. Eight of the Leafs were 37 or older (including Terry Sawchuk—38, and Marcel Pronovost—37), and three were in their forties (Bower—43, Kelly—40, and Stanley—41). The number of seasoned veterans on this team earned them their legendary status as the "Over the Hill Gang."

As the season got under way, Mahovlich wondered if he had made a mistake. The circumstances that had driven him to complete exhaustion persisted, and there was no indication of change in the near future. Carl Brewer, who went through much of what Mahovlich dealt with, recalled being a Maple Leaf during the Imlach years: "They'd use ploys and threats like, 'Take what we give you or go to the minors.' If you were good they would let you go, and if you continued to hold out, they would give you what you were asking for—which was never a great deal. In the process you would become an emotional wreck. And then they'd demand even more from you because you got a raise. For Christ's sake, I was nineteen years old and Imlach was beating up on me." Prior to Mahovlich's leave of absence, Brewer had had no idea that anyone else felt as he did. "I wasn't aware of Frank's problems other than he hated Imlach. But I knew that every guy on the team hated Imlach. Well, Frank had to take a break from it all, as you know. I also needed a break. The only difference was, they wouldn't let me have it.'

A combination of factors confirmed that Mahovlich was no longer suited to the Maple Leafs. Aside from the personal conflicts with the Leaf management, Frank made little progress in Imlach's defensive game. The 1966–67 season exemplified the Maple Leafs' defensive approach, which relied on a bare minimum of offense. Stan Mikita, of the Chicago Blackhawks, finished the season as the league's leading scorer with 97 points (35 goals, 62 assists). In contrast, the Leafs' leading scorer, Dave Keon, amassed 52 points (19 goals, 33 assists), barely over half of Mikita's total. Hockey Hall of Fame member and retired N H L referee Red Storey spoke on Imlach's strategy with the Maple Leafs: "Punch took the material he had and used it to the best advantage. If you have a racehorse, you don't ask him to haul a load of coal. Well, the Leafs had a lot of guys that hauled coal. They had some guys who put the puck in the net, but basically their game was defense. I think an injustice came to Frank by being with the Leafs. They played a defensive style of hockey and Frank was an offensive hockey player. If he'd have played his entire career with Jean Beliveau, which would have been a possibility, he would have approached one thousand goals."

In January and February of 1967 the entire Maple Leafs team was in a rut. The players struggled to win a game, and after every defeat Imlach worked them harder than before. When they lost an away game, they would have to go straight to Maple Leaf Gardens for a practice, having spent all night traveling home. The low point of the season came when the Leafs lost their tenth consecutive game. Fittingly, if not ironically, the tables had turned and the pressure was now on the coach. In February of 1967, Imlach himself succumbed to what was reported to be exhaustion.

Brian Conacher remembered how the losing streak affected Punch, and consequently the whole team. "Punch got sick, I think he had an angina attack [he was suffering from a duodenal ulcer at that time], and ended up in the hospital. Because we were losing, Punch wasn't getting in a better mood and I'm quite sure our performance affected his condition. I mean, he was pulling out the remaining hair that he had—and the practices got more and more oppressive. We weren't losing games because we weren't conditioned. We were losing games because we had practiced too hard, quite honestly. When Punch was gone, so was the oppressiveness. Clancy came along and that was like a breath of fresh air. All of a sudden the attitude became more positive and we played our way out of the slump."

With King Clancy filling in as interim coach, the roller-coaster ride took a turn for the better. Over the next ten games in the Leafs' schedule the team played without the burden of Imlach's regimen. The difference it made in the team's spirit and performance was phenomenal. Clancy just let the boys play hockey. Mahovlich remembered Clancy's stint as coach with a certain fondness. "A team is like a musical instrument. You tune it up, and that's as good as it gets. If you tighten it, it will break. And that's what happened to us—we broke. So, in comes Clancy and he was the opposite to Imlach. After losing ten, we won ten in a row. He just let the reins go. Everybody did what came naturally."

Eddie Shack concurred with his teammates. "When Clancy took over for ten games, we won them all! When you're on the ice it's all yours. You can do whatever you want. It was absolutely fantastic— and he didn't work the crap out of you."

Near the end of the season, after Clancy had returned to his regular duties, Mahovlich suffered a charley horse and took a day's rest.

He needed to clear his mind of all things related to the pressures of hockey and went on a weekend excursion with Marie, Eddie Shack, and Eddie's wife, Norma. The two couples headed to Port McNichol to relax for the day.

On the way to Port McNichol, the group stopped at a gas station to fill up and stretch their legs. The friendly attendant happened to own a snowmobile that was parked at the side of the garage in plain view. Before he knew what was going on, Shack had fired up the snowmobile while Mahovlich jumped on the back. The two sped off with the sled's owner chasing them on foot. After a short tour, Frank and Eddie returned with the snowmobile in one piece. The gas-jockey was a good sport, and the two pranksters kindly thanked him with a tip before they went on their way. Later that evening, the couples enjoyed an authentic sleigh ride with a horse and cutter that Frank had arranged for with a friend. Just getting away for the day made Mahovlich realize what was missing in his life. "When I got that one day off and went out with Eddie Shack, having a good time, I came back like a new person—and I started to play much better. It was something I never did enough of in Toronto, to go out and have a good time."

The Maple Leafs managed to finish the season in third place despite the return of Imlach. However, heading into the playoffs, there was still considerable discontent among the players. Imlach credited the Leafs' ten-game winning streak to the hard work he had made them do before his leave. The situation was like an inside joke between the Leaf players—except no one was laughing. Of the team leaders, Mahovlich felt that Allan Stanley had the best perspective to offer the tortured bunch. "We'd get together to have a meeting, and guys would be peeved off at the way management was. Stanley would say, 'Let's win in spite of them!' He was with four or five teams, and he never thought it was any better with those clubs. So his attitude was, you come by this way just once. You might as well win it because, if it goes by the boards, you'll never win it again—which is true. There's only one year that is 1967—did you win it or not? Well, we won it. And we went through a lot of hardships and it was a bugger, but we did it. If Imlach takes the credit, who cares? My name is there by 1967, and that was Allan Stanley's attitude. Let's win in spite of him."

Allan Stanley's sound advice was taken to heart by the entire team, and so the 1966–67 Toronto Maple Leafs entered the playoffs with a will to win. Aside from the desire to overcome their plight with Imlach, many veterans felt that it might be their last kick at the can, so they had better make it a good one.

The Maple Leafs were slated to play the Chicago Blackhawks in the first round and were heavy underdogs by all accounts. It was the textbook version of having nothing to lose and everything to gain. The Blackhawks, who had finished the season in first place, were an offensive powerhouse. However, this meant nothing to the Leafs now that it was playoff time. Throughout the season the Maple Leafs played a disciplined tight-checking game that was boring to watch, but it was playoff hockey. If the Leafs could shut down Bobby Hull and Stan Mikita, they felt they could outlast Chicago in a seven-game series. Mahovlich was quick to point out that this was made possible due to a pair of veterans named Johnny Bower and Terry Sawchuk. "When you looked at our team, it wasn't really an All-Star team. I mean, who did we have? A bunch of guys that were near forty years old. But we had these two goalies."

At the beginning of the season Brian Conacher roomed with Sawchuk at training camp. Come playoffs he could hardly recognize his roommate from training camp. "A nervous wreck. By the end of the hockey season, Terry Sawchuk looked like he'd been through the wars. He was all skin and bones. He had a bad arm, a scar in the middle of his back for eight inches. But when he was on, you couldn't get a pea past him. And he hated practicing."

Mahovlich remembered how Sawchuk used to leave his net at practice when faced with the Big M's shot. "We would do a lot of shooting and you'd skate the length of the ice and let your shot go. Well, some of my shots were pretty wicked. But this is what we were forced to do, to shoot the puck hard, because Imlach played the practices like he wanted you to play in a game. Sawchuk would see me coming and leave his net and go to the corner. And Imlach would get madder than hell. So one day I let a shot go and it hit Sawchuk on his way to the corner." Mahovlich laughs. "Well, he got so mad that he came after me with his goalie stick. I had to skate like hell to get away from him."

After years of punishment from pucks, Sawchuk's behavior in practice was more than understandable. This, however, was no reflection on how he performed come game time. On March 4, 1967 Terry Sawchuk recorded his 100th shut-out when Toronto blanked Chicago 3-0. Although no record in hockey is unbreakable, Sawchuk's 103 career shut-outs is as close as they come.

In the 1967 playoffs, Mahovlich felt that the Maple Leafs had the two finest goalies in the game. "Terry Sawchuk was a great goalie. He was under a lot of strain, like goalies are, but as far as goaltending he was the best. He would come up with the big save, the save that would break the other team's back. He'd stop Bobby Hull and once he made that save, they were beat, and they knew they were beat. Because if they didn't score that time, they ain't gonna score, and that was it. He'd shut the door on them. Now Johnny Bower had a different personality from Sawchuk. He had a George Armstrong kind of personality. They were two of a kind. They worked their butts off and you knew they were going to be there every night. That was Johnny Bower—solid. He came to us when he was thirty-four years old and he was leading the American League in shut-outs with forty-something. The record still stands today. Between him and Sawchuk, if you counted their shut-outs and put them together, there aren't two goalies that can match it. And we had these two goalies in 1967—and that was a big part of why we won."

The series that was supposed to be a cakewalk for Chicago started out with a decisive 5-2 Blackhawks victory. Mahovlich had scored the only goal for the Leafs until Jimmy Pappin added another with only seconds to go in the game. The next two games belonged to Toronto, or you might say, they belonged to Terry Sawchuk. In back-to-back 3-1 victories, the Maple Leafs netminder was outstanding. Offensive help came from the veteran Leaf captain, George Armstrong, who scored his first goal of the series in game two, while Mahovlich got his second marker in game three.

The bigger story however was the contribution of the younger players who began to complement the veterans. Mahovlich felt the balance of youth and experience was another key ingredient to their success. "We had Ron Ellis, Mike Walton, Brian Conacher, Jim Pappin, Peter Stemkowski—they all played a prominent role in 1967, winning the Cup." Pappin and Stemkowski were the hot hands against Chicago and the Leafs headed into game six leading the series 3-2.

Once again it was the contribution of a rookie that made the difference in the deciding game. When Armstrong got hurt in game two, Conacher was moved up to play the right side with Kelly and Mahovlich. He was a left-handed shot but enjoyed playing the off wing—only now he had the responsibility of containing Bobby Hull. "In that series I was covering Bobby Hull and I just followed him all over the rink. I ended up getting two goals in the sixth game, but if it had of been somebody else covering Bobby Hull they would have got the two goals. It was just that they kept trying to get the puck to him and I was there." Conacher was awarded the first star for scoring two goals and the series winner. With the 3-1 victory in game six, the aging Toronto Maple Leafs advanced to the Stanley Cup final to face the Montreal Canadiens.

The 1967 Stanley Cup was of historical significance for three reasons. The first was that Canada was celebrating its centennial year, and what better way to toast the country than to have its two greatest teams competing for the Stanley Cup. The second reason was that Montreal was hosting Expo '67, and every Montrealer felt the Stanley Cup would be a perfect feather in the city's proverbial cap. The third and most important reason was that the Original Six era was nearing its end. In the 1967–68 season the NHL expanded to twelve teams, adding the Los Angeles Kings, the Minnesota North Stars, the Oakland Seals, the Pittsburgh Penguins, the Philadelphia Flyers, and the St. Louis Blues. The Toronto Maple

Leafs and the Montreal Canadiens, the greatest rivalry in hockey, would play the swan song for an era, in one final series. The series remains the last meeting between these two teams in a Stanley Cup final.

The Montreal Canadiens had swept the New York Rangers in four straight games. In their opening match the Rangers led 4-1 in the third period, and appeared to have the game in hand when the explosive Habs rallied with five unanswered goals to win the game 6-4. And the Canadiens never looked back. The city of Montreal was feverish in anticipation of a Stanley Cup as they awaited their next victims.

When Toronto defeated Chicago, it was considered a miracle. Looking to the next series, on paper the Leafs had a lousy season and hadn't won a game in Montreal that they could remember. All predictions had the Canadiens steamrolling the Maple Leafs on their way to a Stanley Cup victory. And it wasn't just Montrealers who were confident about the forecast. At Expo '67, Red Kelly discovered that the Maple Leafs were international favorites for second place. "Czechoslovakia had beautiful crystal to present to the Montreal Canadiens and we saw this ahead of time. It kind of peeved you off. Crystal for the Canadiens, as if they had already won the Stanley Cup. Well they didn't win, we did. But I didn't see any crystal."

Game one was similar to the first game Toronto played in the Chicago series. Montreal trounced the Leafs 6-2 in a display of their offensive strength. Henri Richard got a hat trick, Yvan Cournoyer netted two, and Jean Beliveau added another. Jimmy Pappin and Larry Hillman scored for the Leafs in the sobering defeat. If the Leafs were going to beat Montreal, they would have to get the kind of goaltending that Sawchuk provided in the previous series.

Prior to 1967 Red Kelly had won seven Cups in total with Toronto and Detroit and knew what it would take. "I figured it was my last shot at it and there were others that felt the same. But the goaltenders had to play well because without the goaltending, you're not going to win anything anyway. Then we had to score the goals when we got the chances."

After Sawchuk's shaky start, Bower took over in game two and showed the Canadiens why he was called the China Wall. The Habs were stymied through three periods of shut-out goaltending and the Leafs skated to a 3-0 win.

Back in Toronto, the Leafs took game three 3-2 in another display of great goaltending. The Canadiens coach, Toe Blake, had veteran Gump Worsley at his disposal but chose to go with rookie netminder Rogie Vachon. In game four, Vachon held the Leafs to two goals allowing the Habs to tie the series at two games apiece, in a 6-2 triumph. Once again, it was anybody's series. Because the Canadiens were headed back to the Forum, they were predicted to win game five. Also working in their favor was an injury Johnny Bower suffered in game four's pre-game warm-up. So, despite the shelling Terry Sawchuk had taken in game four, he remained between the pipes for Toronto. The Maple Leafs got goals from Pappin, Conacher, Keon, and Pronovost, which was enough to shock Montreal in their own building—the final score was 4-1.

Now Toronto was one win away from the Stanley Cup and set to play in Maple Leaf Gardens. Game six would be the most important one of the year. All the Leafs knew that returning to Montreal for a seventh game was not an option. Brian Conacher described their situation. "We won game five in Montreal on a Saturday afternoon and came back to Toronto for game six. Punch basically said to us, and it was probably the only time I have any clear recollection of him really coaching, 'If you're going to win the Stanley Cup, you're going to win it here, tonight.' Everybody realized that when we stepped on the ice for the sixth game, we were either going to win the Stanley Cup here, or if we had to go back to Montreal for a seventh game, our chances would be slim and none."

On May 2, 1967, Punch Imlach entered the Maple Leafs dressing room with a carrying bag stuffed full of one dollar bills—one thousand of them to be exact. He began his pre-game speech by opening the bag and spreading the bills across a table that stood in the center of the dressing room. Imlach frequently used money for motivation, albeit by way of fines rather than bonuses. Prior to game six, the Maple Leafs coach showed his players the individual reward for winning the Cup in hopes of inspiring them to pull off the upset of the century. For most players, getting their name on the Stanley Cup was inspiration enough. Mahovlich, for one, felt that Imlach's presentation was inconsequential to the outcome of the game. "The money never motivated me. I mean, if you can't get up for the Stanley Cup final, you wouldn't be there to begin with."

After the first period the game remained scoreless due to superb goaltending at both ends of the rink. Now that the Habs faced elimination, Toe Blake decided to go with the veteran, Gump Worsley, but the Leafs would get to him, too. Ron Ellis struck with the first Toronto goal, and Jimmy Pappin followed with another. At the end of the second period the Leafs led 2-0. Still, the game was far from over. Ex-Leaf Dick Duff proved this early in the third, when he brought the Canadiens to within one, after which the game went scoreless for a while. Then, in the final minute of the game, George Armstrong sealed the victory with an empty-net goal.

Thus, the roller-coaster season ended in a most memorable series—one that is mentioned in Toronto every spring when Leafs fans ask, when did we last win the Stanley Cup? Oh yeah, it was the Over the Hill Gang in '67.

For ten great Maple Leafs—George Armstrong, Bob Baun, Johnny Bower, Tim Horton, Red Kelly, Dave Keon, Frank Mahovlich, Bob Pulford, Eddie Shack, and Allan Stanley—it was the fourth Stanley Cup they had earned together in Toronto. Red Kelly summed up the feeling after winning his fourth Cup as a Maple Leaf—his eighth in total. "Everything is great when you win. It was hard work, but the hard work paid off. I'm not great at putting into words how one feels, but we were all happy. It's like being in the sunshine every day."

When Eddie Shack looked back on the Leafs years he laughed at how they went about it the hard way simply because no one knew any better. "We were never allowed water on the bench. If you drank water, it meant that you were out of shape. Nowadays you can drink water during the game, and at practice! And the day of the game it was always steak. They didn't know about what you should eat, and what you shouldn't eat. Nobody has steak now—it's pasta and you eat very little. Well, we used to just jam ourselves thinking that it would make us stronger. So we did everything wrong and came out not bad."

———————

Despite having won the Stanley Cup in 1967, the Maple Leafs were in dire need of change. The era of the last great Maple Leafs team was over and management was rightly looking toward the future—a future that would not include Frank Mahovlich. November of the 1967–68 season marked the beginning of the end for the Leafs' number 27. "I found it very difficult playing for Punch Imlach and the Toronto Maple Leafs. I don't think I could have kept it up much longer."

In the first week of that November, Mahovlich was once again admitted to the hospital. Dr. Alan Walters, the physician who had treated Frank during his first bout with depression, was quick to diagnose his condition. Marie recounted what the doctor told her husband. "The way Dr. Walters summed it up was basically, Frank, there's nothing wrong with you. You have an allergy, and the allergy is to Punch Imlach—and that's all that is wrong with you." The prescribed remedy at the time was to ignore Imlach, and as difficult as it was, that was all he could do. Mahovlich commented on the conclusions of Dr. Walters and the situation as a whole: "In the end Dr. Walters said, you can't work for that man, and he just threw up his hands."

Whatever the cause, severe depression is a difficult illness to overcome. Both friends and family credit the fortitude of Marie for helping her husband through those times. Playing in Toronto was a tough experience for both Marie and Frank, but before long the Big M would bounce back.

In retrospect, Frank's brother Peter could see why his older brother struggled with the Maple Leafs. "You have to know him, you have to have played with him, to understand that he was a very honest person, and that's how he wanted to be dealt with. Just very up front, very honest. He didn't want people playing games, and coaches had a tendency to do that. Even today they try to use different means to motivate people. And sometimes they'll do silly and stupid things to try to motivate people, rather than being honest with them. I think it was definitely the case in Toronto—especially in Toronto."

Mahovlich returned to the line-up at the end of November and was once again welcomed with an ovation from appreciative fans. He played well, but that wasn't going to change his fate. Management had realized their inability to maximize Mahovlich's potential, so they began looking for a trade. Mahovlich wasn't the only one on the block. Several Leafs were rumored to be trade bait, and it was apparent that the team's future was up in the air.

This instability plagued the Maple Leafs in the standings, but that was only part of their problem. The team's shaky ground had as much to do with developments in the NHL as with trade talks specific to the Leafs. Alan Eagleson had recently formed the NHL Players' Association, a move that didn't sit well with team owners and management. They knew the creation of such an association would lead to higher salaries for the players. After the swelling of payrolls that resulted from expansion, the owners weren't about to welcome another round of salary inflation.

The representation and organization that the NHL Players' Association would provide were long overdue in the NHL. Nonetheless, not all the players were immediately interested in joining. This was especially the case with the Maple Leafs. The veterans on the team wouldn't benefit from a union, because they were at the end of their careers. Rather than oppose management on the issue, which would cause them grief without benefit, they shied away.

To prevent the younger players (who supported Eagleson's group) from swaying any of those who hadn't joined, the Maple Leafs management tried to keep the two groups separated as much as possible. The imposed division on the Leafs quickly reached comedic proportions. Imlach would have all the players who supported the Players' Association practice at one end of the rink, while he stayed with the veterans at the other end. Not the best recipe for team spirit.

The Toronto Maple Leafs were heading into the dark years. Not only was the league changing but the Leafs organization was going in all the wrong directions. Unscrupulous business dealings would land Harold Ballard in jail, while Stafford Smythe effectively drank himself to death. Eventually, Ballard would end up on top as principal owner of the Maple Leafs, and he went on to prove himself a successful businessman, if nothing else. Mahovlich remembered Conn Smythe at this period, in the twilight years of his life, expressing regrets about his son's involvement with Ballard. "We had friends who owned horses and they would invite us to Woodbine to the races, and we'd have dinner at the clubhouse. I saw Conn Smythe at the racetrack a few times. [Smythe owned horses and spent a lot of time there.] I think he was upset in the end. He shook his head at what was happening when Harold Ballard took over and Stafford died. He said, 'I couldn't talk to my son. He wanted Ballard around there—and it ended up just terrible.'"

Chapter Six

Day 6—Evening

Today's game was in a terrific old barn in Kelowna, which happens to be a lovely town. The game, like the town, was fairly subdued. The dinner and reception after was a different story. The tales seemed never-ending, and as usual, the guy garnering the most laughs was Bobby Hull.

Somehow the topic at dinner got around to how cheap the owners were in the days of the Original Six. Hull broke into a story about Blackhawks chief Bill Wirtz who, in Bobby's estimation, was "tighter than a buzzard's ass in a power dive." After a visit from a building inspector to the old Chicago Stadium, Wirtz was told that there weren't enough water fountains in the building and that more would have to be installed. Miffed, Wirtz replied, "What for? There's a bar here, one over there," and so on. Although Wirtz had concessions for paying customers, fans expecting a free drink of water were out of luck. Eventually Wirtz had to provide the required number of fountains. After the inspector was satisfied with the number of fountains Wirtz had them fixed so hot water ran through them.

Back at our hotel Dad and I close the evening out with a chat while I write in the journal. My final thought on the day is of the great evening we had. I'm sure the folks in Kelowna don't know it, but the reception they gave us meant a lot to the guys. Most nights, the team is sent to a standard banquet room in the arena where the fellows have chicken wings and a cheese platter to nibble on while they spend an hour after each game with the fans. Being in a restaurant, as was the case tonight, and sitting down for a great meal of pasta and salad is appreciated immeasurably. During previous tours when Dad would call me from the road he had mentioned being "cheese-and-crackered" to death. Now I know what that feels like.

Day 7—Morning

Early this morning I did an interview with Red Storey. Red truly is a wonderful guy with a dozen stories about anyone you can think of. I know that Dad really enjoys his knowledge of the game and its history, but since they are friends, Dad makes a point of telling him he knows nothing. We're now on the bus preparing to leave for Kamloops. Red is making his way to his seat and, before Dad can get in his morning abuse, Red grabs him by the throat and gives him the claw. The bus pulls out and the players pass around sections of the morning paper. Once again a conversation arises of what might happen with the excess from the pension fund that Carl Brewer has so diligently worked on. Dad suggests that they use the money to build a retirement home for old hockey players in which the lounge could be modeled after the inside of a bus. The guys start howling at the thought of it.

In 1967 Frank and Marie became close friends with Brian and Susan Conacher. Brian was one of the younger players on the 1967–68 Maple Leafs. Conacher described how their friendship began. "My first year pro, I sat beside Frank. I think Frank was on my right if I'm not mistaken, and Red Kelly was on my left. I was this rookie sandwiched between two great veterans. That's how I first got to know Frank. I used to feel that he was like a radio sometimes. He would come in, and if the atmosphere wasn't right or whatever, he would just turn it off—like you'd turn off a radio. Then he would be quite introverted in the sense that he didn't talk a lot in the dressing room. But when Frank left the room, when

Susan and I would see Frank and Marie socially, they were great together.

"I think a lot of people might not acknowledge how important a part Marie played in Frank's life. She brought an aspect to his life that gave him a life outside of the arena. And a lot of hockey players have struggled with that. She's very artistic, and Frank became very involved in art. We'd go out and you'd realize that Frank was a multi-dimensional person with a lot of interests and abilities beyond that of a hockey player.

"Frank was a player blessed with a gift that he might have been better off not having. He might have been better off if he was an artist, so he could have done his thing in a solitary sort of way. But his gift, among others, was being a great hockey player—one of the greatest. And he had to do his thing in front of 15,000 or 16,000 people judging him all the time. So, when he went through the doors of Maple Leaf Gardens, he was in a persona to do that job. But when he left, it was like the radio got turned back on. Frank and I would leave the arena, and we weren't talking about hockey. We were talking about something else, like there was more to the world than the end of a hockey stick. That was how our friendship developed."

After their victorious season, the friends of the 1967 Stanley Cup team soon began bidding one another goodbye. The Maple Leafs' hunt for new blood was successful, and within eighteen months of winning the Cup the majority of the players from the Stanley Cup team were traded or let go. For some of the players it was difficult to accept, having been in the organization for so long—in some cases, since they were fifteen years old.

In late February of 1968, rumors were circulating that Peter Stemkowski and Brian Conacher were going to Detroit. Mahovlich heard the talk and approached Conacher to offer his friend support. "Frank, as sort of a big brother, came and said, 'Don't be upset, Brian. If you're traded, it could be the best thing for you.'" In the back of his mind, Mahovlich thought—assuming the rumors were true—how much he'd like to be in Conacher's shoes.

Days later, when Frank's name came up in the rumor mill, he

didn't give it much thought. He had heard similar gossip before but the Leafs never had dealt him. Then he got the call. "I was at home and the phone rang—it was Clancy. They always used Clancy around there to do all the dirty work. He said, 'We've made a deal with Detroit.' So I said, 'Okay King, it was nice knowing you,' and I went to Detroit." For Mahovlich, the news of the trade was a relief. Frank hung up the phone, turned to Marie who was standing nearby and said, "Well, now I can use Northland sticks."

The reaction in Toronto was outrage. The Maple Leafs were having a miserable year with no reason for optimism—and now the Big M was no longer a Maple Leaf. Many felt that by deporting Mahovlich, Imlach had driven the last nail into the Maple Leafs' coffin. But sentiment aside, the move made perfect sense. The fact of the matter was that Punch's efforts to motivate Mahovlich had failed, and to prolong their standoff wouldn't benefit anyone. Toronto management finally conceded that moving Mahovlich would serve both parties better.

On March 3, 1968, Detroit gave up Norm Ullman, Paul Henderson, and Floyd Smith in exchange for Frank Mahovlich, Pete Stemkowski, Garry Unger, and the rights to Carl Brewer. While Leaf fans cursed the trade, Frank Mahovlich fans in Toronto and else-where celebrated it. Frank Mahovlich was a talent being wasted in Toronto, and now he was set free. For that reason, Brian Conacher—fan, friend, and teammate (who was not traded after all), eagerly awaited the next time he would see the Big M.

When that time came, Conacher, as one of the young players on Imlach's blacklist, had been benched and thus relegated to spectator status. "I can remember the trade happened early in the week, and we were to play against Detroit on Saturday night. It was obviously going to be Frank's first night back. Now, trading Frank Mahovlich was a real big trade. So he comes back into the Gardens and I'm sitting in my favorite spot on the end of the bench—Punch and I weren't getting along. Frank gets out there and you just knew that he had come to play. He got those big strides going, and when Frank was on the move was he hard to handle. He scored early in the game on a great backhand and he came back to center ice. I was sitting at the end of our bench with a big grin on my face, and Frank and I made eye contact. Then I looked down our bench and Imlach was looking right at me—and I knew I was finished."

Susan Conacher: "I remember when Frank scored Brian applauded by banging his stick against the bench. The trainer Bobby Haggert turned to him and said, 'You're gone.'" (At the end of the season Brian Conacher was let go by the Maple Leafs.)

Because the trade happened in mid-season, the players involved were forced to relocate on short notice. The morning he got the call, Mahovlich went down to Maple Leaf Gardens to pick up his skates and other personal belongings. The dressing room, usually full of teammates, was now empty and quiet. His days as a Maple Leaf were over, but with him he took the memories of eleven years, both good and bad. From the Gardens there was one memento that he wanted for himself, although he thought it wouldn't be easy to get. In those days it wasn't customary to allow a traded player to keep his jersey, for no other reason than that the team recycled them to use in practice. Every piece of equipment had to be accounted for by the equipment manager. The Maple Leafs organization was so thrifty that they made a point of collecting all the sweaters immediately after the last period of the year.

Nevertheless, as a favor to Frank, trainer Bobby Haggert retrieved the jersey with number 27. On his way out, Frank stopped to thank a few of the old ushers who came to wish him well. They shook hands and said goodbye.

Later that evening Frank and Marie packed a week's worth of clothes, got in their car, and drove to Detroit. Peter Stemkowski had asked to get a ride with them and they were more than happy to oblige. "Stemmer" had a great sense of humor that was more than welcome around Marie and Frank. The drive from Toronto to Windsor took just over three hours to complete, a straight line headed west. Between Canada and the United States runs the Detroit River, the natural border. The group arrived at the Windsor–Detroit tunnel and surfaced in Detroit at about 1 a.m. It was just after the

Detroit riots and they found themselves driving in a neighborhood that little resembled their safe surroundings in Toronto.

Their plan was to check into a motel for the night and meet the team the next day. Mahovlich remembered surveying a terribly grim scene. "We were driving through downtown Detroit looking at these abandoned buildings, steel grates covering the store fronts, and absolutely no signs of life. It was like a ghost town. Stemkowski looks out the window and says, 'Home at last!'"

The newly acquired players joined the Red Wings for the last thirteen games of the season, in which Mahovlich tallied 7 goals and 9 assists. The team was also rebuilding and had struggled through the 1967–68 season. Frank recalled the situation around the time of his arrival. "It was right near the end of the season and Detroit was out of the playoffs. I was delighted that my brother was there, we finished off the season, and the games were pretty good. I remember we beat Boston 7-6 in Boston, and they had a pretty good team in those days. I think Peter got two goals but they traded him the next year. Detroit decided he couldn't make the team so Sam Pollock picked him up." Peter Mahovlich became one of Sam Pollock's best acquisitions; a trade that would later be called a steal.

Despite being sorry to see his brother go, Frank felt great in the Red Wings uniform. A dramatic change in his spirits was about to take place.

While Frank finished out the season, Marie returned to Toronto to look after Michael and Nancy. The couple agreed they would rent a house in Windsor and keep 211 Strathallan Wood in Toronto. Although residing in Windsor meant that Frank would have to cross the border to get to work every day, the Detroit Olympia was just on the other side of the bridge. In fact, it took less time for Frank to get there than it took most of his teammates who lived in the suburbs of Detroit.

At the conclusion of the Red Wings' schedule, Frank joined Marie for a date they had in Toronto at the maternity ward of St. Michael's Hospital. On April 16, 1968, Mark Edward Mahovlich was born. Frank had hoped to name their second son Mark, but Marie was fond of the name Teddy. The discussion ended with a compromise suggested by Marie, who said, "Fine, we'll name him Mark Edward—but we'll call him Teddy." The family spent the summer in Toronto and moved to Windsor for the hockey season that fall.

Mahovlich had shown signs of promise at the end of the 1967–68 season, and the Detroit Red Wings management looked for the Big M to pick up where he left off. Although they were confident this would happen, their expectations were intentionally understated in the press. By remaining low-key, coach Bill Gadsby and the Red Wings management hoped to avoid the distractions that had hampered Mahovlich's game as a Maple Leaf. They knew that if Frank were allowed to play without the trials he went through in Toronto, he'd be capable of far more than the Leafs ever saw.

Gadsby matched him with two other veterans, centerman Alex Delvecchio and right winger Gordie Howe. The combination allowed that one superstar didn't have to carry the team offensively on his own. Without the spotlight focused on the Big M, Frank was able to fit in as another member of the team, a role he was more comfortable in. In this relaxed setting he led by example with his linemates Howe and Delvecchio. This powerhouse became known as "Production Line II," as they were reminiscent of the original unit of Ted Lindsey, Sid Abel, and Gordie Howe. The newly formed Production Line proceeded to break the NHL record for the most points by a line in one season (264 total points in 1968–69). In Frank's first full season wearing the sweater he wore as a kid in Schumacher, the Big M found the passion he hadn't felt in years.

After their years of toil Marie was ecstatic to see her husband enjoying hockey again, though it's difficult to imagine not enjoying the game on that line. "When Frank played on a line with Gordie and Alex, they were like one person on the ice. They could read each other's minds. One of them would give a no-look pass and the other would always be there. It was fabulous, wonderful hockey." What was considered spectacular from a layperson's point of view,

Frank saw as the natural sum of the parts. "I had known Gordie for quite a while and always had respect for his ability. The guy was a pretty good athlete—one of the best athletes in the world. It wasn't any surprise when we formed that line with Alex Delvecchio, myself, and Gordie Howe. I knew how good they were."

Recently, one afternoon prior to a Maple Leafs game, Mahovlich was with Walter and Wayne Gretzky at a private table in Gretzky's restaurant; Wayne ("The Great One") was playing that night against Toronto. The group traded stories of the old times over lunch. Wayne expressed a genuine interest in eras past and quizzed the Big M on various players, requesting comparisons of Doug Harvey to Bobby Orr, wondering if Frank knew Bill Barilko, etc.

Walter, who was the same age as Frank and quick to offer his own opinions of those times, recounted a story that harkened back to when Mahovlich and Howe were together on the same line. "Wayne's grandmother was a big hockey fan and her favorite player was Frank Mahovlich. She'd always watch when Frank was on television. Wayne would sit beside her and she'd say, 'Now Wayne, you keep your eye on number 27.' Wayne would tell her that he liked Gordie Howe and mother would say, 'Never mind Gordie, you watch Frank!'" To the surprised Frank Mahovlich, the Great One, laughing, declared, "That's a true story."

With the Red Wings the change in Mahovlich's game was remarkable by all accounts. "When I got to Detroit, I found their system was completely different and it suited me just fine. They played me different, their practices were different, everything was different. I never really felt I reached my potential with Toronto. Detroit just opened everything up and my output doubled. It was like a piano had been lifted off my back—I finally felt like playing."

Mahovlich was a perfect fit for the personality of the Red Wings. The team spent time together outside of hockey, which was a pleasant surprise for the newcomers. Both Marie and Frank were shocked to find that after games, the Red Wings would go out for dinner as a team, with their wives and girlfriends. It was something that virtually never happened in Toronto. Marie compared what happened in Detroit with the scene after a Maple Leafs game: "My most acute memory is of everybody leaving Maple Leaf Gardens tense and tight-lipped, going their separate ways home. That's how it was under Imlach—everyone uptight and tense. And it didn't matter if they won or not. When Frank got traded to Detroit, it was just fabulous. We drove miles after a game to go out with the rest of the team. We were so thrilled to be invited, number one—number two, that the team did go out together. We wouldn't think of turning it down." The team usually dined in the suburbs of Detroit, and although it took 45 minutes to get back to Windsor, it was a drive they were happy to make.

Day-to-day life in Windsor was great for the Mahovlich family. In their rented house on Riverside Drive they immediately felt at home, especially Frank. Marie began to notice her husband doing things that were totally out of character, but at the same time, were welcomed improvements. "He wasn't relaxed in Toronto. Now he gets to Detroit and somebody says, 'How would you like to see the Detroit Lions play?' It was a Sunday afternoon game and the Red Wings played Sunday nights. This was so unlike Frank, so he wore a bala-clava so nobody would recognize him—but he didn't look out of place because it was a very cold day. He ate a couple of egg-salad sandwiches or something at the football game, and that night went on the ice and scored a hat trick. I was so thrilled I said, 'See, you don't have to have a steak, peas, and baked potato!'" Frank confessed that it was good to be free of the old routine. "I saw the Detroit Lions play the Oakland Raiders at Tiger Stadium. I went by myself and sat way up in the stands. The fresh air was great and then I went home, got changed and went to our hockey game—no problem. You'd never go out before a game in Toronto. They'd hear nothing of it."

On another occasion Frank went skiing with Gordie Howe and their families. It was Mahovlich's first time ever on the slopes. Gordie recalled the afternoon he gave Frank his first ski lesson. "I wasn't an expert skier, but I had been taught before; so I was giving some of the basics to Frank at the bottom of the hill. This is how you turn moving both skis, do this to slow down, and so on. Well, a crowd started to form around us and people seemed to think I was an instructor giving lessons. So I took off and left Frank at the beginner's hill and I remember he fell in front of his kids and was all upset." Howe laughs. "After, I told him, 'Frank, the first thing they do is tell you to fall so you can learn how to get up—it's part of the fun.' Well, Frank's enjoyed skiing ever since."

Along with his teammates Mahovlich became very appreciative of the fans in Detroit. "The Detroit Red Wings had the greatest hockey fans. They were very enthused, but they never booed their players. We'd practice at a rink out of town and it would be full of fans getting autographs after practice, and then they'd throw us a luncheon—they were great fans." Feeling that support made all the difference to players. It's a natural reaction to want to perform well for those who take care of you.

And the press in Detroit made life a lot easier being a Red Wing than the press did in Toronto. The sports media wasn't solely focused on hockey, as was the case in Toronto. This made all the difference in Mahovlich's mind. "I don't think the newspapers influenced the fans in Detroit as much as they did in Toronto. In America they let the newspapers control themselves. In Toronto, the team management controlled the press. When you got to training camp in Peterborough, the newspapermen would stay there for three weeks—and the Leafs would pick up the tab. They'd be drinking and eating and it was all looked after, like they were on the payroll, and that's how they lived. There were three papers and three reporters from each paper. So, you've got nine guys around you all the time, each wanting a different story. Same thing would happen, but nine different takes on it."

After years of being grilled by the press in Toronto, Mahovlich was surprisingly comfortable with the newsmen in Detroit. Near the end of the 1968–69 season, writer Paul Dulmage wrote a piece on "the new Frank Mahovlich" that appeared in the *Toronto Telegram* on March 22, 1969. It accurately described the changes in the Big M that had fellow ex-Leafs, now teammates in Detroit, shaking their heads:

The brooding, introverted mess of psychological hang-ups he had become under Punch Imlach has vanished. [Mahovlich] is enjoying life to the fullest. He smiles and laughs and is a part of a team. He is wanted by management, his teammates, and his fans.

"The guys have been marvelous," he says. "They've really helped me. It took about six months for me to get adjusted. You know, they'd heard all the Frank Mahovlich stories and they were wondering if they were true. And I was never the kind of guy who tried to sell myself.

"Gordie Howe wouldn't let me be a loner. There's more fellowship here than there was on the Leafs. We're more of a unit. The Leafs used to break up in different groups and go their own ways.

"They've made me feel wanted here in Detroit. Just by the way they do things, they make you want to do your best. I'm not criticizing Punch. It's just that different people have different methods.

"I could take it for the first four or five years in Toronto, but the last few years, I shouldn't have been there. It was like beating my head against a wall. If I had to play there one more year, I'd have probably retired from hockey. I couldn't do anything."

"His scoring has been important to us," says coach Gadsby. "But there are other things. Geez, he's exciting. Some nights, he'll make one of those rushes and lift the whole team. Or lift the two guys he plays with. On the nights he's going, he's unbelievable."

Mahovlich was leaning forward in his seat on the bus. The only passengers were assistant trainer Dan Olsevich, Bob Baun, Bruce MacGregor, Hank Monteith, and Wayne Connelly.

Baun stopped the bus and bought coffee and donuts. "Listen to him," Baun said, referring to a lengthy conversation he was having with Mahovlich. "In eleven years in Toronto, I don't think I ever said more than twenty-two words to him. I've spent the last year finding out what a great guy he is."

Guarding the puck.
(Courtesy of Mike Leonetti)

Surrounded by legends. The 1969 All-Star team.

Susan Conacher and Marie.

Frank with Gordie Howe, ski instructor.

The Production Line II: Gordie Howe, Alex Delvecchio, Frank Mahovlich.
(Courtesy of The Hockey Hall of Fame)

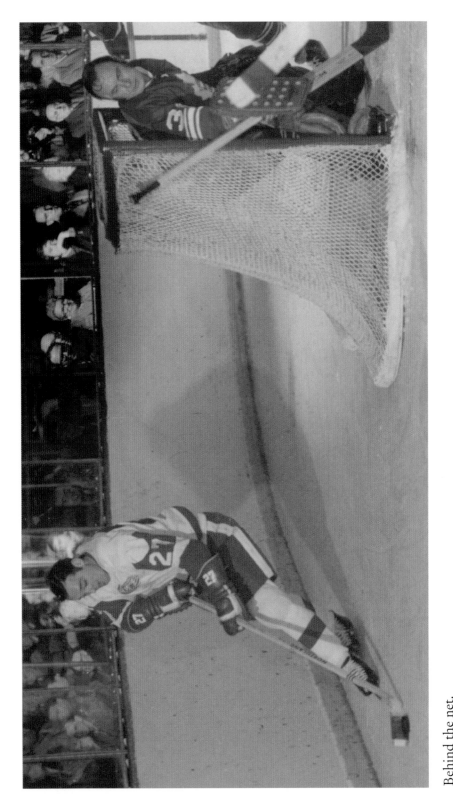

Behind the net.
(Courtesy of The Hockey Hall of Fame)

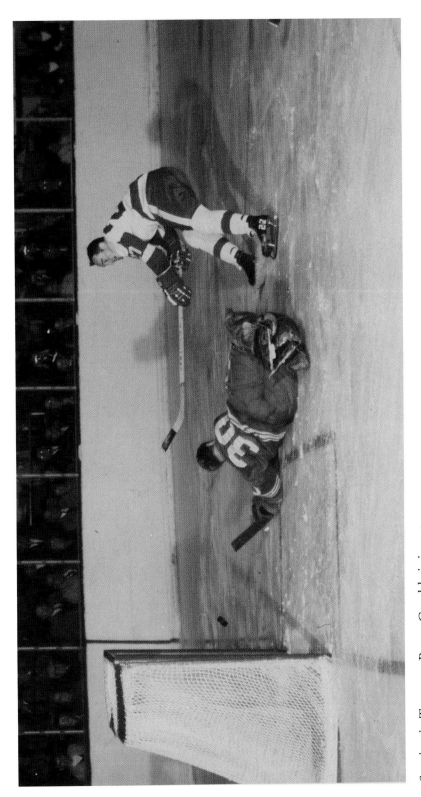

Scoring in Toronto. Bruce Gamble is in net.
(Courtesy of The Hockey Hall of Fame)

On the move. Bill Barber is behind the Big M.
(Courtesy of Denis Brodeur)

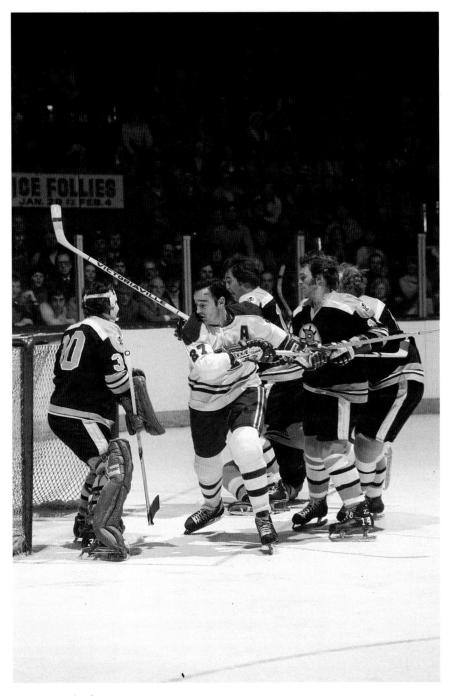

In a crowd of Bruins.
(Courtesy of Denis Brodeur)

Clearing the zone.
(Courtesy of The Hockey Hall of Fame)

In alone.
(Courtesy Denis Brodeur)

The Big M. Frank Mahovlich in a Manhattan button-down from the Contemporaries Col...

Modeling Manhattan shirts.

At the family cottage.

On vacation in Nice, France, after winning the 1971 Stanley Cup. Marie is sporting fashionable eyewear.

The Mahovlich brothers, Team Canada 1972.

Frank with relatives in Croatia.   In Moscow with Team Canada—1974.

Frank having fun at Toros training camp, 1975. (r.) Sailing in the Baltic Sea with Paul Henderson.

Wearing the "C" for the Toronto Toros. (Courtesy of The Hockey Hall of Fame)

(l.) With Vladislav Tretiak—Russia's greatest ambassador and a family friend.

(r.) The Big M and the Roadrunner with the Yankee Clipper. Frank recalls: "It was an honor to meet Joe DiMaggio, a great American."

In the South of France.

Red Storey applies the claw.

Gilles Gilbert's
birthday. (r. to l.)
Gilles, Frank, Wilf
Paiement.

Linemates: Ken Linseman
between Ted and Frank.

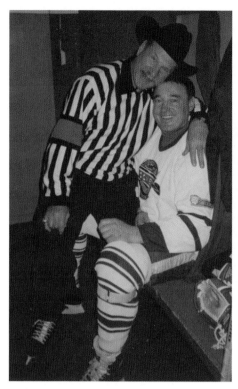

The final game in Vancouver with Guy Lafleur.

Shack being Shack.

On the slopes, Whistler, B.C.

The Prime Minister introduces Senator Mahovlich to Nelson Mandela.

Meeting with Prime Minister Jean Chrétien.
(Both photos courtesy of J.M. Carisse, Office of the Prime Minister)

In Detroit, Mahovlich was in high demand as a sports celebrity, so much so that there wasn't enough time to fill the requests for appearances. One unforgettable appearance that he did make was for a local radio show; it is one of his favorite stories. "There was a fellow by the name of Dave Diles, a sportscaster. Dave had a program in Detroit called 'Dial Dave Diles,' where fans would phone in. He would have hockey players on, and people would call and ask questions. So, 'Dial Dave Diles'—it's Frank Mahovlich's turn. I go out to the radio station one night and I'm answering calls. Callers are asking different questions about the team and all of a sudden there's a call and some guy asks 'How come a high-paid NHL star like yourself can't skate backwards?' Boy, did I ever get hot under the collar at this guy. He kept going on and on about me not being able to skate backwards. I said, 'If you don't think I can skate backwards, why don't you come down to the Detroit Olympia in the morning. We'll have a little race around the rink, and we'll find out who can skate backwards!' Well, Dave Diles looked at me and could see I was getting pretty mad. Then he kind of waved at me, and whispered that it was Peter Stemkowski on the line." Mahovlich laughs. "Stemkowski was a joker."

Near the end of his first season in Detroit, Mahovlich, for the second time in his career, was closing in on 50 goals. The final game of Detroit's season was against the Chicago Blackhawks and Frank had 49 goals going in. When Bobby Hull recorded his first 50-goal season, he remembered playing against Detroit and Gordie Howe encouraging him. Hull recounted the occasion when he did the same for Mahovlich. "I remember the evening well. We all wanted Frank to get his fifty goals. When we started the game, I know I talked to our guys and I said, 'Now c'mon, this game doesn't mean anything to us. Sure, it always meant something to our goaltenders, but one goal didn't mean anything. When I first came up, we used to check when we'd go into the different cities, and guys needed a point for a bonus, or they needed a goal for a bonus. We'd always go to the other team and say, 'Okay, who needs a point, or a goal for a bonus?' That night we said, 'Hey now, big Frank needs a goal.'

So, I get out there, and I'm on the ice with him. I said, 'C'mon Frank—GO, GO! I'm on the ice, GO ON!' You know, you weren't going to lay down and say, 'This way to the goal', but—GO!"

In his NHL career, Frank Mahovlich never scored the elusive 50th goal. But although it would have tied up that loose end, so to speak, it was just a small disappointment in a season full of personal triumph. The 49 goals matched the Red Wings club record (set by Gordie Howe who scored 49 in 1952–53) and was a new career high for Frank.

The creation of Production Line II also restored Mahovlich to his position as one of the league's top goal scorers. The individual statistics of the record-breaking season were: Gordie Howe, 44 goals and 59 assists; Alex Delvecchio, 25 goals and 58 assists; Frank Mahovlich, 49 goals and 29 assists. Playing in Detroit, Mahovlich finally got the ice time he never saw in Toronto. The result was a jackpot of offense. "I can't take all the credit for scoring that many goals because I had these great players with me. I never had that much power on one line in Toronto. When the three of us got together in Detroit, you could tell we had something. We just dominated on the ice. I was quite thrilled, the way the season went for us. It was disappointing not getting into the playoffs, but boy, we certainly played well. We proved a point, and I proved my point—that I could be much more prolific as a hockey player." Aside from the immeasurable contributions of Howe and Delvecchio, Mahovlich was grateful to his old rival, Bill Gadsby. In Gadsby he found a coach who respected his players and believed in him personally. Playing for Gadsby enabled Frank to make a full recovery from the demons that haunted him in Toronto—perhaps his greatest achievement of all.

Despite the domination of Production Line II, the Red Wings did fall short of making the playoffs in 1969. The lopsided split of the league that had all the expansion teams in the same division allowed inferior teams to make the playoffs. Mahovlich discussed the situation with Allan Stanley, who was playing for the new

Philadelphia Flyers at the time. "I remember I met Allan Stanley at the train station. We met for lunch prior to a game. He was investing in a hockey school near Lindsay, Ontario, and wanted me to go in on it. I wasn't interested because I was busy with my travel business—I think Timmy Horton and a few other players got in. Anyways, Allan was playing for Philadelphia at the time and he couldn't believe that they were still in contention for the playoffs with the minimal amount of wins they had." Philadelphia finished with 20 wins, 35 losses, 21 ties—and a playoff berth. Their total of 61 points was good enough for third place in the western division, while in the eastern division Detroit missed the playoffs with a far superior record that totaled 78 points. Mahovlich continued, "It was a big problem. The league should have split it up so three of the expansion teams were in each division. Then it would have been balanced and the proper teams would have had the right to be in the playoffs. So instead, you had teams that didn't deserve be there, making the playoffs. That was Clarence Campbell [president of the NHL] and those guys not structuring it properly."

The problems the Red Wings had making the playoffs could not be blamed entirely on the league. The team was making deals trying to get the right players to fill out their roster. Mahovlich described the shortcomings of the Red Wings. "We just didn't have the depth. Our goaltending and defense were lacking and we only had two good lines. Gordie, Alex, and myself, and Bruce MacGregor, Dean Prentice with Stemkowski or Unger. We really needed two more defensemen, and two more forwards."

At the onset of the 1969–70 season there was cause for hope. In the deal that brought Mahovlich, Stemkowski, and Unger to Detroit, the Red Wings also secured the NHL rights to Carl Brewer. With the return of Brewer to the NHL, and the late-season acquisition of right winger Wayne Connelly, the Red Wings were going to be playoff contenders.

The season began with Bill Gadsby behind the bench and after two games Detroit had two wins and were looking strong. But for some unknown reason, an axe was about to fall. During the second game Mahovlich suffered a minor leg injury. The next day at the Olympia he went to see the coach about it. "I went up to Gads and said, 'Bill, I don't know how well I'm going to be able to play on this leg.' He said, 'Don't talk to me.' I said, 'What's the matter?' He said, 'I got fired!' I wanted to tell the coach I was hurt, and there was no coach. We had just won two games, and we beat Chicago, in Chicago. And it was a great game. When you win two games and a guy gets fired, you want to know what the hell for. And what's the reasoning behind it. I was doing well with Bill Gadsby, and all he needed was a couple more players, but sure enough, he got fired. Everybody was walking around in a daze wondering what was going on. So I said, 'Well, I don't know who the hell is running this show, but I've got to know.' So I went over to Baz Bastien [the assistant general manager for the Red Wings]. I said, 'Baz, can I talk to you for a second.' He was like King Clancy—but for Detroit. So he said, 'Yeah, come on over here.' We went over by the ice and I started telling him about my problem, and I asked if he knew what was going on. I thought he was the assistant general manager so maybe he'd know. He got all upset and said, 'Look, don't ever ask me what is going on around here! For Christ's sake, Frank, you've got a big career ahead of you. I'm just hanging on. So don't get me involved.' And I apologized: 'Sorry, Baz, sorry I asked.'"

For the remainder of the 1969–70 season the Red Wings general manager, Sid Abel, took on the coaching duties. There was no explanation given for the dismissal of Gadsby. The move resulted from what Mahovlich described as a power play. "I liked Bill. I liked the way he coached, and I thought we were headed in the right direction. There must have been an argument upstairs with management. Maybe he didn't see eye-to-eye with what was going on. I think, to this day, Bill still doesn't know why he got fired."

The Red Wings worked hard through the changes, and the standings showed their progress. In a tight race to the end of the season, Detroit finished in third place in the eastern division (with a total of 95 points) behind Chicago and Boston (both of whom finished with

99 points). Production Line II fronted the Wings with another impressive year. Gordie Howe was the team leader with 31 goals and 40 assists, and Mahovlich ran a close second with 38 goals and 32 assists. Alex Delvecchio added 21 goals and 47 assists making them one, two, and three on the team for the second year in a row.

One of the improvements that made Detroit a better team in 1969–70 was their second line of Nick Libett on left wing, Garry Unger at centre, and Wayne Connelly on right wing. In particular, Garry Unger scored a career high of 42 goals, which put him second to the league's leading goal scorer, Boston's Phil Esposito (43 goals). Along with the increased productivity of their offense, the team's defense was bolstered by the return of Carl Brewer. Mahovlich liked what his old Leaf teammate brought to the Red Wings. "Carl certainly helped our defense. He stabilized it quite a bit. We all knew what he was capable of. In key situations you could put him out there and he would slow the game down, and hold the other team off until we regrouped. You could see the improvement in the team that year. It was getting better."

But even with the stronger offense and shored-up defense, Detroit still lacked depth. This became a problem when their starters got injured. As far as Mahovlich could tell, this was something the Detroit management neglected. "There was a guy by the name of Larry Jeffrey that they picked up from the New York Rangers. We were playing at training camp and he got hurt, and he ended his career. But they never replaced him. You've got to have depth. You've got to fill your holes, then you can build a championship team."

The Detroit teams of the fifties that boasted stars like Ted Lindsey, Red Kelly, and Terry Sawchuk were long gone. That was another era, a time when Jack Adams, the Red Wings' general manager, employed tyrannical methods but put together a winning team. The rule of "Jolly Jack" ended when Bruce Norris took over the Red Wings, and later on fired Adams in 1962. Mahovlich noticed the difference in the Detroit organization under Norris. "Bruce Norris ran the team through Sid Abel. Now Sid Abel was no

Jack Adams. Sid didn't run roughshod over everyone. I don't think Adams would have taken orders from Norris."

Detroit's new regime may have had a calmer disposition without Jack Adams, but Abel and Norris still got rid of Gadsby. Having spent his entire career in Detroit up to that point, even Gordie Howe was puzzled by the move. "They fired Gadsby for no apparent reason—and I remember that really upset Frank." To Mahovlich, the misguided decision suggested that there was something wrong at the top. And whatever's at the top filters down throughout the organization. "Sid Abel was a pretty good coach, but what we needed was good management. I don't think that was stressed enough in Detroit. Management doesn't have to make a move every day, but they have to think about the future of the club all the time. This is where they were lacking. They didn't have the vision. This is why they didn't make the playoffs for seven years in a row [from 1971 through 1977]. They weren't managerial—they didn't know what the word meant. They had a team, they had Gordie Howe and Alex Delvecchio, two of the greatest players in history. But someday, they were going to move on and they should have prepared for that day."

Although that day had yet to arrive, it wasn't far off. At the end of the 1969–70 season, the Red Wings clinched a playoff spot and were heading to New York for their final regular-season game. On the flight to New York, Mahovlich's concerns about management were realized. The problems he suspected at the top filtered down through the team, and literally so—in the form of champagne. When several bottles of chilled bubbly were presented compliments of Bruce Norris, Mahovlich felt that management was acting prematurely. "I didn't agree with it. We got in the playoffs, and we deserved to, but that shouldn't have been cause for celebration. We started to celebrate before we accomplished anything. We had just played in Detroit and got on the plane to finish the season in New York, and we're drinking champagne just because we got in the playoffs. I'm thinking, we should be preparing ourselves for the playoffs. We hadn't won anything yet. That was the difference in

Toronto. You didn't start smoking cigars and drinking beer until it was all done—until the fat lady sings."

For the Red Wings, the outcome of the game in New York would not affect their standing. However, the Rangers were fighting the Canadiens for the last playoff berth in their division. Should Detroit lose to the Rangers, it would put Montreal in fifth place behind New York, and out of the playoffs. Mahovlich never said the team was ordered to tank the game, but there was no indication that the Red Wings management were playing for the win, and this was a strategy Mahovlich was sorry to be a part of.

"It was one of the saddest things I've seen. We had made the play-offs but the season wasn't over. The Montreal Canadiens could still get in if we beat New York. Well, for the first two periods of the game they benched our top line of Howe, Mahovlich, and Delvecchio. Maybe they were trying to rest us for the playoffs, but to me, the season wasn't over. Something wasn't right. Anyways, in the third period our goalie is getting bombed, so finally Abel decides to play us. I get on the ice and I'm going behind the Ranger net, I don't even think anyone was near me, and my blade got caught in a rut. Because we weren't playing I was cold and ended up with strained ligaments in my knee. I always went out to win a hockey game, but that night our owners let us down. We never even gave it a shot." The New York Rangers won the game, and as a result Montreal was out of the playoffs.

When the celebrations ended the team addressed the upcoming series. Detroit had played well against Chicago throughout the year and were optimistic about facing them in the first round. To beat the Blackhawks they'd have to solve the goaltending of the stingy Tony Esposito. Mahovlich remembered a game from that season in which Esposito was unbeatable. "That year we played a game against Chicago in Detroit. I'll never forget it. I had three or four good chances, but they beat us 1-0. Tony Esposito played one of the greatest games I've ever seen a goalie play—he stopped everything! It was a hell of a game."

The Blackhawks won the first two games in Chicago by scores of

4-2 and 4-2. And both contests were played as close as the scores indicated. Back in Detroit there'd be no more champagne for the Red Wings who lost their home games in identical fashion, 4-2 and 4-2. Carl Brewer remembered the series as very close. "Every game we lost to Chicago in the playoffs, we could just as easily have won." After being played sparingly on a bad knee, Mahovlich felt, as did the rest of the team, that the outcome was short of the team's potential.

In response, the Red Wings management decided to make changes that they felt would better the team. The first of these was to hire a young coach named Ned Harkness.

In the summer of 1970, Marie and Frank returned to Toronto with their kids and resumed management of the travel business. On weekends the family went to their cottage on Lake Simcoe. Near the end of the summer Frank and Marie invited Ned Harkness to dinner at their home. They wanted to welcome the new coach with the same kindness the Red Wings had extended to them. Harkness, who was going to be in Toronto on business, graciously accepted the invitation. Prior to that evening, all Frank knew about his new boss was that he coached at Cornell University with reported success. Beyond that, he didn't know what to expect.

"The first time I met Ned Harkness he came over to our house for dinner. This was in the summer before the season started. I didn't know what to make of him. We were in the living room before dinner and he pulls out these hockey magazines from his briefcase—and he's looking up information in these magazines. I'm wondering, is this how he's going to coach our team? Marie made dinner for us, and we sat down in the dining room. I recall that he said, 'There are three players that won't be traded from Detroit—Alex Delvecchio, Gordie Howe, and Frank Mahovlich.' And I said, 'Uh-oh!' Right there my antennae went up. This fellow doesn't know what I know." The mention of three players being safeguarded from trades told Mahovlich one thing and reminded him of another. One, that trades were about to take place, and two, despite what Harkness said, everyone was fair game.

The first change Mahovlich noticed was the absence of Carl Brewer from training camp. With no word of a trade, Frank wondered if Carl knew something else about their coach that he didn't. Then there was training camp itself. Ned Harkness brought in a new approach of coaching that was foreign to the veterans who had missed out on the collegiate experience. Mahovlich recalled the reaction to Harkness' style that ultimately led to resentment followed by more change. "At training camp, things didn't go the way Ned Harkness thought they would. And there were disciplinary measures that he was going to take. So, he started making trades because he couldn't discipline some of the players the way he wanted to. They weren't the 'rah-rah' type. He was coaching like it was still college. I mean, you couldn't get Gordie Howe to be a cheerleader. Gordie Howe wasn't that type. We went about our work like professionals. What happened was that some of the players started to laugh at practice. It was the way Ned would yell and shout, and Stemkowski would pick up on it and imitate him."

On October 31, 1970, after playing just ten games under Harkness, Pete Stemkowski was traded to the New York Rangers for Larry Brown. After eleven games, Bob Baun was let go and found himself back with the Toronto Maple Leafs in mid-November. The anxiety over who would be next and the adjustment to new players made the atmosphere around the team uneasy to say the least.

After a game in Toronto, the culmination of these pressures got to the young Detroit netminder Jim Rutherford. The Maple Leafs had beaten the Red Wings badly and Rutherford had a particularly weak outing. On the way to the airport following the game Mahovlich noticed how troubled his teammate was. Having been through years of frustration with the Leafs, Frank thought he might be able to help. "The bus was pulling up to the airport and we were going to get on the plane. Rutherford was very upset and he was ready to be sick to his stomach. So I said to our coach, 'It's okay, I'll talk to him and calm him down, and we'll meet you on the plane.' The bus was going on the tarmac with all the equipment and the players. So I thought we'd walk through the normal procedure, and

I'd talk to him and settle him down. Sure enough, we got off the bus and I tried to get his mind off what happened. We talked about his girlfriend, his family—everything but hockey. Well, before you know it we're walking on to the plane and he says, 'Geez, I feel pretty good.' He got rid of the sick feeling and the anxiety and was quite calm. Then he looked at me and said, 'You know, you remind me of a doctor.' I said, 'Yeah? I remind you of a doctor? What doctor is that?' He said, 'Dr. Zhivago!'" Mahovlich laughs. "He was in good shape after that." (Frank wore a fur hat that reminded Jim of the character in the movie.)

After experiencing the worst of times in Toronto, which may have indeed strengthened his outlook, Mahovlich maintained a caring attitude. Gordie Howe spoke of his linemate's endearing nature, which won his friendship and respect. "I used to bring my son Mark to practice; he was twelve or thirteen at the time. One day Mark was sick at home and Frank asked, 'Where's Mark?' I said, 'He's at home sick.' Frank said, 'Well, what are you doing here?' I said, 'Frank, it's my job. Colleen's quite capable of taking care of him and if she can't the doctor will.' So that week we headed out west to play and we were back at the hotel in Oakland when Frank asked me, 'How's Mark doing?' I said, 'I don't know.' Frank says, 'Well, call home and find out!' So I called, spoke with Colleen and Mark was doing fine. I told Frank that he was outside playing hockey and Frank said 'Good.' That's the kind of person Frank was. He cared about people and family."

Whatever concerns Frank Mahovlich had in his life, the well-being of the Red Wings under Ned Harkness became a priority with him. In his short time as coach, Harkness had done little to gain the confidence of his players. He repeatedly showed himself to be an amateur, using profanity excessively, while continuing to methodically cripple the team. It was clear where things were headed. So, before all of the Red Wings' quality players were shipped out, while they still had the guys to win a Stanley Cup, the team decided that the person in need of a travel agent was their coach. Gordie Howe described a rare occasion when he heard Frank Mahovlich speak aloud in the dressing room. "Our team had a meeting before a game in Buffalo. The players wanted to get rid of Harkness as our coach and decided to go on strike and not play the game. I thought that our predicament had nothing to do with the people in Buffalo, so let's address the issue when we get home. I remember Frank was adamant and said, 'Gordie, either you're with us or you're against us.' Well, we worked it out so Harkness was no longer our coach—they went and gave him a position with more power!" Howe laughs. "They made him the new GM. After that I was sitting in the dressing room next to Frank and I turned to him and said, 'They really screwed us, didn't they.' We laugh about it now."

Confident that Harkness could help his team, Bruce Norris promoted the failing coach to general manager. Mahovlich recalled how the decision to promote Harkness enabled the dejected coach to finish dismantling the team. "They moved him upstairs, so everybody got traded one by one. But some of the trades were made out of spite and he didn't get the value back for the quality he gave up. And there were a lot of sharp guys around the NHL. Emile Francis, the New York Rangers' general manager, took Stemkowski and gave us some guy with a concussion. We really got taken." The "housecleaning" continued until just four players from the previous year remained.

After playing 35 games of the 1970–71 schedule for Detroit, Mahovlich was moved for the second time in his career. "My number came up on January 13, 1971. When Detroit was ready to trade, Sam Pollock wanted me. Well, Montreal wanted me way back in the sixties when Frank Selke Sr. would approach Conn Smythe. And Smythe would say, 'I don't know what's the matter with Frank.' And Selke said, 'Oh yeah? I'll take him off your hands.' Because Selke knew me, he knew I couldn't work for those guys."

Over the years many people had told Mahovlich he'd be great with the Montreal Canadiens—among them Jean Beliveau—but until he arrived and got to play with Beliveau and a cast of other future Hall of Famers, he never knew just how accurate that prediction was. However, the trade (Mahovlich to Montreal for Mickey

Redmond, Guy Charron, and Bill Collins) didn't have the same immediate appeal as the move to Detroit. Frank was pleased to be a Detroit Red Wing and was sorry to see the break-up of what he thought was a decent team. "I thought I did real well in my first two years in Detroit. And we were improving every year. You know, we finished with 95 points in 1969–70, got into the playoffs—so we're improving. When I left Detroit it was upsetting. I wanted to prove something and take aim at the Stanley Cup."

Sam Pollock called shortly after Mahovlich found out he would be joining the Montreal Canadiens. "I told him how upset I was and he said, 'I understand. When you get to Montreal we'll have a meeting. In the meantime, go up to Minnesota.' There was a game in Minnesota the next night." On the flight Mahovlich sat quietly and thought about the trade. It had come as a bit of a blow to him. Although he understood that no hockey player was indispensable, to accept that Detroit didn't want him wasn't easy. But after the shock wore off, Mahovlich saw the deal in a different light. "They made a pretty good trade. They got three younger players for one."

And although his new team had struggled in the previous season and missed the playoffs, there was an upside to joining the Canadiens. They still had a number of great players, as well as some younger talent that were showing signs of coming into their own—among them Peter Mahovlich. Being reunited with his brother was reason enough to welcome the move. Frank resolved, if he wasn't going to help Detroit win a Cup, he'd win one for Montreal.

Chapter Seven

The arena in Kamloops was an impressive complex and the fans there loved the game. It was also a special night for the team, it being Gilles Gilbert's birthday. In the first intermission the guys presented him with a chocolate birthday cake that had a little hockey net and goalie on it and we all sang "Happy Birthday."

I played on defense with Gilles Marotte, who is a great source of entertainment. When it comes time for the standard pranks that are part of the Greatest Hockey Legends show, Marotte is a master. He has two prop hockey sticks. One is like an extension ladder that allows him to make a poke-check on a rushing forward from ten feet away. The other, which he had custom-made by Sherwood, has a blade that is like a 1-by-6-inch plank. When Marotte takes that stick out and he gets the puck, it is virtually impossible to take it off of him until he unleashes a lethal wrist shot that he lets fly from the blue line. Ultimately the puck rattles off the glass a few times before the opposing goalie eventually catches hold of one. Jean-Guy Talbot and Marotte are good buddies and have the schtick down pat. We are now on the ferry to Victoria where we play tonight.

Day 8—Evening
Both good news and bad news resulted from the game in Victoria tonight. The good news was that I finally got to play an entire game on a line with Dad, an opportunity I've been

patiently waiting for. It was great, although it came about after a fairly serious accident—the bad news part. Two players joined us today, Ken Linseman and René Robert. On Robert's first shift, the flat side of a deflected puck slapped him in the face and shattered his jaw. The poor guy had spent all day traveling to meet the team, and he was with us for all of five minutes, and now he's in the hospital.

Because the show must go on, I was moved to a line with Dad and Ken Linseman. Kenny is a great guy who played with my Dad at the end of his career in Birmingham in the WHA. Between periods Dad pointed out to Ken that he had played with Ken's father at St. Michael's. And now I'm with the two of them and it's a regular father-and-son-fest. Before I go overboard on the family-tree thing, I'll mention that it was a great game. I must have gotten five assists but couldn't bury one, though it was nice to hear several folks tell me that it was my best game yet.

Day 9—Afternoon

Today is a travel day that will take us to Spokane, the first of three cities we will play in the United States. Ken Linseman is a refreshing addition to the team and the fact that he is a music enthusiast has given us plenty to talk about. At this moment he and Eddie Shack are engaged in a friendly generation gap-related discussion that reminds me of a number of talks I've had with Dad over the years. Eddie thinks Ken's hair is too long and Linseman, being the individualistic sort that he is, tells Shack something that is the equivalent of mind your own business—but with more zest.

It is nearing lunchtime and there's talk about pulling into a restaurant. As the suggestion makes its way to the back of the bus, the question of when to stop is put to Maurice Richard. One of the nicest things I've witnessed on this trip is the love and respect all the guys have for the Rocket. He sits quietly at the back of the bus and the decision when to stop is rightly his to make. Gilles Marotte sits next to Maurice and keeps the Rocket and the rest of the guys in the cigar circle smiling. I should mention that the fellows who smoke cigars are considerate enough to keep a hockey stick jammed in the faulty ceiling vent for the sake of the non-smokers. And if they forget, Don Awrey is sure to remind them.

Day 10—Morning

Last night Ken Linseman and I furthered our musical bond by visiting a Spokane blues bar called the Big Dipper, where we shot pool and took in the Sunday-night jam. After conversing about Jimmie Vaughan, Duke Robillard, and various other acts, Kenny told me that he got a kick out of seeing Dad play on a line with me. He also emphasized the fact that every time Dad had the puck he tried very hard to get it to me. Thinking about what Kenny said makes me realize just how much that means to me. To lace up the skates with Dad, and play well— to me, that is something very special. In my life I've done everything from attending major events in my father's honor to washing the dishes with him after supper. But of all the things we've done together, the best of those, bar none, has been playing hockey with him. I hope Jean-Guy Talbot keeps our line intact.

I'm now off to interview Guy Lafleur in his room. I've been looking forward to the Montreal years. Dad is most fond of his days with the Montreal Canadiens.

At the airport in Minnesota, Canadiens assistant general manager Ron Caron and coach Al MacNeil greeted Mahovlich. Frank was pleased to see the familiar face of Al, whom he had known through Al's affiliation with the Toronto Marlboros. Prior to that night's game, he was also introduced to several more familiar faces, those of the men he had battled with for over a decade. Among them was his new centerman, Jean Beliveau. For Mahovlich it was a great honor to play with Beliveau, a player for whom he had the utmost respect.

A well-documented story came out of that evening when the two got a chance to speak in the dressing room. Frank reminded Jean of a conversation they had had during a break in a game at Maple Leaf Gardens years ago. Beliveau knew that Mahovlich felt stifled in Toronto and told him that "his style would fit in beautifully with the Canadiens." That was something Frank had never forgotten and finally the time had come for Mahovlich to test that theory.

That night the Habs played the North Stars to a 3-3 tie and Frank salvaged a point for his new team when he scored the tying goal. It was credited to number 10. "They didn't have a number 27 sweater, so I wore number 10, and I think I wore it the next night at home—for two games. Then I got number 27."

Since Frank was mostly a quiet person, some found it took a while to warm up to him. This didn't seem to be a problem in Montreal, where there was no shortage of guys adept at breaking the ice. Longtime friend and jawing partner Serge Savard described the character that joined their team in January of 1971. "I was fairly close to Frank when he came to us. And I think it was a great trade for Montreal at that time. It probably gave us two Stanley Cups, the addition of Frank. I think I had the right approach with him because Frank was a bit of a loner. You have to go and get him; he wouldn't come to you and start a discussion. So I would provoke him all the time by starting an argument—and we used to have a lot of fun with him."

Savard's method worked so well that the two friends carry on in this fashion to this day. "The last argument I had with Frank was in Vancouver two years ago. He started to talk about George Chuvalo who fought Cassius Clay—Muhammad Ali was Cassius Clay at that time. I said that Cassius Clay didn't fight Chuvalo in Toronto—he fought Clay in Houston, Texas—and I was there! And so the argument starts. I got him thinking and worried a little bit that he might be mistaken. A month later I saw a note in the *Montreal Gazette* that he had called up Red Fisher and said, 'That Savard doesn't know anything about sports and he gave him the date, the place—he had all the details. I was never sure myself, but personally, with him, I do that all the time to get him going."

Among a group that welcomed him with open arms, Mahovlich immediately felt like part of the team. And shortly thereafter he began to prove Sam Pollock and Jean Beliveau correct as the Habs tore through the second half of the schedule. "Right off the bat I found things very settling in Montreal. I think we only lost four games from January 13 to the end of the season. It was a good hockey team. We had some young players and some veterans—the mix was great. Henri Richard, Jean Beliveau, and myself were the veterans. We had a good young defense—Guy Lapointe, J. C. Tremblay, Jacques Laperrière, Serge Savard, and a good goalie in Rogie Vachon. I didn't know it at the time, but we also had the young Ken Dryden down on the farm team."

While getting settled in Montreal, Sam Pollock called Mahovlich in for the meeting he promised the day of the trade. Talking with Pollock instilled confidence in Frank and he was reassured to learn that Montreal was committed to winning. During their meeting the two casually discussed hockey, old players, coaching, and the trade that brought him to the Canadiens. Everything that was thrown on the table the two saw eye-to-eye on. Frank even mentioned the situation with Detroit benching their top line against the Rangers, which helped Montreal miss the playoffs the previous year. Sam replied, "A team that can't get in on their own merits doesn't deserve to be in the playoffs."

Mahovlich had never experienced someone so straightforward in all his years of playing hockey. "It was more businesslike than any other team. It was all business! And that's the way Sam Pollock ran it. Very professional, and they had a lot of pride—which other teams don't have. Their outlook was very positive and they believed in tradition. In the dressing room there was tradition all over the place. You went to a hockey game and you'd see Dickie Moore, you'd see Maurice Richard at the game. It affected the players and it showed them the way. Sure, Montreal had good teams and good players, but they always did things right."

The Montreal organization helped the Mahovlich family find a suitable apartment that was conveniently located near the Forum. Then, while the Canadiens took to the road, Marie was faced with the difficult task of moving from Windsor to Montreal in the dead of winter with their three children. She had packed all their belongings and was anxious to go, but a record snowstorm hit Montreal in 1971 and the trip was delayed. Six weeks later, they remained stranded in Windsor, living among the boxes, waiting for the movers to arrive. When weather permitted, the team sent a moving van to Windsor to gather the Mahovlichs' belongings. The family joined Frank in their new residence in an apartment called Mac-Gregor Place. Once the eldest of their kids, Michael, was enrolled in a new school, life returned to normal.

February 1971 boasted a special event in the history of the Montreal Canadiens. In what promised to be his final season in the NHL, Jean Beliveau was approaching his 500th goal. To score that many goals was a great achievement, one that only three players had accomplished—Gordie Howe, Maurice Richard, and Bobby Hull. On February 11, heading into a game against the Minnesota North Stars, Beliveau's career total was 497 goals, but before the halfway mark of the second period he had joined this elite group.

Mahovlich had been playing on a line with Beliveau at center and Phil Roberto on right wing. The goal came on a play that started when Mahovlich picked up the puck at his own blue line. Skating his familiar route up the left wing into North Star territory, Mahovlich left a drop pass for Roberto who cut wide on the right side. While the Minnesota defender chased the puck carrier, Mahovlich headed for the net. This opened a lane in the slot where Beliveau arrived to take the feed from Roberto. With nothing but daylight, the puck, and Mahovlich planted at the left side of the crease, Beliveau closed in. The goalie for Minnesota was a young Gilles Gilbert who recounted the milestone marker with perfect clarity. "I've got the picture at home. Beliveau scored three identical goals that night. In the picture, my God, you see Frank wide open on my right side by the post—with no Minnesota defensemen.

And Beliveau had the long reach like Frank. So, I tried to set a trap but it didn't work. Like I said, you see the Big M and Beliveau. And I'm saying, 'Oh my God, here we go—look out Gillo!' But it's not a dishonor."

Gilbert played the pass while Beliveau shifted and slid it by the Minnesota goaltender—Beliveau from Roberto and Mahovlich. The longevity of Mahovlich's career allowed him to play with many great players, from both the pre- and the post-expansion eras. Even so, the opportunity to assist on someone's 500th goal was extremely rare—an experience Mahovlich remembers with great fondness. "It was a beautiful three-way passing play with Phil and myself, then over to Beliveau, and he put it behind Gilles Gilbert. I feel great about it now. I feel quite proud to have my name associated with some of the greatest hockey players and having assisted on their big goals.

"The same thing happened in Detroit for Gordie Howe's 700th goal. Alex Delvecchio and myself set him up. And then Guy Lafleur tells me the other day that the first point he got was an assist on a goal I scored. It's trivia—but it's nice."

Along with fitting in on a personal level, ultimately a player had to fit into the team's system. Jean Beliveau recalled the ability of Mahovlich and Montreal's policy in such cases. "He fit right in. When you have a player the caliber of Frank Mahovlich, you let him play. You don't try to convert the player's style." This approach reflected how knowledgeable the management was at every level within the Canadiens organization.

It's no coincidence that when Peter Mahovlich was asked, "Wouldn't Frank look great in a Montreal Canadiens uniform," he answered without hesitation, "Sure—he'd love it here!" To be among people who understood the game of hockey the way Montreal did was a treat for Frank. Peter knew what it would mean to his brother to play with the likes of Jean Beliveau, and what could be better company for winding down an extraordinary career. For spectators, watching Beliveau and Mahovlich work together was a rare thrill. Of Frank, Peter Mahovlich said, "I always had a tremendous amount of respect for my brother," and then went on to compare him to "Le Gros Bill." "They were mirror images of each other. They had a class and an aura about them and that's the way they were. Very well respected, honest people. They were both gentlemen and that's the way they played the game."

In his last season, Beliveau led the team in scoring with 76 points (25 goals and 51 assists), followed by Yvan Cournoyer with 73 points (37 goals and 36 assists). Although Mahovlich arrived mid-season, his contribution was no less significant, a combined total of 73 points (14 goals and 18 assists for Detroit, 17 goals and 24 assists for Montreal). After missing the post-season the previous year, the improved Canadiens secured a playoff spot, finishing in third place in their division. Exclusion from the playoffs was simply unacceptable in Montreal. Third place was not only a relief to the team but to the entire city.

The downside was they'd have to play Boston in the first round. The Bruins were the big story that year, and although Mahovlich thought the Habs were good, Boston appeared to be unstoppable. "They were breaking records. I think it was 32 records they set that year, and they were running away with everything." The Bruins had finished with an incredible 57 wins, 14 losses, and 7 ties—12 points ahead of the second-place New York Rangers. Of the league's leading point scorers, the top four were all Boston Bruins. Phil Esposito won the scoring title with a record-breaking 76 goals (along with 76 assists), followed by Bobby Orr with 139 points, John Bucyk with 116 points, and Ken Hodge with 105 points.

Mahovlich recalled that aside from the finesse play of Bobby Orr, the Bruins accomplished their success through size and grit. "They were all big guys. Wayne Cashman was great in the corners and he was pretty tough. Esposito was great in front of the net. He was big and had a long reach and Orr would give him the puck in front of that net and he was quick to put it in. And of course there was Hodge, he also made things happen. But Bobby Orr was great. Gosh, I wish I'd have played with him. He would carry the puck up the ice and in two strides he'd be flying—great speed, great ability.

He would make things happen. I mean, the doors were wide open."

Although Mahovlich's style was different from Orr's—Frank's speed was based on momentum compared to Bobby's great acceleration—the book on stopping them was identical. Mahovlich recounted the game plan when his team played Bobby Orr and the Boston Bruins. "You'd have to catch him early before he got started. You'd poke-check him and try to get control because if he got up ice, there was no stopping him. He could motor, and our defensemen wouldn't have time to turn around."

No one expected the Canadiens to defeat the Bruins after their dominating season. But Montreal being Montreal, well, you can never entirely dismiss the Habs on principle alone. Along with the acquisition of Frank Mahovlich, Sam Pollock made another key move that changed the equation for the Habs. He borrowed from within, summoning an unknown from the farm. Up until that point, Mahovlich had never heard of the goalie that arrived at the end of the season—someone named Ken Dryden. "With six games to go, Ken Dryden joined us. He was down playing with the Voyageurs. Because he was new, Ken was a surprise—and he surprised everybody, including the opposition. They didn't know what to make of him because they'd never seen him before. So it's to your advantage if you've got somebody that the opposition is unfamiliar with. The other teams don't know his weak spots—if he has any."

In March of 1971 Ken Dryden made his NHL debut with the Montreal Canadiens. The call came for a road game against the Pittsburgh Penguins. For Dryden, the most vivid memory of his first game was not of the game itself, but of the scene in the dressing room beforehand. Hockey players do many different things to make sure they are ready come game time. Preparing their sticks is one of those chores, and it requires a personal touch. Often players tap a "powder-sock" (a long cotton sock filled with talcum powder and taped shut) on the blade to negate the tackiness of the hockey tape. This allows the puck to slide off the blade. While trying to focus in preparation for the game, Dryden witnessed another use for the powder-sock.

"They'd start firing this powder-sock around the room trying to hit the other guy's clothes—especially if he had a dark suit. As soon as it appeared, everybody would just start scrambling, grab their clothes and run them into the trainer's room and try to hide them. So I'm sitting there trying to get myself ready for this game—and this is the dressing room of the world-famous Montreal Canadiens. And, of course, the Canadiens were different from any other team with the way in which they approached games. The seriousness of what they were doing, the passion of it—and here's this bloody powder-sock and it starts flying around the room. Everybody is laughing, grabbing their clothes, and running out snarling threats at the next guy. The other part of the powder-sock routine was, you fire it, hit somebody's dark suit, and then the other players come in with this great sympathy. 'Ahhh geez, poor Fergie. Look at his suit.' So then, they'd grab the cotton batten and use it to take the powder off the suit. Well, of course, what the cotton batten does is just stick and makes a complete mess. This was the whole routine that's going on. It's like, holy cow! What is this? We've got a game to play. And not only that, I've got a game to play—and it's my first game."

Whether or not Dryden felt it at the time, the powder-sock routine was a tactful method of keeping the team loose, and that it did. With his sensational play through the end of the season, Dryden won each of the six games he played. But waiting in the wings were the mighty Boston Bruins, and so the Canadiens management had a crucial decision to make. Who would start in goal? Like a pitcher in baseball, a goaltender can single-handedly win a game. But the Habs needed better than a typically good game to beat Boston. Rogie Vachon had played the majority of regular season games for Montreal and earned a respectable 2.65 goals-against average. In the six games Dryden played, his goals-against average was a stellar 1.65. One thing is certain about playoffs; you must have great goaltending to win. Dryden was hot, so Dryden got the nod.

In front of Ken Dryden was a group of defensemen that made his job a lot easier. Having played with and against them, Mahovlich believed the Canadiens' blueliners were second to none. "The defense was the key to Montreal's teams over those years. They were good skaters, they were good offensively and they were good defensively. And it really helped my play. [Midway through the season] Serge Savard broke his leg, so he was out. Bobby Baun of the Leafs hit him at the blue line one night here at the Forum. But still, we've got a great defense. We've got a young Guy Lapointe, J. C. Tremblay, Jacques Laperrière—better defense than I've ever had. Each one of them played their own game and Montreal lets you do that. They don't say, 'Stay here' or 'Do this.' They let you do what you think is right. And if it works, they let you do it. With J. C. Tremblay I was amazed at how good he was because he never stood out in my mind until I played with him. Then I knew just how good he was."

Montreal's defense was put to the test on April 7, 1971, in the opening game of the post-season. As predicted the Bruins won. Although it was a low-scoring affair, the Habs struggled to keep it close. The final score was 3-1. Game two in Boston was more of the same. Montreal's Yvan Cournoyer opened the scoring but after that it was all Bruins through the first and second period. They thrashed the Habs, scoring five unanswered goals before the end of forty minutes. It was the kind of drubbing Beantown fans relished—especially when the victims were the proud Montreal Canadiens. Unfortunately for the Bruins, just when they appeared to have victory clinched, the fat lady was nowhere to be seen or heard. In a tremendous display of one-upmanship, the Flying Frenchmen rallied, surpassing Boston's five goals by scoring six consecutive goals in the face of certain defeat. Henri Richard scored at the end of the second, then Beliveau in the third, Beliveau again, then Jacques Lemaire, John Ferguson, and Frank Mahovlich. The clutch play of these veterans was something the Bruins could not deny.

Truly one of the great playoff series of all time, the seesaw battle went the distance. After their record season, fans were shocked that the Bruins didn't walk all over the Habs. While Boston did physically dominate the play, the Canadiens continually bounced back. Ken Dryden recalled the strength of his resilient teammates. "The Bruins would have the puck in our zone, and all of a sudden we'd break out on a two-on-one. When it was Frank, or Cournoyer, or Lemaire, going in two on one, we'd score goals. It was so terrific. It just gave heart to everybody else who was under the gun, and under this kind of pressure. Knowing that if we could hang in a little longer, we were going to get the reward. Because these guys were going to score."

As in Boston, the teams split the games in Montreal. The Habs took game three 3-1 before the Bruins evened the series with a 5-2 victory. After games five and six the series came down to a seventh and final game in the Boston Garden on April 18. Mahovlich remembered heading into Boston. "I didn't expect to beat Boston. No one expected us to win. We had come back to Montreal leading three games to two, and Boston beat us 8-3. Now we've gotta go back into Boston and it's Sunday afternoon. The series is tied three games apiece and we're the underdogs. I can always remember that game. I had two goals and an assist, and with seconds to go they pulled the goalie. I got the puck and Bobby Orr was in the net. I let the shot go and it hit the post. However, we won 4-2, which was unbelievable."

Knocking off the Boston Bruins made the Canadiens serious contenders for the Stanley Cup, but they were far from favorites. The Chicago Blackhawks finished first in the western division and swept their series against Philadelphia. They too would be tough opponents.

In the semifinals, Montreal faced Minnesota, and New York played Chicago. In the latter series, the Rangers fought hard, but in seven games, three of which went into overtime, Chicago outlasted New York. Montreal also advanced to the finals by taking the North Stars in six. Their run with Minnesota was less taxing than their series with Boston, but as Jean Beliveau recalled, they didn't go down easy. "I know we had a very hard time beating them. It was a very tight series with Minnesota." Mahovlich concurred in his recollections of the 3-2 victory that ended the North Stars' playoff run. "Minnesota was no cakewalk. They had a pretty good team. We're in the sixth game and we've got a one-goal lead. I can remember being on the ice with seven seconds to go and I'm thinking we've got 'em. The funniest thing happened. The puck was in their end so I thought I'd go in and pressure the fellow, force him to throw it away. Well, he threw it to his blue line, a player at the blue line threw it up to the red line and this guy at the red line skated and took a shot from our blue line. Dryden does the splits and the puck hits the post, deflects behind him, and comes out the other side. We almost lost the grip on things. And then the game was over. It's amazing how quickly with only seven seconds left this game can change. I think Ken kind of misjudged the shot and it just dinged off the post. And I thought holy smokes! But we won the series four games to two."

The Stanley Cup finals began in Chicago on May 4. As always, the man the Canadiens had to watch was Bobby Hull. After Jacques Lemaire scored the icebreaker in the second period, Hull answered for the Blackhawks in the third. The game remained tied at one until Frank's old teammate from Toronto, Jimmy Pappin, won it for Chicago in the second period of overtime. Game two was another disappointment for Montreal. Lemaire and the Mahovlich brothers each scored for the Habs but it wasn't enough. In the third period Lou Angotti netted a pair of goals and gave the Blackhawks a 5-3 win.

When the Canadiens returned to the Forum they were in a must-win situation. Down two games to nil in the series, and trailing 2-0 in the second period, the Mahovlich brothers put the Canadiens on the board. Peter scored first and then Frank rallied with the tying goal while Ken Dryden, who was outstanding through the second and third periods, shut the door on Chicago's offense. It was Yvan Cournoyer that got to Tony Esposito for the winning goal while Frank added his second with nearly eight minutes to go. Dryden held on and the Habs were back in the series.

In the spring of 1971, Frank Mahovlich was in top form. Coach Al MacNeil gave him the ice time he needed and it was paying off. Scoring goals at a record pace, the Big M led overall in playoff points. His success, which he's quick to point out, was largely due to the wealth of talent Montreal had down the middle. "They played me with Beliveau, Henri Richard, Peter, and Jacques Lemaire. We had four good centermen, so they mixed me up with everybody. They were tough to beat. Any one of those guys could turn the game around."

Frank was especially delighted to work with his brother. "I couldn't believe how well we clicked. We killed penalties together, played on the power play together. Peter was just coming into his own. He was a tall kid who wasn't very coordinated when he was young. He had some moves but his strength wasn't there—like a young deer. All of a sudden he's twenty-three years old and is starting to play hockey. He could take the puck from end to end, stickhandle, make some great plays. He was really developing into a great hockey player."

The Canadiens took game four in Montreal with a convincing 5-2 win. Pete Mahovlich, Harper, Laperrière, Beliveau, Cournoyer, Frank Mahovlich, Lapointe, Houle, and Richard all made the point sheet. With their big guns producing and their sharp rookie goaltender, the Habs felt confident for game five in Chicago. And goaltending was the difference. Although Dryden played well, Chicago's netminder was superb. After letting in five goals the previous game, Esposito responded by blanking Montreal 2-0. Chicago was a win away from the Stanley Cup while the Habs faced elimination.

Back in Montreal the heat was on Al MacNeil. MacNeil was under fire for his spotty use of fan favorite Henri Richard. Richard, the consummate competitor, did not take kindly to riding the pine. Mahovlich remembered the Pocket Rocket's reaction and the panic that followed. "The players came first in Montreal. It was great for the player. The fans stuck up for you and the reporters would too—which I liked. So Henri made a comment to the press about MacNeil being a bad coach. After that

MacNeil had police detectives guarding him all the time. The people were very emotional in Montreal. When Maurice Richard was suspended for swinging his stick back in 1955, a fan actually bombed Clarence Campbell. And the riots! The emotion was so high they broke every window down Ste. Catherine Street. When Henri spoke out against MacNeil, well, that was the end of MacNeil's career as a coach in Montreal. [In recent years] I asked Henri, I said, 'What the hell did you do that for? I thought he was a good coach!' Henri said, 'I got mad. It was just a spur of the moment thing.'" Mahovlich laughs.

Game six. The tension in the Montreal Forum was tangible in every narrow seat. Would the fans' hostility toward Al MacNeil surface during the game? Could the Habs stave off defeat one more time? The possible scenarios intensified with every passing minute. At the end of the first the score was tied 1-1. After two periods Chicago held a 3-2 lead.

That year, having played just half a season with the Habs, Frank Mahovlich had already established himself as one of the team's leaders. Ken Dryden, the rookie, remembered him as a veteran when he joined the team. "Frank was past his prime in terms of his most dominating years. He was still a scorer, but he was becoming more of an all-around player, which also worked very well in Montreal." As the series with Chicago continued, so did Frank's scoring tear. At 5:10 of the third period, when the Habs desperately needed a goal, the Big M netted his 14th of the post-season and in doing so broke the NHL record for playoff goals. "I scored the tying goal and Pete got the winner. If they win that game, they win the Cup. That put us in good position going back into Chicago." (The lone assist on brother Pete's winner also tied Frank for the league record of 27 total points in the playoffs set by Phil Esposito the previous year.)

The mood in the Montreal dressing room was very positive. It was the place where Canada's greatest heroes prepared themselves, and sharing that legacy was something Mahovlich loved being a part of. He described the demeanor reserved for the sanctum of hockey's winningest team. "You never looked for anybody to say too much, other than fun things to keep people loose. People would crack jokes or tell funny stories. Henri wouldn't say too much. What you saw on the ice was how they showed their leadership. Beliveau would say, 'Let's do it together, as a team!' This is how we won—a good team effort. We go back to Chicago for the seventh game and anything can happen, and it did. I remember Lemaire fired that puck from outside the center red line. A blistering slapshot, right through Tony Esposito's legs. It stunned everybody. That was a key goal." After Lemaire's rocket-blast, the question Montreal fans pondered wasn't "Will a Hab score next?" but "Which Hab will it be?"

They were behind 2-1 in the second period, but a storybook finish had been written for the previously benched Henri Richard. "Henri, after tying the game at 2-2 went and scored another beautiful goal. He broke down the side, went around the defenseman, and then stickhandled by the goalie. He made a great move—and that was the winner." After four Stanley Cups with the Toronto Maple Leafs, the feeling of winning the Cup as a member of the Montreal Canadiens overwhelmed Mahovlich. "In Montreal you felt like cheering, you felt like having a party—it was very enjoyable." And the team had plenty to celebrate. Henri Richard was a hero, as was rookie goalie Ken Dryden, who won the Conn Smythe trophy for his remarkable playoff debut. Frank Mahovlich's first playoff as a Hab resulted in a new league record for playoff goals, all while the Canadiens reveled in the great Jean Beliveau's farewell performance.

It's 1999. Now in his sixties, an incredibly young looking Frank Mahovlich rummages through a box of old photographs. From the faded relics he draws a picture of himself taken in the summer of 1971. His eyebrows rise on his forehead as he nods with approval. "You see that." Frank hands over the photo. Mahovlich is seen standing on a beach, but it's not the beach he wants noted. "That was the best shape I've ever been in." The chiseled physique of the man in the photo prompts the Hall of Famer to take a quick bodily inventory. With pride intact, he pats his belly. "I gotta lose ten pounds."

Looking back on his career, Mahovlich thinks of 1971 as the benchmark—and understandably so. The Habs gave up three players to acquire him and he responded by playing a major role in the team's Stanley Cup victory. This did wonders for his spirits, as did being part of the Canadiens family. His teammates were great, the fans were supportive, and Marie and the kids were ecstatic to be in Montreal.

———————

In 1971 the Mahovlich family found a small downtown house to rent. A block away, the children learned to skate on a public rink. A few more blocks and Frank was at work. On special occasions he'd take his sons to practice at the Forum. The players were always happy to greet the young ones and offer a stick of Wrigley's Spearmint chewing gum from the family-size pack fanned out on a table next to the skate laces and hockey tape. Life in Montreal was a blessing for everyone.

With the departure of veterans Jean Beliveau and John Ferguson, and the hiring of new coach Scotty Bowman, the 1971–72 season became somewhat of a building year. Through the shrewd business dealings of Sam Pollock, the Habs secured a young player who would become the team's future. To ensure their investments paid off, it was customary for management to bring their top prospects along slowly. One of the standard practices was to room a rookie with a veteran to give him confidence. In the case of the French-speaking Guy Lafleur, he was paired with the English-speaking Frank Mahovlich.

Lafleur laughed when he recalled the unusual experience that broke the ice. "We were in Victoria playing an exhibition game, staying at the Empress Hotel. I was very shy and impressed to have a roommate like Frank—and I didn't speak much English. So we're having breakfast in our room, and there is a guy hanging outside, cleaning the windows. Frank looks at me and says, 'Why don't we

invite him in for a cup of coffee?'" The window washer recognized
the gentlemen extending the invitation and gladly accepted. The
teammates helped the fellow through the window in his harness and
enjoyed an early morning cup.

Joining a team that included no fewer than eight future Hall of
Famers was intimidating even to a talent like Guy Lafleur. "I was
the youngest on the team, surrounded by guys that had three, four,
five Stanley Cups—and more! Frank was telling me, don't be
impressed by that, you'll get there one day." With all the eyes in
Montreal waiting to see greatness from number 10, the pressure he
felt was immense. "The first game I played, I played center between
Frank and Yvan Cournoyer. I was very, very nervous because I
knew if I played center, I had to feed Frank or Yvan—because these
guys had to produce."

Having been the top rookie in Toronto, Frank was able to offer
Guy reassurance with a voice of experience. "There was a lot of
pressure but I remember Frank often told me not to worry about it.
Just play your game and things are going to go well. He was very
good at that. He didn't talk much, but when he had something to
say, it was the right thing." The Canadiens management also recognized this and had an "A" sewn onto Frank's sweater.

As always, Frank's example on the ice spoke louder than the man.
In 1971–72, his first full season with the Canadiens, he led the team
in scoring with 43 goals and 53 assists. The contribution of 96 points
was a career best that helped solidify the Big M's place in Montreal's
glorious history.

As a veteran on the Montreal Canadiens, Mahovlich continued
making his regular appearance at the All-Star game, the NHL's
annual event that Frank played in for an incredible fifteen consecutive seasons. By 1972, the tradition of the All-Star game taking place
in October was no longer, having ended with expansion in 1967.
The All-Star break became a mid-season affair that, in 1972, was
slated for Minnesota.

Asked about his favorite All-Star experience, the Big M paused
for a moment. To single out a particular highlight is very difficult

for a player who had been honored to play so many All-Star contests—an incredible feat in itself. On two separate occasions Frank was named the game's most valuable player, something many would consider a career highlight.

But even more memorable was a unique incident that followed the 1972 game in Minnesota. With a smile Frank commenced the story. "The All-Star game was in Minnesota—I was with Montreal. There was a group of us who were on that All-Star team. So we were coming back to meet the team in St. Louis for a game. We're at the airport, walking down this long corridor, and I see these servicemen in their coveralls sitting down having their lunch. Then I look up and notice this man, all dressed in black, coming towards us. He's got an entourage of nine or ten people following him all carrying attaché cases—like businessmen, well dressed. Except this guy in front who wasn't wearing a tie. He was a very tall man and gosh, I took a second look, and it was Johnny Cash. I was amazed so I just stood there and observed. As he walked by the workmen sitting down for lunch, one of the men looked up at him and said, '*Hi-ya, Sue!*' As soon as he said that, I knew it was Johnny Cash. So Cash turned to the workers and in his low voice he says, '*Hi-ya, men!*' He continued walking and these guys thought it was great that he'd say hi to them.

"Over at a ticket counter between myself and this procession were Serge Savard and Guy Lapointe. They were trying to fix something with their plane tickets. As Cash was walking by them I yelled, '*Hey, Serge. It's Johnny Cash, right behind you!*' Savard turns around and he doesn't know what the hell's going on. Cash looks at him and says, '*Hi-ya, Serge!*'"

Chapter Eight

Day 10—Afternoon

My interview with Guy Lafleur went extremely well. When I entered his room, Guy offered me the seat by the balcony door, which he had thoughtfully opened. You've gotta love a considerate smoker. We discussed the Canadiens organization, the years he played with Dad, Uncle Peter, and all aspects of the game of hockey. It was fascinating to hear Guy talk about the role of the goal scorer and how it felt having to carry that burden. Enormous amounts of pressure, attention, glory, or frustration were all part of what that player had to contend with on a daily basis. When I probed for a description of Dad from that perspective Guy suggested that it was characteristic of most goal scorers to be a quiet presence in the dressing room—especially when the chips were down. He said that he was like that, too.

After my chat with Guy I strolled downtown Spokane with time to kill before our evening game. After a few blocks I found a park that had several arts and crafts vendors where I ran into Dad. We sat down on a bench to enjoy the sunshine and he told me that he ran into a lady selling homemade chocolate. Her name was Thelma Fisher and she was a great fan of Bobby Hull so she gave Dad a box of chocolates to share with the team. As we continued our walk through the park we came upon a carousel that was open for business. It was funny because Dad and I looked at each other simultaneously with expressions that said sure, let's take a ride. We mounted our horses and went around trying to grab the brass ring laughing hysterically. After that we found an Italian spot and had a fine pasta lunch. It's prior to game time now and we are resting in the hotel. It's been a great day so far and I'm looking forward to tonight.

Day 11—Morning

We are now on the bus on the way to Seattle after last night's eventful proceedings. The game was played at the Spokane Veterans Memorial Coliseum, and it was the last function prior to the historic building's retirement. The national anthems were sung by a fantastic barbershop quartet before we played one of the better teams on the tour, which included several old Senior A players. Once again I was matched with Dad and Kenny and we had an even better outing than the game in Victoria. I set up Dad on a nice goal and netted a hat trick for myself.

Feeling in good spirits following dinner, I joined Eddie Shack and Bobby Hull for a beer in their hotel room down the hall. Eddie and Bobby had their chairs out on the balcony that looked out upon an indoor courtyard where they could shout and laugh with other teammates and guests. After an hour or so of carrying on I thought I'd turn in, but when I returned to my room I found that Dad had locked me out. Immediately I understood why. He was angry that I was with the guys making the racket on the balcony. Before long he got up, slid the chain across the door and let me in. "After two beers you should turn in. I don't want people saying what's Ted doing with those guys." I explained to Dad that I was just trying to soak up as much of the road experience as possible when he repeated, "After two beers you should turn in."

So this morning I really felt bad that Dad was cross with me, which I especially regretted after having such a great day yesterday. Well, I've just learned that the night before, when Kenny and I were being respectable patrons of the local blues bar, the shoe was on the other foot. Dad was found guilty by association when he and Bobby and Eddie and a few of the other fellows all got tossed from a bar for being too loud—which explains his reaction to my hanging out last night. All the same, I'll avoid any further indiscretions that might cause him grief.

Jean-Guy Talbot has just walked to the back of the bus and is chatting with Dad. He knows that Dad and I are happy to be headed to Seattle because we'll see my sister Nancy who is living there with her family. Mom is out visiting Nance too, so it will be great to hook up with all of them. Jean-Guy was joking with me the other day and said "I'm gonna bench you in Seattle like Scotty Bowman because your mother and sister are going to be there." I howled and asked if Bowman really used to do that. Apparently he was known to do so on occasion.

It's quiet on the bus now, which is perfect as I'm about to conduct an interview with Don Awrey. Awrey is a well-spoken individual who played on Team Canada '72 with Dad. He should have some interesting input on that ever-popular subject. In contrast to your typical Canadian hockey fan, Awrey's recollections about the series seem less romanticized. I suspect, from what I've seen of Don Awrey, his account of the Canada/Russia Series in 1972 will be honest and factual.

Frank Mahovlich: "I guess the announcement about the series against the Russians was made in July, and we had August to get ready. On August 15th our training camp started. We were told Eagleson arranged everything. We were going to play the Russians but we didn't know what they had." In September of 1972, Frank Mahovlich and 34 other NHL players found out.

The schedule and format of the series was eight exhibition games that pitted two fundamentally and politically opposed cultures against one another in the sport of hockey. People understood that the series meant a lot more than two All-Star teams playing for hockey's ultimate bragging rights. However, what nobody could predict was how the series would swell to take on intense political importance that far surpassed the gravity of what any of the players could have imagined. Team Canada '72 member Serge Savard summarized how important it was from the Russian standpoint: "It was political because the Russians were trying to show the world that their system was better. Talking to them now, like to Tretiak, those guys were training away from their families for eleven months maybe."

And so, for their country, the victors would prove whose way of life was superior, North American or Russian—democracy versus communism. When the Canadian players realized what was at stake, they found themselves with their backs up against the wall.

Today, the 1972 Canada/Russia Series is recognized as the greatest hockey series of all time. In many ways it was, certainly in the eyes of most Canadian hockey fans. This, however, was not the case for all the players involved, especially if one looks past the political drama. Because it was the first of its kind, the series was full of kinks, some of which got ironed out, some of which didn't. Thus hockey was often secondary to the politics (internal and external) of what was supposed to be a great exhibition of the sport.

For the most senior player on Team Canada, Frank Mahovlich, the first sign of trouble had to do with the number of players invited to camp. "We had thirty-five players, the equivalent of two teams. So right off the bat, if a player doesn't play there's dissension. Management should have picked twenty players and stuck with it. We'd have been far better off."

With a team chock full of All-Stars, coach Harry Sinden had the unpleasant task of deciding who would play and who would sit out. The result was that players who sacrificed their time and energy were justifiably upset when they were reduced to being spectators. As the series progressed this issue became a serious problem.

The first four games of the series were scheduled for Montreal, Toronto, Winnipeg, and Vancouver respectively. The remaining four games were played in Moscow. Keep in mind that in 1972 international relations with Russia were far from the amicable terms, if not perceptions, that exist today. It was the time of the Cold War, during which an insecure fear of communism was very much a reality in North America. It's no surprise, then, that mistrust between the hosts and the guests pervaded the series. Nevertheless, it was a golden opportunity to learn about one another, though neither side cared to show a weakness. While most of Canada assumed their team would be schooling the underdog Russians on how the game was played, the Russians came prepared for the series.

Game one in Montreal started out with Canada dominating, but in the end, as Frank recalled, it was the Canadian team who received the lesson. "We went into Montreal and we weren't prepared. Guys were walking into the dressing room ten minutes late for practice. We weren't keen. In the meantime, the Russians *were* ready. They were ready months in advance. So the game started and boom, we got two fast goals. And then the Russians took over the play."

Peter Mahovlich knew that Frank was uneasy with several aspects of the series. Considering their family background, coming from parents whose immediate family had lived under communist rule, Frank maintained a cautious mistrust of communist authorities. Peter Mahovlich offered some keen insights into his older brother regarding such matters and the 1972 Canada/Russia Series in general. "If anybody was paranoid about the Russians, it was Frank. He hates the communist system. He felt the whole thing was a scam, and in a lot of ways he was right. If they didn't feel they could beat us, they wouldn't have played us. That was Frank's assessment—and he was right."

Canada lost the series opener 7-3 to a Russian team that was anything but amateur. Coaches and players alike were guilty of underestimating their opponents, and they knew it. The result was a storm of criticism on the team's performance from the media and the public. Needless to say, Team Canada had plenty of incentive for improvement. After the embarrassing outcome in Montreal, Mahovlich suspected that the Russians had toyed with them. "I can remember talking to Harry Sinden about the Russians and what they were doing. We were in Montreal, and we were supposed to be on the ice at 11:00. And there were three Russians still on the ice and they wouldn't get off. The Zamboni driver wouldn't go on the ice because the players were still on. I guess no one cared. So then we arrived in Toronto. I said to Sinden, 'You leave two or three players on the ice and see what happens.' He says, 'All right, I'm going to do it!' I said, 'You can't do it because it's not the way we do things.' He says, 'Ah, to hell with them. I'm gonna do it.' I don't even think Harry Sinden realized what they [the Russians] were up to.

"So sure enough, we practiced and now it's the Russians' turn to get on the ice. Esposito, my brother, and Ken Dryden are still out there. And out comes Kulagin, their coach. He sees the three players on the ice so he puts up his hand. It was like an army. The Russian team halted and one guy bumped into the next all the way down the line. Kulagin didn't know what to do now that he was confronted. So he puts his hand down and orders his guys on the ice. They start skating around the rink and Esposito and my brother are shooting pucks. And the Russians are skating around the net behind Dryden. Esposito lets a shot go and it missed a guy by two inches. The guy didn't even blink! He just kept skating around and around. But sure enough, it upset them a bit."

In Toronto, Team Canada bounced back with Tony Esposito in net. Brother Phil scored the opening goal in the second period followed by Yvan Cournoyer who made it 2-0 in the third. On a Russian power play, Aleksander Yakushev brought his team to within one. Then Pat Stapleton drew a minor penalty 21 seconds later that gave Russia the opportunity to tie the game. The crowd at Maple Leaf Gardens felt the game's momentum shift. Canada had blown a two-goal lead in Montreal and were in danger of doing it again. To kill the penalty, Sinden used Phil Esposito and Peter Mahovlich. It was a must-win game for Canada and the Russians were making their move. What happened next was arguably the most spectacular goal of the series.

Peter Mahovlich was returning to his own blue line when Esposito banked a clearing pass off the boards. Pete turned, gathered the loose puck, and headed for the Russian end in hopes of getting a shot on net. At their blue line, Pete wound up. The Russian defenseman Paladiev braced himself to block the shot. At the last moment Pete held up. With a shift to the right the younger Mahovlich froze the defender, skated past, and found himself in alone with only Tretiak left to beat. "I went in on goal and made a real good move, went to the backhand. As I was crashing the net I was able to put it past Tretiak. That was my Mona Lisa—it brought a smile to my face." The fans in the Gardens witnessed one of the most memorable goals in hockey history and exploded with cheers of recognition. The short-handed marker was indeed a critical goal. It restored the team's confidence and put Canada back in the series. Just over two minutes later brother Frank iced the victory with the final goal of the game.

With the series tied at one, Frank was relieved to see the team back on track. "Everyone woke up in Toronto. We had to win that game and Pete scored the big goal. It was a fantastic goal. The 4-1 score didn't indicate the play. That was a very close game—very even. After the game the Russians went to Winnipeg and we stayed in Toronto. They practiced on the Winnipeg ice and we practiced in Toronto. They were one step ahead of us."

Team Canada recovered from the defeat in Montreal but still had a great deal to learn about the Russian game. Like Canadians, Russians never quit. The third game in Winnipeg showed the resilience of the Russians, who never held the lead, but battled back to tie the match 4-4. In this contest the Canadians also learned their opponents had been trained exceptionally well. Mahovlich was impressed. "I can remember a few things they did that were outstanding as a hockey team. They had set plays. If a fellow was in the corner he could fire the puck to the opposite side, the puck would hit the boards and a guy would be there to pick it up. Esposito and I were on for a power play. We were forechecking in the Russian end, and both of us were about to hit this guy in the corner when he fired the puck. I'm wondering where the hell is he passing it; there's nobody there. The puck hit the boards, bounced to center ice, and Kharlamov picked it up in full flight. Esposito and I are taking this guy out in the boards behind their goal and the puck was in our net! That's how quick it was. Kharlamov, with his speed, he was like Cournoyer—a great hockey player."

From Winnipeg it was on to Vancouver where the plight of Team Canada took a turn for the worse. The calamity began with the ceremonial gift exchange, which unexpectedly wreaked havoc on the team. Mahovlich laughed when he recalled the scene in the dressing room before the game. "Usually we present gifts before the game. In Vancouver they gave us these wooden dolls, the ones that fit into one another. First there's a very tiny doll that fits into another tiny doll, and the dolls become bigger and bigger. They are hand-painted like a Russian peasant woman in a beautiful dress and a kerchief around her head. So they bring these out as gifts, and the number-one guy got the biggest one, whereas a guy with a higher number got a tiny one. We got into the room and the guys were arguing about the dolls. No one had their mind on the game. We were all fighting—'I want a bigger doll!' Anyways, Eagleson came and picked them all up—I think he still has them. So there we were before this big game, arguing about dolls."

However silly the subtle psychological ploy was, its intent to disrupt the players was in part successful. But the team had more serious problems that became evident as the game progressed. Fatigue set in. Their abbreviated training camp wasn't enough for the level of play the Russians put forth. After Boris Mikhailov gave his team a 2-0 lead, the Canadians were unable to pose a real threat. At the end of the second period Russia led 4-1. They went on to win 5-3. The disappointment expressed by the Vancouver crowd made the final score seem much worse than it was. Team Canada had been greeted with a round of boos prior to the opening face-off, and the booing continued throughout the game. It was hard on the players who were committed to winning.

Mahovlich remembered how the team was both infuriated and dejected. "That's when Esposito gave his speech to the press about how terrible the fans were. 'We're trying as hard as we can,' which we were, but it didn't look like it because we were tired. We trained, but training is a funny thing. If you over-train, you become tired. We were trying hard but it wasn't coming easily for us."

As much as the fans wanted to see Canada win, the players themselves wanted to win—and more. After the abuse from the Vancouver fans, the players' disillusionment with the series turned to resentment. If they were going to win in Moscow, they'd do so not for any fickle hockey fans, but for the team.

Before the series resumed in Moscow, Canada played two exhibition games in Sweden. By this point the problem of too many players had become an obstacle to the team's success. Players that weren't getting played bitched to other players who in turn felt bad for them. Morale suffered and the situation had to be addressed. Harry Sinden hoped to appease the frustrated personnel by playing them in the games versus Sweden. He also wanted the alternates to experience the European-sized rinks so they'd be ready if called upon to play in Moscow.

But although the week spent in Sweden was supposed to be a time of relaxation prior to the coming battle in Russia, it ended up being a battle in its own right. After an ugly 4-1 victory for Team Canada, a crowd of police prevented the team from entering their hotel. Through the commotion it was learned that the holdup was due to a bomb threat. On what was supposed to be a holiday for the team, the atmosphere went from boos to bombs.

When the bomb threat occurred, Mahovlich was on his way to Sweden from Canada. He wanted to recuperate and collect himself on his own time. The enormous pressure of the series was something all the players had to deal with. For some, this was more easily done than for others. Frank had a tendency to internalize his feelings, as opposed to a fellow like Phil Esposito who could speak his mind and process his feelings. After a few days at home, Mahovlich was able to rejoin the team before their second game against Sweden. Their first match was a chippy affair, so Team Canada came prepared to answer any dirty play from the Swedes. And they did just that.

Game two against Sweden was literally a bloody mess, and regrettably it turned into a media nightmare for the fed-up Canadians. What stood out in Mahovlich's mind from this brutal scene was a ghastly hatchet job performed on his teammate Wayne Cashman. "It got nasty. The Swedes had a defenseman [Ulf Sterner] who got Cashman with a stick and cut his tongue for about eighteen stitches. In his *tongue*! Gosh, we had terrible press. Believe me, things were not going well for us."

The next day the Swedish newspapers depicted a one-sided affair that charged Team Canada as both instigators and goons who were guilty on all counts. Then more criticism came from back home when the Canadian press hopped on the bully-bandwagon. Since his introduction to the international hockey stage, Mahovlich had experienced little of anything that resembled enjoyment. Next stop, Russia.

Frank Mahovlich recalled, "The players' wives and the Canadian fans met us in Moscow. We got off the plane and the soldiers were there and they took us to the hotel. We stayed at the Intourist Hotel. It wasn't the greatest hotel. I mean, Moscow was a gray place."

The city of Moscow was a new experience for the Canadians. In the fall of 1972 the freedoms that Canadians generally take for granted were not part of day-to-day life in Russia. Russian people were very much controlled in their behavior and what they were permitted to do. In this environment Team Canada got special attention. To keep the Canadians in line they were assigned their own escort/watchdog, an older, portly gentleman who quickly earned the nickname "Oddjob" after the character in the James Bond film *Goldfinger*.

Defenseman Don Awrey remembered the Russian influence during their stay in Moscow. "Our movement was controlled by them. When they wanted to take us on a little tour of the city, they took us to see only what they wanted to show us. We couldn't go where we wanted to go." And then the hosts began taking liberties with the supplies the team brought over. Mahovlich was amazed at the lengths the Russians went to in order to upset the Canadians.

"They wouldn't give us our beer and they started to take our food. The food there was strange to us, so we brought our own steaks. They sliced them in half horizontally and gave us half the steak. We started to complain so they cut them in half the other way. We got the thickness but still only half the size. By the last game we went to dinner and finally got our whole steak."

The steak and beer incident reminded Mahovlich of an experience his general manager in Montreal related to him. "Sam Pollock told me a story about the Russians when they came over and played in Verdun. The rink was sold out, two periods were played, and they wouldn't come out for the third period. Sam wondered what was wrong, so he went down to their dressing room to find out—and they wanted to talk to him. They were going to play across Canada and were short of hockey sticks. They wanted six dozen hockey sticks or they wouldn't go on the ice. So Sam gave them the hockey sticks instead of refunding all the ticket money. They didn't have much."

Hoarding was a common practice for Russians. Luxuries like hockey sticks and beer were too precious to pass up, even if it meant insulting a host or offending a guest. In their actions the Russians effectively killed two birds with one stone. They made life unpleasant for their opponents, and became well stocked with Canadian beer.

Whatever inconveniences the team had to put up with, they appeared ready for the first game in Moscow. Canada dominated for two periods and held a three-goal lead at the start of the third. But once again the Russians fought back. After goals by both sides, Russia netted four consecutively to finish the game with a 5-4 victory.

The situation in the Canadian camp was not good. Team Canada looked like a sinking ship and four of the players who weren't playing wanted off. The resentment factor over not playing was now a serious problem. To the disgust of coach Harry Sinden, Vic Hadfield, Richard Martin, Jocelyn Guevremont, and Gilbert Perreault all requested early flights home. The only solution was to get rid of the bad blood, and to do so as quickly as possible.

The press called them deserters and the coaching staff did little to exonerate the group. As a fellow player, however, Mahovlich saw it differently. Team Canada was made up of professionals, men who played hockey for a living. To go to training camp for the chance to represent Canada was a reasonable undertaking, but to expect these men to stay in Russia under the watch of the KGB as cheerleaders for their peers was not. Though it had been made clear that not everyone could play, the entire situation could have been avoided by choosing one team of three lines at the end of training camp.

The players who did stay in Moscow were there because they were committed to the team. If they couldn't contribute on the ice, they'd support their teammates from the stands. And so, each member of Team Canada—a group with an abundance of character—accepted that they'd have to win each of the next three games. To pull it off, they'd have to play as a team. Don Awrey assessed the crucial difference in the two sides. "We were known to be the hockey capital of the world until this series took place. And then we had to wake up and really smell the roses and say look, these guys are pretty good hockey players. They were certainly better conditioned and better skilled, but maybe they didn't know how to win as a team. We were more team-oriented."

In achieving the kind of bond that developed between the Team Canada players in 1972, a sort of mental hurdle had to be cleared. Peter Mahovlich explained: "To know a person by name and having watched him play on another team is not knowing him. I got to know Phil Esposito, Bobby Orr, Wayne Cashman, Bobby Clarke—these are all pretty solid people. But I never liked Bill White and I never liked Pat Stapleton prior to the series. So you had to get rid of all of these other feelings. All of a sudden you get to know them and respect them—and like them. Don Awrey was the same way. These are people that you didn't like. Now you're supposed to like them and support them? And that's what happened."

In game six, Canada cashed in with consecutive goals by Dennis Hull, Yvan Cournoyer, and Paul Henderson in the second period to grab a 3-1 lead. Near the end of the second period, Aleksander Yakushev narrowed the gap but Canada was able to hold on through a scoreless third. After their 3-2 victory the mood surrounding the team began to look up. The players were drawn together; they relied on one another with an absolute confidence and a shared desire to win. From this momentum shift Henderson emerged as Canada's man in the clutch, scoring the winning goal in both games six and seven. Phil Esposito also came up big in game seven with a pair of goals that paced Canada to a 4-3 victory that evened the series at three wins, three losses, and a tie. Emotions were high and this lifted the play of several players.

Frank Mahovlich remembered a few of the standouts. "I think Gary Bergman played an excellent series. I knew Gary from Detroit. Paul Henderson, I think he came out and played the best of his career. Phil Esposito and Yvan Cournoyer both had a great series, and of course we had Guy Lapointe and Serge Savard. Bill White always played a steady game. He was an All-Star and played exceptionally well—along with Pat [Whitey] Stapleton. I never called him 'Whitey' too much because Bill White was always around him."

The games in Moscow were as intense as the scores were close; all were decided by a one-goal margin. Although popular opinion in Canada once pegged the team for losers, the 3,000 Canadian diehards that made the trip to Moscow would have disagreed. And they made their presence felt. For Frank and the rest of the players their spirits were elevated by their fans' enthusiasm, a display that had the Russian fans in shock.

Mahovlich remembered, "At the games in Moscow the Canadian people were very boisterous. Whereas in Moscow, people would applaud—they wouldn't cheer. If the referee made a bad call, they would whistle. The Canadians would be shouting, booing the referee, and it was something new to the Muscovites. They didn't know what the hell was going on because they'd never seen this kind of behavior before. And we'd see the fans in the lobby of the hotel, or walking around to the different museums. They were all over the place making a lot of noise, having a super time. My mom came and was with Mickey Redmond's mother and the two of them had a great time."

Frank Mahovlich joined the spirited ranks as well when he found himself in a rather precarious situation prior to game six. "I wasn't dressed for game six and I was walking around the rink on my way to join our guys when our national anthem came on. Just by coincidence I happened to be right behind the Russian team bench." Serge Savard described the atmosphere in which his Montreal teammate defiantly sang for team and country in the face of the entire Russian unit. "You have to be in '72 to understand all of the reactions of the players; Russia being a communist country, not an open country like it is today. You'd see spies all over the place. I didn't worry about that, but Frank, he saw the bad side of it. So he went behind their bench and stood up for the national anthem."

Yvan Cournoyer, another Montreal teammate, knew what his friend was up to. "If Frank could do anything for the team, he would do it. The Russians used all these different tricks to win, and I think Frank must have said, we're going to do everything to win ourselves." Bewildered, the Russian team turned and took notice of the lone voice singing "O, Canada" at the top of his lungs. When asked if he was a good singer Mahovlich replied with a definitive "No," adding "but I did sing in the Schumacher Public School choir. We won a competition where we sang 'MacNamara's Band.'"

With one game remaining, Team Canada was a tight-knit group fighting with one goal in mind. With the series even, Team Canada's hosts were also looking to gain the edge, and once again it was back to the old trick bag. Frank and several other players received anonymous phone calls in the middle of the night that disturbed their rest. Russian coach, Vsevolod Bobrov, attempted to deny the team their allotted practice time. Worst of all, Joseph Kompalla, the biased referee they had promised not to use in game eight, was brought back to aid the Russian team. Mahovlich recalled the West German referee Kompalla. "He was brutal. The whole series over there was really difficult because the officiating was just terrible. And it upset a lot of our players."

Despite having the deck stacked against them, Canada was optimistic with the momentum of back-to-back wins. Another positive was the overdue support from the home front, telegrams that wished the team success and stated that the whole country was behind them. "We used to post them. You'd come into the dressing room and guys would be reading them, and reading the names. Thousands of telegrams."

On September 28, 1972, all of Canada tuned in to watch what became hockey's most renowned contest.

After twenty minutes, game eight was tied at two. Phil Esposito and Brad Park scored for Canada, Aleksander Yakushev and Vladimir Lutchenko for Russia. Alan Eagleson watched intently, hoping the series he had helped orchestrate would end in Canada's favor. In a good-natured gesture to his Russian counterpart, Alexander Gresko, Eagleson suggested that a tie would be a nice way for the series to end. This itself was wishful thinking on Eagleson's part, as Canada was down by two goals when he made the comment, but to his surprise he was told that in the event of a tie Russia would pronounce themselves the victors. Eagleson was frantic as he told Mahovlich and the rest of the team. "I can remember Eagleson was very upset. The series was tied—we had won three, they won three, and we tied one game. So they said, 'If we tie the last game, we win because we've got more goals. Oh geez, Eagleson was upset—'No, that's no good!' I remember he called me over and said, 'These guys . . .' and I said, 'Yeah—you'll learn.'" But Eagleson was determined to make sure Team Canada got a fair shake the rest of the way.

At the end of the second period Russia led 5-3. Could Canada stage one last comeback? Phil Esposito thought so, and started the ball rolling with a goal early in the third. Next it was Yvan Cournoyer with the tying marker. But for some unknown reason there was no red light to indicate that a goal had been scored. Clearly Yvan had scored, and yet no goal light. For Alan Eagleson the pressure was unbearable. Convinced this was another attempt to cheat Canada, the "Eagle" flew over the rows of seats between himself and the announcer to make sure the goal got announced. Just as soon as Eagleson went into action, a group of Russian soldiers accosted what in their eyes was a dangerous and out-of-control spectator. Frank Mahovlich recalled how his brother Peter, for better or for worse, prevented the army from carting Eagleson off to a less desirable place.

"Eagleson complained about a goal because the goal judge didn't turn the light on quick enough, and these soldiers grabbed him. There was a big hullabaloo. Pete stepped in and raised his stick in front of the soldiers and stopped them cold. They were going to take him off to jail. So Eagleson jumped over the boards and ran across the ice to our bench. I was on our bench and he sat beside me. I looked at him, he didn't say a thing—turned as white as a sheet. He was in shock. I said, 'Al, you're okay now. You'll be all right here.'" Mahovlich laughs. "He thought he was going to jail until Pete let him loose. I'm telling you, Pete was the only guy there to stop them." Cournoyer's goal counted and the game was tied, 5-5.

Six minutes of scoreless hockey followed. In Canada, fans were glued to their televisions, hoping for that deciding goal. The last minute of play arrived. Tension built to the point where fans could hardly stand to watch. But they did, and everyone in Canada old enough to go to school saw it happen. With 34 seconds remaining, Paul Henderson picked the puck out of a crowd in front of Tretiak. He got a shot away in close. Tretiak made the save, but the rebound came right back to Henderson. Sprawled across his crease, Tretiak was down and helpless. With a determined swipe Henderson sent the puck to the back of the net. It may not have been the prettiest goal, but it was certainly the timeliest. His third consecutive game-winner was not only a legendary goal in hockey—it remains and always will be a great moment in Canadian history.

And so, for the average Canadian, the 1972 series was a glorious triumph. It was a chance to bond, a rare occasion that saw Canadians express their nationalism. But as wonderful as this story-book ending reads, on the inside, for the participants, their perspective—distorted by the realities of business and politics—could not help but differ from that of the spectators. It began with the instrumental figure of Alan Eagleson.

Frank Mahovlich: "Eagleson was supposed to be our leader. He was representing the National Hockey League Players' Association. But he was in cahoots with the NHL, making his own deals with them as far as I could see. For the series, they made some kind of deal amongst themselves. The players—well, you kind of felt obligated to play. They didn't ask you if you wanted to play, they kind of told you. You've been picked to play. And there was a lot of ill feeling because Bobby Hull didn't play. He'd just jumped to the WHA. If it was Team Canada, where was Bobby Hull? So it was really Team NHL. And they called it Team Canada."

For Mahovlich, the exclusion of Bobby Hull served as a reminder of the control that the NHL still had, and forcefully exerted, over the men in their profession. In the world of the NHL, exercising one's right to earn a better living was not done without paying a cost. Bobby Hull fumed while recalling the course of action taken against him in 1972. "I was supposedly on the list of guys to come to training camp. But when I signed with Winnipeg of the WHA in July, that's when Campbell, Eagleson, Wirtz, and the whole NHL said 'This guy, we're gonna blackball!'"

Beneath the hype and the flag-waving was a cash cow of a series controlled by the NHL. So it was no surprise to see a traitor of the WHA punished for his new-found allegiance. For the players who did play, yes it was great to win—that's a given. But who, and what, were they really playing for? They were told "Canada," but that wasn't entirely correct. The hidden truth can be condensed to the fact that a smokescreen of patriotism made it easy for the people running the series to exploit the players. Huge profits were generated but it was never revealed to the players exactly where the money went. A portion was supposed to go to amateur hockey. How much did? And how much went to the NHL players' pension fund? These are questions Mahovlich has never heard satisfactory answers to.

On the bright side, if the players overlooked the money that they raised for something or someone else, they were left with the belated gratitude of a country that had offered uneven support. Frank pointed out that the critics and nonbelievers made their victory just that much sweeter. "It was great because Canada kind of wrote us off. They were always told that we were the best, and here Russia was leading the series. So it was a good win."

With the conclusion of the Canada/Russia Series, a celebration was in order. After game eight a banquet was planned in honor of both teams. Mahovlich remembered the gathering, which took place at the Metropole Hotel. "They said win or lose, we're going to have a party after the series at this hotel. But when we went to the party, the Russian players didn't show up. Maybe one or two of their players and that was it. I asked their coaches, 'Where are all of your players?' We would have all been there if we lost. I thought it was very unsportsmanlike at the time." In hindsight Mahovlich realized that the absence of Russian players was a reflection of how much the series had meant to the Russians.

In 1987 a reunion series brought the two teams together once again, this time as friends who had done battle long ago. It ended up being the celebration they had never had. After a game in Montreal a party was held that all the players attended. Food, and more so, drink, were plentiful.

Regrettably for Mahovlich, the latter made it difficult to have the conversation he was looking for. "At the reunion I spoke to a couple of them. We had one or two interpreters there to help us out. I was asking Vladimir Lutchenko about the [1972] series and what they thought when they first arrived. I wanted the Russian viewpoint. He told me that they got off the plane and on to a bus, and they had a police escort—a motorcade. They were all very excited and thought this is really big. Like hey, we better play well. We don't want to let anybody down. They went to the rink in very high spirits and came out smoking. So I was getting some really good answers but I kept getting interrupted by other players. People were making noise and drinking—it was loud. Rod Seiling was there and he started butting in." Mahovlich laughs. "I told him, 'I want to talk to this guy! Shut up and get outta here.'

"But I never got the whole story, the conversation that I wanted to have with him. Although I did hit it off well with Lutchenko. He was knowledgeable, a very conscientious fellow. Tretiak was another smart man. There's some good men there."

Chapter Nine

Day 11—Afternoon

We've just checked into the Ramada Hotel in Seattle and have a couple of hours of free time. Dad is having a nap and I'm going to go find some Gatorade to drink before the game. The bus rides can sure leave you parched. When we pulled up to the hotel another tour bus was parked outside. Immediately I started thinking, maybe that bus belongs to a band. I love going to see live music. So sure enough, as I entered the lobby, sitting in the lounge was the rap artist Ice Cube. I must admit that I'm more familiar with his film roles than his records, but I had a nice chat with him and afterwards his road manager said to call his room if I wanted to see their show tonight. They seemed to be a nice bunch of fellows.

Day 12—Morning

Last night was one of the more diverse evenings I've experienced in a while. It started out with our hockey game, which was attended by Nancy's family, and by Mom, who's been visiting with her for the past few days. Rather than benching me as promised, Jean-Guy Talbot appointed me honorary team captain for the night. This involved taking the ceremonial opening face-off that precedes each game. Then our line of Dad, Kenny, and me got to start, and seventeen seconds in I hit Dad with a pass at the crease for the first of the evening's many goals. We were actually embarrassed at the lopsided score of the game (22-4), but as Tiger said, the fans come to be entertained.

During the first intermission, Mom and Nance came into the dressing room for a visit. We were hoping to have dinner with them after the game but it would be too late for Nancy's young son whom she's still nursing. Mom knows most of the players on the team and was pleased to say hello to Jean-Guy, Maurice Richard, and the other fellows. In the dressing room after the game Tiger turned to me and said, "You've got a very nice mother; I've always liked her." I thought that was pretty nice, especially coming from Tiger who I've noticed doesn't waste a lot of breath on compliments.

Back at the hotel Ken Linseman told me that he was up for going out. Earlier I had mentioned my encounter with Ice Cube and he was interested in checking out the show. Dad had never heard of Ice Cube and predictably declined. So off Ken and I went to this club called Rock Candy. Neither of us had been to a rap show before. I can't speak on Ken's behalf, but I for one was enlightened by the pre-entry door exercise. It included a full pat-down search followed by a thorough scan with a handheld metal detector. There were also plenty of other security guys standing around waving flashlights the size of baseball bats. Inside the venue it was very loud and smoky. We stayed a little past midnight, opting for an all-night diner a cabby took us to. The rap show was a world away from the Greatest Hockey Legends—nothing to write home about, but nevertheless an educational experience.

We're on the bus on our way to Portland, Oregon—our last stop in the United States before heading back up to British Columbia. I'm thinking how nice it was in Seattle that Mom was there. She has spent a good portion of her life watching her husband and then her son play hockey—but has never witnessed the two of us playing hockey together. I know she enjoyed seeing us having such a good time together.

Family is so important. It reminds me of an insight Guy Lafleur offered during our interview the other day. He was reminiscing about the Montreal Canadiens when he first joined the team. "I miss the type of team we had when I first came up with the Montreal Canadiens. Guys like Frank, Jim Roberts, Peter Mahovlich, Ken Dryden, and Yvan Cournoyer—all the guys on that team. We formed a family, and the family we were playing for was maybe more important than the family we had at home. We had a togetherness that I've never seen anywhere else." When Guy said this, I thought, that must have been something else, being on that team. I understood what he was talking about because Dad had always said one of the big differences between the Toronto Maple Leafs and the Montreal Canadiens was the closeness of the players, the Habs being the tight bunch they were.

In the season that followed the Canada/Russia Series, 1972–73, the rebuilding of the Montreal Canadiens continued. The addition of two more future Hall of Famers, rookies Larry Robinson and Steve Shutt, guaranteed the Canadiens would grow stronger through the seventies. In 1975, Guy Lafleur, Peter Mahovlich, and Steve Shutt would emerge as the NHL's most lethal combination, but for the time being Frank Mahovlich, Jacques Lemaire, and Yvan Cournoyer led the way. The 1972–73 season was an exceptional year for the team, even by Montreal's high standards. The Habs finished up in first place overall with a record 52 wins, 10 losses, and 16 ties.

Undeniably, this team had all the earmarks of greatness. And the incredible spirit at the core of this unit carried over to life outside the Montreal Forum. If the change in lifestyle when Frank and Marie moved to Detroit delighted them, the change in Montreal left them ecstatic. For Frank, the memories of that camaraderie spill out in anecdotes that replay the good times they had. One such experience Mahovlich recalled had the team armed and dangerous.

"We went pheasant hunting up north of Montreal, Guy Lafleur, Jacques Laperrière, Claude Larose, Steve Shutt, and a few of the other of guys from the team. We all had these shotguns—I don't think anyone knew how to handle them. I thought somebody was gonna get hurt. And Lafleur! He was into guns at the time. He went out and bought this beautiful shotgun. It was a thousand-dollar gun that had stuff carved in the handle and all of that. I just liked being out in the country.

"So Laperrière and I paired off and we're going through the woods. All of a sudden the dog we've got starts to point and he's wagging his tail. Laperrière says, 'Ah-hah. You go over there and I'll go over here.' So he sends the dog in to get the pheasant to jump up and fly. Well, the pheasant takes off, goes right up in the air. I take my rifle and BOOM—I fire away. At the same time Laperrière lets a shot go. Well, there was nothing left of the bird. There was one feather that came trickling down. We both nailed it at the same time and there was no blood, nothing! Just the one feather.

"The ones I did bring home Marie cooked up and we'd be eating them and spitting out these pellets."

At all times the Montreal Canadiens had a stock of characters that could unleash their humor on the spur of the moment. When the time came for mischief and gags, more often than not Peter Mahovlich could be found with his finger on the trigger. Frank recalled his younger brother's ability to improvise in what would have been an afternoon of airport-confined boredom.

"We're all waiting for our airplane, which was coming in from South America. The team had just played in Oakland and we were on our way to Vancouver. Along with us, there was a large group of people waiting to greet someone from South America that was on this flight. This fellow must have been a prince or a dignitary of some sort because all the ladies had these huge bouquets of flowers and the men were in suit and tie and there were body-guards watching everyone. So we're just sitting there and all these well-dressed people start forming a receiving line. The line alter-nated, man, woman, man, woman, and so on. The dignitary they were waiting for got off the plane and began making his way through this receiving line. It was all very formal. The women handed him their flowers and then gave him a hug and a kiss, and each of the men in line gave him a hug and a kiss, too.

"When this starts taking place my brother decides to join the line. Everybody's looking around to see what was going to happen. Well, this guy gets to the end of the line and there's Pete. Pete picked this guy up, gave him a big hug and a kiss and just dropped him. It was the funniest thing you ever saw. You just never knew what was going to happen with Pete."

In comparing the Mahovlich brothers to one another their team-mates on the Montreal Canadiens shared the same opinion. Serge Savard shook his head and laughed while offering the common response. "Frank and Peter, they were like night and day." But under the surface of their defining characteristics, there was, and always has been a shared love and respect for the individual.

Ken Dryden found the two to be an interesting study and described what he thought was a great friendship. "They were this odd couple, but I think they were more odd couple seeming than odd couple being. There was this sense of real pleasure and bemusement that both had for one another. You could see Frank reacting to Peter's behavior like, God, look at him. There is something that is so strange and sort of wrong about it, but you know, there's something quite right about it, too. The underlying tone was one of humor and brothers. I never had the feeling that either one of them was really treading on the other, or that the other felt as if one was this heavy weight on the other. It was like, I like him as a little brother, and I like him as a big brother. And they both enjoyed playing out their roles."

Being nine years younger than Frank, Peter had both the benefits and the drawbacks of having an older brother close at hand. "One night," recalled Peter, "we were playing Buffalo and I got in a fight with Reg Fleming. Fleming had my shirt and we were struggling with each other trying to land a punch. Well, over my shoulder comes this fist that tagged Fleming—it was Frank. After the fight broke up I was angry and said, 'Hey! I can take care of myself.' But he was looking out for me."

On another occasion Peter had good reason to be angry with his brother. "During a warm-up before a game in Oakland Frank drilled me in the back of the leg with a slapshot. Before I could tear into him he says, 'What the hell are you doing skating in front of the net?' I was at the blue line and he's at center ice trying to shoot the puck into the open net." Peter laughs. "Geez, he was a piece of work."

Another reliable source of entertainment, a teammate that Marie loved to hear stories about, was Guy Lapointe. On his wife's insistence, Frank described a prank Lapointe would routinely play that would have the team in stitches prior to a game. "In Montreal we often had guests come into the dressing room before our regular-season games. When they were important people, like some head of a corporation or a public figure of some kind, they would take these fellows around the room and introduce them to all the players. These guys would be wearing a sharp suit, very impressed and feeling good about being in the Canadiens' dressing room. As the guest would be making his way around the room shaking hands we all knew what was coming. Lapointe would stick his hand in a jar of Vaseline and wait for the introduction to come around to him. When it did, without cracking so much as a grin, he'd nonchalantly offer a handshake and smear this greasy mess into the hand of the stunned guest. Then Lapointe would apologize straight-faced like it was an accident. Meanwhile, the entire room would be laughing while our trainer had to find the guy a towel."

Despite the daily hijinks in Montreal, there was a strict balance of work and play that produced results. Frank Mahovlich reflected on his years with the Habs with this in mind: "I can't remember ever losing a game on the West Coast. In the three and a half years I played with the Montreal Canadiens, we never lost a game in Los Angeles, Oakland, or Vancouver. It just shows you that playing with the Montreal Canadiens, it was very important that everybody be ready to play when it was show time. A lot of teams I played on, we just weren't properly prepared. We practiced too long, or too often, and we wouldn't produce as well. But with the Montreal Canadiens, almost every game felt like the Stanley Cup.

"I remember being in a restaurant with Dave Molson, who was the owner when I joined the team in '71. We were at the Windsor Arms restaurant in Toronto and an elderly couple came up to us and congratulated him on the Montreal Canadiens and what a great organization, and what a great team they were. They said, 'We've been watching them for twenty years and we've always thought highly of the Montreal Canadiens.' And I thought that was just great. And it's so true. I can remember going down and watching Jean Beliveau and Maurice Richard in the fifties, and boy it was electric. The games were so good. Every time Montreal came to town, they were always ready to play."

Another factor in the success of the Canadiens that must be acknowledged is the excellent coaching their teams have had over the years. After the retirement of the great Toe Blake, two brief stints with Claude Ruel and Al MacNeil led to the Habs' dynasty under Scotty Bowman. When he first signed on as head coach with the Canadiens, Bowman was still relatively new to the NHL coaching ranks. After an initial period of adjusting to another new coach's style, Mahovlich found Bowman to be a tolerable man to work for. Which isn't to say that Scotty and Frank didn't have their moments.

"I had a difficult time with him in the beginning, but it was nothing like Punch Imlach. He was all right in a lot of ways, and he spent a lot of time thinking about the game. He knew when to back off if he was getting to certain players and upsetting them. That was my experience. I didn't find him too bad, really."

As a veteran and a team leader, Frank Mahovlich carried a certain clout that the young Bowman respected. Serge Savard eagerly related a story that indicated just how far the elder Mahovlich's presence in the Canadiens dressing room went. "We always thought that sometimes Frank was somewhere else, you know, deep in thought. One day, we were in Oakland, and Scotty Bowman kept us after practice in the room and he started to talk. Well, he talked, and talked, and talked. He went on for half an hour. I remember this because it was after practice. We were all wet and started to get cold in our wet equipment because he'd been talking for so long. Everybody was tired of listening because Bowman wasn't really saying anything. All of a sudden Frank looked at him, everybody was silent, and I remember exactly what he said. 'Scotty, you've been talking for a half an hour now and you haven't said a f—ing thing.' And that was it. Scotty didn't know what to say."

Peter Mahovlich added to the story. "I think it was before practice because we were dressed and ready to hit the ice. After Frank said that to Scotty he got up and the left the dressing room. So everyone was in shock and Bowman turned to the Pocket and asked, 'Henri, what do you think?' Henri gets up, heads for the door and says, 'I think Frank's right!'" (Clarifying the particulars, Frank said the incident occurred between periods of a game, which explains Serge's wet equipment and Pete's recollection of Frank heading out to the ice.)

Mahovlich had reached the stage of his career that Carl Brewer had alluded to when he spoke about the Leaf veterans and their approach with Punch Imlach. Frank had been through so much that whatever Bowman had to say, he had heard it before. After exceeding his reasonable limit with the players' collective ear, Frank had let Scotty know. As direct and critical as his assessment was, in the big picture, it was part of what players and coaches went through in marking their ground, so to speak. Back when Mahovlich was with the Maple Leafs, there was a general misconception on the part of management regarding how to motivate the Big M. They felt that the best way to inspire Mahovlich was to drill him twice as hard as the other players—either that or spur him with insults and fines. Needless to say, this was beneficial to neither Mahovlich nor the team. In Montreal, Frank appreciated being left to his own devices, and in his own quiet manner he let that be known. This seemed to be fine with Bowman, as the Big M proved to require little motivation beyond his own discipline.

In retrospect it is easy to understand why Mahovlich, after considerable success with the Detroit Red Wings, continued to flourish once he joined the Montreal Canadiens. With Scotty

Bowman, Mahovlich established a working relationship that allowed the two men to do their jobs. Besides which, in the Habs dressing room there were situations that got Bowman's goat more than the steady routine of Frank Mahovlich ever did. Terry Harper was one such character who tangled with Bowman's running of the show. While Scotty didn't care for this, Frank and the rest of the team found it to be quite amusing.

"I remember Bowman getting really upset at him. Terry Harper was a guy who could come into the dressing room five minutes before practice and fall into his equipment." Mahovlich laughs. "He'd just jump into his skates and uniform all in one motion and go on the ice. You'd never know if his skates were untied because he looked the same every day. His uniform was always sloppy. It would frustrate Bowman because he liked the players to be on the ice five minutes before practice with everything ready. I remember Scotty Bowman looking at his watch as Harper was coming in with ten minutes until practice time. He was never late, but he was always close."

As the 1972–73 campaign neared the playoffs, the Montreal Canadiens were a win away from first place in their division. The game against the Vancouver Canucks that clinched it was also the game in which Frank Mahovlich reached yet another telling milestone in his career. From a Henri Richard cross-ice pass Mahovlich let fly an awkward shot that wheeled off the heel of his blade. Vancouver goalie Dunc Wilson was fooled by what amounted to a knuckleball shot that found the back of the net. Mahovlich was checked on the play and slid to the boards wearing a smile on his face. Upon getting up, he was jumped by an elated Jim Roberts while the Pocket Rocket retrieved the puck that marked the Big M's 500th goal. The Canadiens bench emptied onto the ice to congratulate Frank while the crowd in the Montreal Forum gave him a standing ovation.

The goal put Mahovlich in an elite group with the four others who had reached the 500-goal plateau—Maurice Richard, Gordie Howe, Bobby Hull, and Jean Beliveau. Beliveau, who was in attendance that night, joined the team after the game and congratulated Frank.

It was fitting that the Montreal Canadiens ended such an incredible season on a joyous note. The only matter of unfulfilled business was the last item on their agenda. With his second season as Montreal's skipper under his belt, Scotty Bowman had a group primed and ready to dismantle any team standing between them and the Stanley Cup. In the first two rounds of the playoffs, the Canadiens faced two of the league's expansion teams. The Habs took the first series against the Buffalo Sabres in six games. In the second round they squared off against the Philadelphia Flyers. At that time the Flyers were on their way to earning their nickname "the Broad Street Bullies." They played a dirty brand of hockey meant to intimidate their opponents; however, this impressed the Habs little.

Peter Mahovlich remembered Frank dealing with one of the Flyers who tried to test his veteran brother. "One night in a playoff game against Philadelphia, Moose Dupont speared Frank in the back of the leg. Without hesitating, Frank cracked him over the head with his stick. It sort of shocked me but at the same time it sent a message. If you want to do it, you're going to pay a price. And that's the way it should be. If you want to play the game, we'll play it. If you don't, here's the message. Not too many people fooled around with Frank."

The incident with Dupont reflected the changes in the league that were a direct result of expansion. With expansion came a new, hungry breed of players. Now those who previously couldn't make the NHL on their hockey ability alone had an opportunity to make it on other, less refined skills. Philadelphia would perfect their approach to the game the following year, but as predicted in 1973, the Habs defeated the Flyers handily, winning the series four games to one.

En route to the Stanley Cup, Philadelphia was a quick stop, but from that series Mahovlich notched one goal that Sam Pollock singled out as a most memorable play. "One game in Philly, Henri Richard and I were playing together and we passed the puck back and forth all the way down the ice. Sam Pollock had a seat behind the Philly goalie at the other end so he could see the play develop from one end to the other. He came up to me the next day and said, 'Frank, that was one of the nicest goals I have ever seen.' We passed the puck like click-click, click-click, click-click, all the way down the ice and I left it on the doorstep for Henri and he just tapped it in."

The Chicago Blackhawks would once again provide the opposition for Frank Mahovlich in the Stanley Cup final. This was a good sign for Mahovlich, who had been very successful against Chicago in the past. Also working in his team's favor was the fact that for the first time since their days prior to playing junior, the Big M's old counterpart Bobby Hull was no longer in the picture. Hull had made the jump to the World Hockey Association, and although his brother Dennis had done a fine job filling his shoes, in the end the Chicago Blackhawks could not match the depth of the Montreal Canadiens. In their seventeen-game quest for the Cup, once again the Big M came through for the Habs by contributing a very respectable 9 goals and 14 assists. Teammate Yvan Cournoyer was also exceptional through the post-season, and surpassed Mahovlich's playoff record with 15 goals and an additional 10 assists. The Canadiens defeated the Blackhawks four games to two.

Because of Montreal's lengthy roster of talent, each and every year seemed to be full of milestone achievements for the team. And so the Stanley Cup of 1973 provided yet another important page for the history book of the Montreal Canadiens. For future Hall of Famers Scotty Bowman, Guy Lafleur, Steve Shutt, and Larry Robinson, it was their first of several Stanley Cups. For team captain Henri Richard, it was his eleventh Cup—a record that he firmly holds to this day. For the Big M, 1973 brought his sixth and last. It was also his second Cup in a Habs uniform, which made Mahovlich one of only three players ever to win multiple Cups for multiple teams (Red Kelly and Dick Duff being the other two, with Bryan Trottier being the only player to do it since).

But more than records, statistics, or details of the games, Mahovlich's strongest memory from his final Stanley Cup is of the bond that existed between the players on that team. "They were all good guys and we had great morale. I can remember in the last game of the Stanley Cup in 1973, Claude Larose went into the goalpost and broke his leg. Well, the guys brought him right home—he was in a stretcher on the plane. When we got to Montreal that night the team thought more about how Claude was going to be taken care of than getting home themselves."

Back in Montreal the city honored the team in royal fashion with a Stanley Cup parade. Each player rode in a top-down convertible, perched on the back deck waving to a sea of humanity and shaking hands of the thousands that lined the downtown sidewalks. When the parade was over, Mahovlich was brushing off the confetti when he was invited to take part in a meeting that remains his fondest memory of a Stanley Cup celebration.

"It was after the parade and we'd come back to the Forum to pick up our cars. One of the players said that Toe was waiting for us, and he'd like us to have a drink. So we went to Toe Blake's tavern, which was like a hockey museum. It had all these beautiful old posters. Gosh, I don't know who has that collection now—I hope the Hockey Hall of Fame does. These posters were great. They went right back to the nineteen-thirties, and they were all around the tavern. Fellows would go into that tavern every day to get Toe Blake's response to the game the night before. It was a watering hole for locals that lived in the area for thirty-some years.

"We walked in and the headwaiter saw us, so immediately he lead us to this private room. And there was Toe Blake. It was in his office and he was opening up a cabinet. He took out a bottle of scotch, a bottle of rye, and he sat us all around and poured a drink for everybody. We all took a seat and you felt so comfortable because there we were, all of us Stanley Cup champions—of course Toe was on eleven Stanley Cups himself as coach and player—and we all knew what it took to win and what it was all about. So we just sat there and enjoyed the moment. Not too many words were tossed around, but we had a lot of laughs. Serge Savard, Jacques Lemaire, Yvan Cournoyer, who were all coached by Toe Blake at one time, and understood him and knew him. To have that kind of admiration for a coach was something special. It was an experience I never had the opportunity to have because of the ill feeling I had towards Punch Imlach all the years I played for him. So I never really sat down with Punch on a man-to-man level my entire career. I had one or two meetings with him but they were volatile, you know, I told him where to get off. But with Toe Blake you could see the mutual admiration was there, among us. He gave us all a pat on the back and didn't want us to leave. He wanted us to have a good time— savor the moment."

After the hockey season, the Mahovlich family remained in the townhouse they had moved to in Beaconsfield, west of Montreal, while the children finished the school year. During the summer they moved back to Toronto where they kept their house. Frank and Marie had also kept up the travel agency business, which they saw as something to fall back on when Frank retired from hockey. With everything going so well in Montreal, retirement was only in the back of his mind, and Frank returned that fall looking forward to the 1973–74 season.

Shortly into their schedule Frank received an injury during a home game. Unaware of the severity of the internal wound he had, Frank went on to play the next game. What followed was a frightening experience. "I got hurt Saturday night and I went to New York for our next game. I didn't realize it but my testicle was swelling and I started to sweat—like I had a fever. I went back to see the doctor on the following Monday and he took a look at me and said you're going up to the operating table. He thought it was cancer. I said, 'Holy geez!' So I went to the operating table. What happened was, I got speared and there was a blood clot that hardened and it formed a big lump. They took a look at it and said, 'Uh-oh, this doesn't look good.' It was so hard they had to chisel the blood clot off my testicle. So they did a biopsy to see if it was malignant. I said, 'Look, I've got cancer—open the window, I'm divin' outta here.'" Mahovlich laughs. "That was scary, I'll tell you. But the tests said I was okay and I was playing again in ten days."

While Frank was in the hospital recovering, Marie got a call from one of the team's owners. "Peter Bronfman phoned me up and said, 'we want to honor Frank.' They picked out a game in the schedule that would be broadcast in Toronto because they knew Frank had so many fans there." The Montreal Canadiens owners, Peter and Edward Bronfman, organized a special evening in honor of Frank Mahovlich and the scoring of his 500th goal. Marie met with Peter at an art gallery to help select an Inuit sculpture that would be presented to Frank on that night.

When the day arrived the Bronfmans took the Mahovlich family and a few of their close friends to dinner prior to the game. Following dinner, in the front-row seats behind the Montreal Canadiens bench, Peter Sr. and Cecilia proudly watched the pre-game ceremony during which their son thanked his parents, his family and his fans. In the Montreal Forum Frank addressed the crowd and read a French version of his speech. Marie and Frank discussed it and felt that it would be a nice way to show their appreciation to the people of Montreal. "I can remember practicing at home on a tape recorder. I wanted to give a speech in French so I wrote the speech and our babysitter translated it for me." Marie recalled her delight with the crowd's reaction. "The moment he began to speak in French they began to applaud in the Montreal Forum. You can see in the picture that Frank breaks into a smile as he's reading the speech. So it was acknowledged and appreciated."

Along with the sculpture Frank received a beautiful plaque commemorating the 500th goal as well as much fond applause. It was a great evening for a justly deserving man, and while the celebration paid homage to the career of Frank Mahovlich, it showed the generosity, kindness and class of the people in Montreal. More so than his 500 goals, what was truly remarkable about Frank Mahovlich standing at the center of the Montreal Forum that evening was the journey through life that brought him and his family to that point. Two immigrants came to Canada, not able to

Cutting the cake, June 13th, 1962.

The wedding party.

Million-dollar offer from James D. Norris.
(Courtesy of The Hockey Hall of Fame)

Clockwise from top left:
Frank and Marie with favorite artist
and friend, A.J. Casson; Michael
Mahovlich and Billy Kyle serve
dinner; summer vacation, Michael
and Frank in Lake Louise, Alberta;
camping trip; Nancy Mahovlich
holds on.

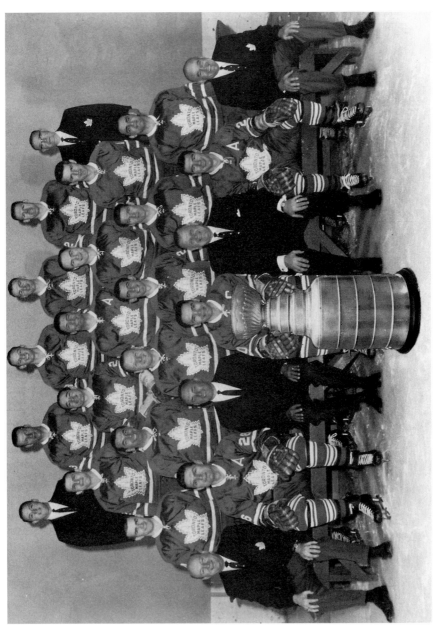

1964 Stanley Cup Champs.

The 1964 Stanley Cup parade—Bay Street approaching City Hall.
(Courtesy of The Hockey Hall of Fame)

Toronto City Hall (left to right): Johnny Bower, Andy Bathgate, Dave
Keon, Frank Mahovlich, Tim Horton (in background), and Tom Nayler.
(Courtesy of The Hockey Hall of Fame)

The follow-through. (Courtesy of The Hockey Hall of Fame)

Slapshot.

Winding up with Bob Nevin in pursuit.

Frank and Red Kelly in alone on Jacques Plante. (Courtesy of The Hockey Hall of Fame)

Frank with brother Pete who was with the Hamilton Red Wings.
(Courtesy of The Hockey Hall of Fame)

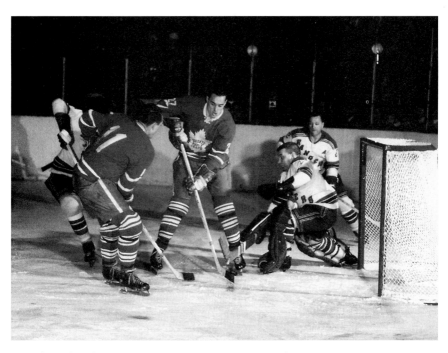

Frank and Bob Nevin team up on Gump Worsley. Doug Harvey
watches. (Courtesy of The Hockey Hall of Fame)

Warming up.

Watching the play.

Mahovlich family, April, 1968.

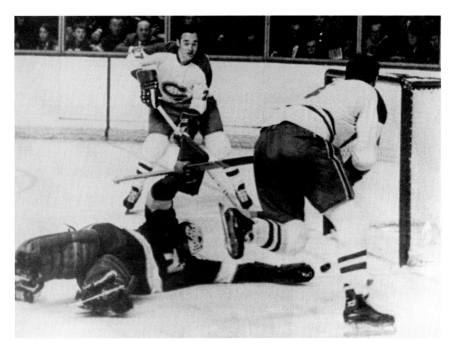

Jean Beliveau beats Gilles Gilbert for his 500th goal.
Frank got an assist on the play.

Ted Mahovlich, age four, and The Big M talk hockey.

The 1972 Canada/Russia series (left to right): Stan Mikita, Frank Mahovlich, Yvan Cournoyer, Serge Savard. The Russian player is Viacheslav Starshinov.

Pete Sr. at Leaside Arena. Frank remembers, "John Candy told me that my dad used to sharpen his skates."

Left: Mr. and Mrs. Peter Mahovlich at the Montreal Forum the night Frank was honored for his 500th career goal.
Below: The Mahovlich family at center ice. (Photos courtesy of Denis Brodeur)

A hunting expedition hosted by Jacques Laperrière (left to right): Guy LaPointe, Larry Robinson, Frank Mahovlich, Steve Shutt, Jacques Laperrière, Wayne Thomas, Chuck Lefley, Claude Larose, Guy Lafleur, Murray Wilson.

Henri and Lise Richard with Frank. Frank makes a point of always calling his friend on his birthday—February 29th.

Marie and Frank pose with the 1973 Stanley Cup.

FORUM XMAS PARTY
1973

Big M with Little M.

speak a word of French or English, and within their lifetime of hard work they lived to see their son being honored in one of the most cherished meeting places in Canada. When casually probed for his thoughts regarding his considerable life accomplishments, Frank characteristically downplayed them. "I haven't done anything yet."

When Marie looks back at the kindness extended to their family in Montreal, she is eager to point out the people who made a difference. "We had never experienced such nice owners as we did in Montreal. Bruce Norris [in Detroit] was also very good to us, but the first and only time an owner came to visit Frank in the hospital was during the time of that operation. And both Bronfman brothers, Peter and Edward, came and they brought Frank a book on Inuit sculpture. So they were very special people, and the Molsons were the same—they were lovely people. Because of that we still have a nice relationship with both of those owners."

For Frank, a professional hockey player, doing business with the people in Montreal was far better than he imagined it could be in the NHL. Because Montreal had great owners, people that cared about the game and the players in it, their honest approach filtered down through the entire system and resulted in a legacy of greatness. Frank Mahovlich praises the Montreal organization, which was an exception to the rule in the days of the Original Six. "I think in Montreal they always tried to be fair. Senator Molson and the Bronfmans and all of the leadership, they tried to be fair. I think that if there were Molsons running the whole league it would have been different, because they knew how to deal fairly."

After the business end of contracts was handled, players in Montreal had a clear understanding of what it meant to be a member of the Montreal Canadiens. Like Mahovlich, Dick Duff played for the Toronto Maple Leafs and later for the Montreal Canadiens. For Duff the experience of playing for the Montreal Canadiens was cut and dried. "In Montreal they expected the maximum best out of everybody, and they wouldn't take anything less. Anybody they had brought there, there was already an assumption that you were a quality player, you were a quality person, and that's what they expected from you."

The results that Frank Mahovlich brought to the team in the 1973–74 season once again proved his worth to the Canadiens. Despite games missed due to injury, Frank had an impressive 80-point season with 31 goals and 49 assists. At the conclusion of their season, the Habs made a disappointingly early exit from the play-offs, losing to the New York Rangers, four games to two, in the first round. Frank felt the performance fell far short of the team's potential. "We should never have lost to the Rangers with the team we had." With the conclusion of their season bringing an end to his first contract with the Montreal Canadiens, Mahovlich was now in the position of having to address his future with the team.

After three and a half exceptional years with the Canadiens, retiring from hockey was not a consideration. Positioning himself for that day, however, certainly was. As a marquee player, the Big M could benefit from a new professional league called the World Hockey Association. Several of the top NHLers had made the jump that Mahovlich was now contemplating while he considered what was best for his family. Prior to the formation of the WHA, professional hockey players had no leverage in negotiating contracts. If a player wanted to play pro hockey there was only one league and the salary earned was determined by powers beyond a player's control. Now everything in the NHL was changing due to the competition.

The good news was that the changes were in the players' best interests. Mahovlich recounted an experience in the Montreal Canadiens dressing room that illustrated the turning of the tide in a subtle way. "Scotty Bowman had called a practice at eight o'clock in the morning. Because we would stay up so late after a game, getting there and being ready for practice at eight was difficult. You're still half-asleep. You're not alert that early. We'd regularly practice at ten o'clock so some of the players were upset. Cournoyer came late and told Bowman that he wasn't accustomed to practicing any earlier than ten. Well, I was surprised. You see, I was brought up in the Toronto organization when the NHL was a monopoly. With the WHA now in the picture I could see the power was shifting. The players were going to have more to say now because of the opposition. They couldn't tell you to jump, whereas before the WHA came along, you'd say, how high do you want me to jump? That was changing. So when Cournoyer spoke out, I thought, aha—this is a good thing."

Frank and Marie kept the family in Beaconsfield while their children finished the school year. In that post-season Frank began making the calls that would determine the future for his family and the end of his NHL career. Aside from the financial benefits of joining the better-paying WHA, the reality that the Canadiens had to start developing their younger players was another key factor steering Mahovlich to the WHA. "There was a lot of young talent coming up—Steve Shutt, Bob Gainey. I didn't want to sit on the bench and finish two years like that, and these kids needed ice time." As always, Sam Pollock was efficient in presenting an offer and Mahovlich was left to struggle with the decision. "I hated to leave Montreal because the best part of my whole career was when I was thirty-three, thirty-four years old—my years in Montreal."

Frank and Marie decided that if they were going to leave Montreal, they would do so only if the circumstances were going to benefit their family. In a nutshell this meant playing in the city they called home, Toronto. Although Frank kept an eye on the new league's progress, he wasn't certain which WHA team owned his rights. Frank's next move was a phone call to Toronto Toros owner John Bassett. "I was watching the WHA develop. Bobby Hull had started it in 1972, and then Gordie and the Howe boys went down to Houston. From what I could see the guys were enjoying it and there was some pretty good hockey. New England had a good team, Houston had a good team, and then Winnipeg started to develop a good team. I remember Dayton chose me in the draft. I think I was number one on Dayton's list—Bill Dineen was the manager. Well the team never formed, it never even got started and it ended up that maybe Houston or somewhere owned my rights. I didn't know exactly who I belonged to so I called John Bassett to find out. He had purchased the Ottawa Nationals and moved them to Toronto. He called me back and said, 'Where do you want to play?' The owners were making deals among themselves, if they were interested in a player they would make a deal to get him. I thought it would be ideal to finish my career in Toronto. The kids were in school there before we moved to Montreal, our house was there so we wouldn't have to move again—everything seemed to point to Toronto."

John Bassett was eager to sign Mahovlich to the Toros and offered a contract that proved it. The offer was a four-year deal that amounted to nearly double the yearly wage the Canadiens offered over two seasons. With the better part of his career over in the NHL, Mahovlich was solely concerned about his family's future and their financial security. "In 1974 I was thirty-six years old, so it was decision time. I had hardly made any money in the NHL, and the pension wasn't any good. Montreal offered me a contract but I had this opportunity to go to the WHA. So it was a money situation."

To be sure he was making the right decision, Frank went to discuss the move with his brother. Marie recounted the final days that included the visit to Peter's home and a decision that was mentally easy but emotionally tough. "Frank talked with Peter and the two of them weighed it, should he go or should he stay. Eventually Frank went down to see Sam Pollock but he didn't want to keep saying to him, 'Well, this is what Bassett's offering.' Pollock sort of gave his last offer and Frank knew that it was still less than Bassett's offer. Then he made the decision that he would go to the Toros. He walked down the hall and he wanted to say goodbye to Jean Beliveau who was working in the offices at the Forum, but Beliveau was on the phone. Frank just waved to him and Jean waved back—and Frank came home."

Chapter Ten

Day 12—Evening

As always, the conversation on the bus provided an afternoon of solid entertainment. I've become keenly aware of the fact that not all the players on the Montreal Canadiens loved Scotty Bowman. After Dad left the team and Bowman established a considerable record as a winning coach, he also developed a few ongoing conflicts with some of the players on his team. Guy Lafleur told a story about the Canadiens having to evacuate a hotel in the middle of the night because of a fire. Once outside, one of the players Bowman had been riding that year shouted with alarming concern, "Where's Scotty?" Another voice yelled, "I'm surprised you care!" Then the first voice answered, "I don't give a shit about Scotty, I just want to find his plus/minus sheet!"

Before the game here in Portland, the folks running the tour had me interviewed for a promotional video they've been working on. Along with questions related to the appeal of the old-timers games, I was asked about my experiences as a guest on the tour. I explained that I was writing a book on my father, interviewing the other players on the trip, and having a ball in the process.

Then I was asked what I had learned about Dad, and I replied as best I could, but this is a question I'd like another shot at answering. I have to say that most of what I've been told by the others about Dad's personality, his ability as a hockey player, and so on are things I'm well aware of. My purpose in doing the interviews is to gather different stories that illustrate the facts. So before answering the question I would like to amend it to, What have I learned from this experience with Dad? More important than discovering something new about my father, I believe I've gained an appreciation for something very significant in the big picture of life—his life, my life, everyone's lives. It's about family, loved ones, and taking time to enjoy oneself. Together Dad and I have had a great time doing what we love to do, which is something both simple and precious.

After the game, the team was tired and thirsty and we gathered in our hotel's restaurant bar. From the late-night menu Dad and I each ordered a glass of beer and a garden salad. Scattered around small cocktail tables the team conversed over a nightcap while the local evening news came on the large-screen television that dominated the lounge. Dad and I were feeling content after another particularly good night for our line. One thing you could say I learned about him is that, for his age, the Big M is in tremendous shape and can still play hockey better than I could ever hope to.

We had won the game 7-4, and our line had scored five of the seven goals. As we were being served our salads, Dad and I began discussing one of the nicer goals we'd scored. Dad had gone to the corner to gather the puck with a defenseman checking him. Anticipating the play, I had circled over from my wing to give him an open man. As soon as I moved to Dad he dished a pass that drew the second defenseman away from the slot and a trailing Ken Linseman. Skating my arching route I had given a tidy backhand pass to Ken, who with expert precision had roofed the puck over the goalie's shoulder.

While I was indulging myself in this verbal replay a similar goal was being broadcast on the sports news. As I watched, I was about to say that the play was exactly like our goal when I realized that it *was* our goal. Another one of those "Fantasy Island" moments that I've had a few of on this trip! I thought that any moment now Ricardo Montalban would appear in a white suit to announce in that slow, exaggerated voice, "Nice, nice pass, Ted—your fantasy is over. Please board the pontoon plane waiting at the end of the dock."

Day 13—Morning
We're on our way back to Canada to play in Chilliwack tonight. Earlier this morning Bobby Hull had been good enough to chat with me some more. The topic I had wanted to cover was the second and less recognized series between Canada and Russia that took place in 1974. Hull had been a member of the team that in 1974 was made up of WHA players. After Dad made his decision to sign with the Toronto Toros, he too became eligible to play.

In the summer of 1974 Frank and Marie had packed up their rented townhouse, made arrangements for the shipping of their accumulated antique Quebec pine furniture, and bid farewell to Montreal. While Mahovlich looked forward to resettling their home in Toronto, plans were being made in the WHA for a pre-season trip that wasn't on the Big M's wish list. "As soon as I signed my contract they were negotiating for another series with Russia. So there I was off to Russia again and I hadn't even played a game with the Toros. I didn't actually want to go, but the league was starting out and there was great coverage. It was good exposure for the league and that year the WHA must have signed ten or fifteen NHL players. The publicity the league was getting was worth millions, so we had to participate."

In a similar situation to Mahovlich's, Paul Henderson was considering signing with the WHA that same summer. Henderson was a member of the troubled Toronto Maple Leafs, and with his family in Toronto and a generous offer on the table, joining the Toros would be a logical career move. Knowing that Mahovlich was on board with the Toros, Paul met with his old mate from Team

Canada '72 and expressed his reservations about leaving the Maple Leafs and the NHL.

"I have a vivid memory from when I was considering jumping to the WHA. I talked to Frank about it and I said, 'You know, Frank, I've never won the Stanley Cup, and geez I want to get my name on there. I'm just not sure this is the right move.' One of the great disappointments for me was that I've not won the bloody thing. Frank looked at me and he said, 'Paul, as long as you are a member of the Toronto Maple Leafs you are not going to win the Stanley Cup. It is impossible for Harold Ballard to have a Stanley Cup-winning team.' And I specifically remember saying to Frank, 'Frank, do you not think that if he gets a good general manager and a good coach, that a good general manager and a good coach can overcome this?' He said, 'Paul, that will never happen because he will never let them run the team. His ego is too big. And first of all, if he gets a good man, a good man will leave.' I sat there, and I thought about it, and I said, you know, I think Frank is right. That was the thing that sealed it for me to jump to the WHA. Now, hindsight is 20/20. Do you think that wasn't prophetic? I mean, Frank predicted that and I was naïve, I thought, oh geez Frank, I think if we just got a really good general manager and a good coach. And he said, 'Paul, it ain't gonna happen!' So I decided to go to the WHA and it was the best thing I ever did."

Once Paul Henderson signed with the Toronto Toros, he too was obligated to boost the WHA in their series against the Russians. Having been there before, Henderson was also less than keen on a second visit to Russia. "I didn't want to go. That was one of the things that I was reticent to sign with because I didn't want to go back there. I hated Russia with a passion. I had no desire to go back there whatsoever. It was just such a desolate, dismal country. There was nothing that I liked about it. The oppression of the people—I just couldn't wait to get out of there after the series."

The format for the 1974 series was basically the same as in 1972, eight games, four across Canada and four in Moscow. Game one of the 1974 series took place in Quebec City as opposed to Montreal, the one variation from 1972, followed by Toronto, Winnipeg, and Vancouver. To gear up for the series Team Canada headed out to an Edmonton-based training camp.

As part of their preparation for the main event they played a series of exhibition games against Canadian juniors. While the team worked on a cohesive line-up, the press speculated on what Team Canada '74 might be able to accomplish. Of particular interest in the analysis of the squad was the father-and-sons presence of the Howe family. Offering a teammate's perspective, Frank Mahovlich was delighted to be back playing on a team with Gordie and was further impressed by his boys. "Mark and Marty, they were just great. I can't say enough nice things about the Howe boys, and they stood up well." Another item in the plus column was the inclusion of the "Golden Jet," Bobby Hull. After being denied eligibility to play in 1972, Hull was eager to play the Russians this time around. However, despite the fact that Hull liked their chances, he could see where the team might run into trouble. "We had a good team, a very good team. But our defense core wasn't as good as the 1972 team because they had Serge Savard, Guy Lapointe, and Billy White— that group of guys knew how to play."

Understandably, and undoubtedly by design, Team Canada '74 and the series as a whole would be compared to 1972. Since the newer version of the team was made up solely of WHA players, this allowed only three players from Team Canada '72 to return: Frank Mahovlich, Paul Henderson, and core defenseman Pat Stapleton. Aside from the other former NHL stars—Gordie Howe, Bobby Hull, goaltender Gerry Cheevers, and defenseman J. C. Tremblay—the bulk of the 1974 team was made up of lesser-known talent. As a result the expectations were nowhere near those that existed for the All-Star team of 1972. This second-fiddle factor, WHA to NHL, put Team Canada '74 in the favorable position of having nothing to lose and everything to gain. This was also the case for the WHA owners, who had created the series to showcase their upstart league on an international stage. And so, with the experience of some great veterans, the knowledge gained from the 1972 series, and some fine young players, Team Canada '74 was ready to take on the Russians.

The opening game in Quebec City was not the hockey extravaganza the 1972 series was in Montreal two years earlier; it couldn't be. Nevertheless, on both a personal and a professional level, the Canadian players had an opportunity to earn respect and credibility for the league they supported—and they were determined to do just that. Paul Henderson, the hero of Team Canada '72, recalled the feeling heading into the series and the shape they found themselves in early on: "To me it was very important that we beat them, and we were fired up for it. I was on a line with Bruce MacGregor and Mike Walton. The first game in Quebec we tied. Then we came to Toronto and won. So we had a tie and a win and I was feeling good about this and we were playing really well. Then we went into Winnipeg and Billy Harris the coach said, 'Everybody is going to play.'"

For Mahovlich, the call Harris made reminded him of the turmoil Team Canada ran into in 1972. "After the second game in Toronto, then, as always, politics got involved. Certain players play, certain players don't play. The same problems were there in 1974 as in 1972." In fairness to all the players who committed themselves to the team, Harris decided that everyone would get ice time during the series. To facilitate this gesture of good faith, six players from the 4-1 Toronto victory line-up were replaced. One of the six missing players was goaltender Gerry Cheevers, a move that Gordie Howe, who was also rotated out of the line-up, saw as a critical factor in the outcome of the third game. "Cheesy was playing well for us but in Winnipeg our coach took him out and put Don McLeod in—and the Russians really got to him." The upshot of the decision was an 8-5 shelling of Canada, but even more damaging was the loss of confidence the players felt. Bobby Hull expressed the general feeling among the veterans: "He took Cheevers out of goal, benched Howe and one or two of our other good players— gave them the night off! You don't give anyone the night off in a series where you need to win or tie every game."

The next game in Vancouver saw the return of Frank Mahovlich, Gordie Howe, and Gerry Cheevers to the line-up. Frank and Gordie both scored, along with Bobby Hull who netted a hat trick, all of which took place in the first period. But what should have been a victory for Team Canada ended in a 5-5 tie. Canada had squandered an opportunity that would have put them ahead in the series and restored their confidence. For Mahovlich, the situation the team was in felt like shaky ground. "We went back to Russia in better shape than Team Canada '72 went back with. But with the mixing of the line-up and who would get to play, there was a lot of doubt in everybody's minds. We didn't know what the next move would be."

With the series even in games, Team Canada prepared for the trip back to Moscow where little had changed since the last visit in 1972. Communist Russia was still very much a harsh alternative to the North American way of life. Going in, the Canadian players were aware that good treatment and comfort would be at a minimum.

Although Mahovlich maintained his dislike for the oppressive society in Russia, he made the trek in a more relaxed mood than in his last journey. Paul Henderson, who had first played with Frank in the 1972 series, recalled the difference in his teammate on their second trip: "Frank sort of went with the flow—and I think most of the guys did."

Appropriately, Team Canada was expecting to roll with a few punches, and as soon as they disembarked from their plane the tampering the Russians became famous for commenced. Marie Mahovlich recounted the ordeal orchestrated upon their arrival: "We flew from Finland to Moscow. Billy Harris had scheduled a hockey practice for about two hours after the team arrived, but when we got to the airport the hockey bags of Gordie Howe, Bobby Hull, and Frank Mahovlich were nowhere to be seen. The coaches decided that we'd wait, and they kept hoping the bags would appear off the plane. Of course they were purposely removed and the end result was that Team Canada did not practice that day. So the Russians effectively threw them off their game plan."

Trying to prepare mentally and physically for a series that was supposedly of international importance became next to impossible with the planned Russian interference. Although Mahovlich attempted to put a good face on it, many of his previous experiences from 1972 were being relived and it wasn't something he cared for. Gordie Howe, who discovered a book of figures relating to his cattle business had gone missing from his hockey bag, had more of a laissez-faire attitude. As soon as Gordie and his wife Colleen checked into their hotel room they seized the opportunity for levity on the off chance that the Russians might be listening in. "They said that our rooms would be bugged so Colleen and I just had fun with it. We would walk around our hotel room talking to them. 'The bedspread in our room has a hole in it which allows us to see the lovely floral pattern on our sheets, which is nice, but there are terrible urine stains in the bathroom that you should really get rid of.' Well, years later I spoke to someone that was in the KGB and I found out that each of our rooms were definitely bugged and they would randomly listen in."

After losing a close game five in Moscow 3-2, the remainder of the 1974 series was a disappointment for Team Canada. When game six resulted in a 5-2 loss, the best Canada could hope for heading into the final two games was an overall tie. Although a disallowed Bobby Hull goal at the buzzer of game seven might have made for an interesting finish, the 4-4 tie marked the end of the series for Team Canada. With no heroic performance left to be played out, Team Canada '74 came home tired and frustrated after losing the final game 3-2.

Paul Henderson summarized his thoughts regarding the forgettable series of 1974. "To me it was over at the third game. I mean, you get up, and obviously you go out and play, but it had lost all its intensity. As soon as I saw the line-up I said, 'This is throwing in the towel.' There was no way on God's green earth that you could win at that caliber by putting that many new guys in the line-up. They absolutely blitzed us that game and I thought to myself, if that's the way it's going to be, I will not let myself get so emotionally involved as I did the last time. It took all the heat off as far as I was concerned."

Upon returning home Mahovlich and Henderson reported to the Toronto Toros where they met their new teammates. Over the first few days Mahovlich felt a little awkward joining a dressing room full of players that he had never even heard of, let alone met before. Nonetheless, with an open mind he welcomed the challenge of building up another hockey franchise in his old hometown.

Part of what made the opportunity so attractive was the prospect of building a new arena that would rival the shop run by Harold Ballard. But to Mahovlich's dismay, the Toros owner John Bassett made a deal with the competition. "When I signed on with the Toros they were playing their games at Varsity Arena [the University of Toronto's existing venue] and I thought they would build a new rink. So Harold Ballard gave Bassett a phone call. You see, he was already concerned because Bassett was getting a team together that maybe could compete, and he didn't want another big rink in Toronto. Well, John Bassett fell for the trap—and his father warned him, 'Stay away from Ballard!'"

Rather than spend the initial investment on an arena that the Toros could have managed to an eventual profit, Bassett's team became tenants of Ballard's, the landlord of Maple Leaf Gardens. This arrangement allowed Ballard to control the activity of the team he wanted to see fail. Mahovlich described typical ploys of Ballard. "So now we're playing in Maple Leaf Gardens and the Winnipeg Jets are coming in with the two Swedes and Bobby Hull, and I mean people are lining up for tickets. So for that game Ballard only allowed one ticket wicket to be open. He closed all the other wickets. Three of my buddies came down to see the game and they couldn't get in because the line-up was down to Yonge Street! They ended up watching the game on television at the Westbury Hotel. We had over 10,000 people, which was our best attendance, and we could have filled the rink. So these were the things Ballard would pull. Now the lights. When the Toros started to play at Maple Leaf Gardens we were playing in shadows because Ballard wouldn't turn the TV lights on. So it was like back to 1957 when I started. John Bassett got all upset and he said, 'We want the lights, turn the lights on,' and Ballard said, 'That'll be another $3,000 per game.'"

After Mahovlich's years in the Toronto Maple Leafs organization he knew the outcome of doing business with Ballard, but John Bassett was determined to learn the hard way. While Bassett was fair with Mahovlich as an employer, his lack of experience in running a hockey team became another hindrance to the team's success. The firing of the coach that Bassett so desired for Team Canada '74 was a clear indication of the uncertainty in Bassett's mind involving hockey matters. Mahovlich recalled the total disregard the Toros owner had for management planning—as though it was of no great importance. "The Toros coach was Billy Harris, and it was John Bassett that put him in as the coach of Team Canada '74. You see, all the WHA owners were trying to get along, and John Bassett wanted *his* coach to coach the 1974 team. Then he goes and fires him six months later. So I heard these rumors going around that something was up, so I went to John, 'Well, wait a minute, who are you going to hire to replace him?' Because I had some guys in mind—Al MacNeil in particular. If it had of been possible to get Al MacNeil that would have been great. Well, Bassett was right off the wall, he hired a player with a broken arm and no previous coaching experience, Bob LeDuc."

LeDuc was a journeyman player on the Toros who was out of the line-up due to injury. Rather than incur the expense of hiring a qualified person, Bassett simply handed over the coaching duties to the most available person already on the payroll.

After the first half of the season had gone by, Mahovlich was amazed at the number of critical decisions Bassett made without seeking his advice. "I thought I would have some influence with John— but I had none. This guy would make a move and he wouldn't even ask you. I thought he might consult with me because of my experience. You know, who do you ask? You ask the veterans on your team, right? Where do we go from here? After about four months into the season I knew it was going to be difficult. The WHA didn't have the same philosophy as the National Hockey League yet. It was just building. You had managers and coaches of a different caliber who didn't have the experience that a lot of the NHL management had."

If the owners of the WHA wanted their league to be considered on a par with the NHL, then developing a respectable level of professionalism would be key to its success. This was the standard Frank Mahovlich brought to the table, but over time he learned that even the most requisite details were not a priority for the league. "We were practicing one day in Cincinnati and we got on the ice and there was about two inches of snow on it. So I went over to Jacques Demers who was the coach for Cincinnati at that time. I said, 'Jacques, when we were in the NHL, oppositions came in for practice and this ice was nice and clean for them.' He said, 'Frank, you're not in the NHL now.' This was a little thing but it was typical of the learning process that these teams needed to go through."

On a more critical scale was the situation of the Toronto Toros' revolving door: players came and went with such frequency that they'd have departed before Mahovlich got to know their names. "It was trial and error. One year we had something like 64 players—so management was always trying out different players. An NHL team would be chosen before training camp started. Sure, other players came to training camp, but after two or three days that was it. The guys that didn't make it went to the minors, here, there, everybody was placed. Once the team was set, there was peace of mind and you went out and played hockey. With the Toros, it was like training camp all year round—guys were coming and going. We had a lot of players that would last maybe two weeks. In the middle of the season a guy would be given his walking papers. I can remember being on the bus in the morning to go to the plane and three players were told to get off the bus because they were being sent to the minors. It was humiliating."

Without a doubt the Toronto Toros organization was the short end of the stick in many ways. But not all the hockey franchises in the WHA went about business in such a haphazard manner. The teams that had success in the WHA had the experienced people. In particular, Mahovlich thought highly of the Houston organization and their man Bill Dineen. "Bill Dineen—experienced in the NHL with scouting. He put a team together and they were together. I can remember more Houston players than our players. They had the same team for five years and it was a good all-around team. They wouldn't make a move unless they got a better player to take the guy's spot. We had Vaclav Nedomansky, Paul Henderson, myself, but other than that our management was just guessing."

The part of the Toros' line-up that was painfully suspect was their defense. Up front the forwards had no problems scoring goals, which Mahovlich recalled from a memorable game, but the defense was another story. "We didn't have any experienced defensemen. Gosh, I remember we had an 8-3 lead in Cleveland one night and I think we won the game 9-8." Mahovlich laughs. "I mean, if Doug Harvey was on that ice, the score would have been 9-1. This is what a good defenseman does for you. We never had it."

Concurring with Mahovlich, Paul Henderson expanded on Bassett's strategy. "He went with all firepower. Vaclav Nedomansky, I mean the guy was a fantastic hockey player. Of course big Frank and him were out there and they were like two men playing among boys. When they turned it up and wanted to go it was incredible. But you look at our defense core and you knew we were in big trouble back there, which we were. What Bassett should have done, he probably should have looked at a goaltender. If you don't have goaltending you've got problems, and we had a fruitcake for a goaltender, I mean Gilles Gratton was out of control. He was a space cadet from another era. A lot of nights he couldn't stop a football. Les Binkley, our other goaltender, was right at the end of his career, and then we had a very young defense. We never had an NHL defenseman on the team, so there was just no way that we were going to be able to compete with what we had."

It was clear to the NHL veterans that a league in its infancy, as the WHA was, would have certain shortcomings. With an understanding of this predicament and an appreciation of the benefits,

Mahovlich took his new job as captain of the Toros in stride. Paul Henderson complimented the relaxed approach Frank had with their predominantly young team. "It was like Frank was on a picnic. He enjoyed himself. I think that Frank had got to a place in his life, he had won his Stanley Cups and that kind of stuff, so he came with just a great attitude. He was as loose as a goose. I remember he got a hat trick the first bloody game."

Entirely at ease with leading the team, Mahovlich conscientiously showed the younger players the ropes on and off the ice. Pat Hickey, one of the youngsters on the Toros, recalled what the arrival of Frank Mahovlich meant to him when he first heard the news. "Reports came on the radio back then, that's where you got that type of stuff, it wasn't on TSN. My Dad and I discussed it that summer afternoon, how lucky I was. Playing with the best left winger in the NHL at that time, it was going to be a great experience so I'd better pay attention."

While all his teammates knew who the Big M was, Frank had to get to know an entire roster of unfamiliar faces. In doing so he planned to kill two birds with one stone, and thus he began his work of making them into a team. Hickey remembered the direction of their captain, which allowed the team to take in all the years of experience their veterans had to offer. "With Frank the first thing he wanted to do was spend time together. He'd lead the way by teaching us how to go out to dinner together, how to travel on a plane together, what we did in airports. He'd say, 'The team's going out to dinner tonight,' and we all, especially the younger guys, promoted going out to dinner with Frank and Henny. And we'd bring Vaclav along and hear stories about Czechoslovakia and ask how the heck do you handle the puck like that, and why do you tape your stick that way, and why do you curve your stick like that? We would have discussions like that over dinner."

A generation apart from most of his teammates, Mahovlich could see the gap that coincided with the new era in hockey. Along with the obvious changes of a new league and improved salaries, cultural advancements such as the introduction of rock and roll on a dressing-room stereo created a different atmosphere from the one Frank was used to at Maple Leaf Gardens. Although he was unacquainted with the hits of Bachman-Turner Overdrive, Frank kept his place and took things as they came.

Indeed, the players were given plenty of freedom by John Bassett, who seemed to thrive on the youthful character of his team. For Mahovlich, this would explain, at least partially, the employment of the likes of Gilles Gratton in the midst of more serious players. "Pat Hickey, Wayne Dillon, Tom Simpson. There were some pretty good hockey players that came through there, young guys. Some of them went on to play in the NHL. But Gilles Gratton, he was cut from a different cloth—but for some reason John Bassett identified with him. Bassett liked the movies and show business, and I guess he liked this guy because he played the piano."

Gavin Kirk, a Toro centerman and linemate of Mahovlich, was with the franchise from its inception when they were the Ottawa Nationals. He was quite familiar with "Gilley" Gratton and offered a stockpile of anecdotes that more than qualified the man as an eccentric. "I guess it started, him being a little different from most of us, when he got a puck in the ribcage just underneath his padding. Gilles was down on the ice and our trainer Larry Ashley went out to see him, and then they called for the doctor. Gilles said, 'I got the puck right here in my ribs, in behind my padding, and it hit the same spot where in my earlier life somebody hit me with a sword when I was a Spaniard.' They're looking at him and the doctor said, 'What's that, Gilley?' 'In my earlier life I was a Spaniard and during a war I got stabbed with a sword—this is where it hit me, in the same spot. The doctor, who was an orthopedic surgeon, said, 'Gilley, I think you've got the wrong type of doctor here. You need one with a couch.'

"So Gilley was a little wacky. I mean, he went on the ice at George Bell Arena at practice wearing skates and his goalie mask and that was it, buck naked! He was just a different cat." Kirk continued with a story from Gratton's stint in the NHL where he gained further notoriety for having the first painted mask. "Gilley went to the New

York Rangers. He had that mask which became quite famous. He was a Leo, he believed in the stars and astrology. Leo the lion, I guess that was a lion's face he had on the mask for good luck and good vibes. When he went to the Rangers after the Toros, John Ferguson was the coach there. Gilles told Fergie, this was about the first week of November, he said, 'I won't be able to play well until December 16th. And John Ferguson said, 'What's the matter, Gilley, are you hurt? Do you have an injury?' He said, 'No no, the moon is rising over Saturn and I just won't be able to play good until then.' And Fergie's not the most sensitive guy in the world."

If Mahovlich wasn't accustomed to the behavior of his team's more colorful players, it certainly didn't cause him to react against them. In Pat Hickey's recollection of his time with Frank, this was perhaps his greatest gift. "Sometimes the best doers aren't the best teachers, but you can learn a lot from them. In hindsight, Frank probably taught me more about acting like a man than anything else—to act with class, and to be professional. I learned that just by being around him off the ice. Never ever, could I ever remember Frank talking down to us for the new ways of the time. And there were a lot of new ways. I mean Gilles Gratton, every hotel we went into, if there was a piano in the lobby or on the mezzanine he'd jump on it. In Frank's way he would say, 'It's okay to play the piano, Gilles, but let's ask first—permission?' And Gilles didn't understand that you had to do that. So we would get it done and ask permission and the next thing you know Gilles was playing "Disco Duck" on the piano and we were all dancing around. And Frank was there and he would dance with us. You know, very accepting and supportive. We inspired him as much as he inspired us. In music, when I see Neil Young helping out Pearl Jam it's the same idea. There's a lot to learn on both sides of the coin, for the rookie and the veteran."

Without a doubt, for everyone involved, the WHA was a learning experience—especially for those on the Toronto Toros. As time passed, Mahovlich was learning more about their owner's limitations and how he was going to compensate for them.

John Bassett, although lacking in hockey knowledge, was committed to the success of the Toros. Mahovlich watched, unconvinced, as the man he called "the promoter of all promoters" gave his all with what he knew. Along with setting the standard in exploiting the boards at Maple Leaf Gardens with corporate advertising, Bassett pumped out every kind of merchandise, from replica jerseys and hats to wristwatches with a referee going around as the second hand. In this aspect of the game Bassett truly was a pioneer. And it didn't stop at souvenirs. To maximize the entertainment value at their home games, hockey was but one of the many pleasures he could offer.

In one of his more creative stunts Bassett brought in world-renowned daredevil Evel Knievel for a celebrity shootout. Between periods Evel donned the blades to test his skill against Toros goalie Les Binkley. Paul Henderson, another apprehensive veteran, described the merciless scene. "Oh God, it was so embarrassing it was just awful. Evel got out there and he could hardly stand up on his skates. He misfired twice and poor Les Binkley was ready for a hockey player to shoot the puck—and Evel actually scored twice. I felt so embarrassed for Les it was just unbelievable. If the guy had gone out there and looked like a hockey player, but he looked like a drunken sailor. I understood what they were trying to do, showmanship and all, but bringing in Evel Knievel is not going to sell hockey. As players we just shook our heads and said, 'What the hell is this?' After a while nothing surprised us."

After recurring experiences of this sort, Mahovlich's reaction to the ongoing circus in the Toros organization was to take it for what it was. As a result, when Frank's expectations for his team were not met, he, like the freewheeling management, was left to improvise. Paul Henderson recalled Mahovlich aiding the team for a practice in which they were going to be short a goaltender. "One of our goaltenders was hurt. So Frank was on his way to practice walking down the parking lot and there was this guy walking beside him and they started talking. The guy told Frank that he was a goaltender. Frank said, 'Well, isn't that ironic, one of our goaltenders is hurt.

Why don't you come on in and we'll see if we can get you on the ice.' So help me God, he brought this kid in and we dressed him up. I walked into the dressing room and I didn't know the story. This guy was putting on his skates and I said, 'Hi, how are ya?' I figured he was a goaltender we brought in from somewhere because you know, hell, I didn't even know half the guys on our team—never heard of them. So we got out there and the guys were just teeing them up, Tom 'Shotgun' Simpson and so on. Well, this goalie was huffing and puffing and I could tell he was struggling so I skated over to the net—and it was obvious that he was hurting bad. I said, 'Are you a little out of shape?' He said, 'I haven't had the pads on in five years!' I said, 'You haven't had the pads on in five years? What the hell are you doing out here?' He said, 'Well, I was walking by the rink and Frank asked me if I had ever played goal, and I played goal.' He told Frank he was a goaltender, Frank took him at his word, got him out there, and he was just awful. It was a wonder we didn't kill him. I mean, it wasn't his equipment he put on and by the end of it the guy was so black and blue it was unbelievable. He could have sued us."

At the end of Mahovlich's first season of fun and games with the Toros, the team finished second in their division behind the Quebec Nordiques. For the most part, the decision to leave the NHL had worked out well for Mahovlich, who had a fine year scoring 38 goals and 44 assists. This put him second in a powerful offense between Wayne Dillon and Vaclav Nedomansky. Shotgun Simpson was another force that season, having a career year notching 52 goals. But despite their arsenal around the net, the Toros lost in the first round of the playoffs to the San Diego Mariners, four games to two. This ended a season that could best be described as a work in progress.

In the off-season that year Frank and Marie purchased a new cottage for the family where a pocket of their friends had summer homes, including Billy Kyle who helped them find the spot. The cottage offered their kids plenty of summer sports to keep them busy while Frank and Marie pursued their interest in gardening.

Since his days with the Leafs, Frank has developed into a respected horticulturist. Today their cottage boasts a magnificent tiered rock garden of shade plants that has matured over twenty-four years of hard work, knowledge, and love.

Following that first summer at their cottage Frank resumed his journey down the Toros' rocky road. In the 1975–76 season the next round of coaching changes would determine the direction the team was heading in. As was the case in the 1974–75 campaign, Bassett appointed another ex-Leaf as head coach, and was the case with Billy Harris before him, the tenure of Bob Baun as head coach would be relatively short-lived. Gavin Kirk described the conditions the old-guard Baun faced in what were changing times. "Bobby Baun, who I have the utmost respect for as a person and a player, was a bit of a dictator as a coach. And that was the start of when the old boys' club no longer worked. You couldn't rule by the hammer. You had to understand players and talk to players, and actually coach a team rather than just send them out there. So Bobby, who was from the old school, was used to: 'I tell you to do this and you do it, right or wrong.' In the mid-seventies, that's when players said, 'Hey, wait a second. This doesn't make a lot of sense. I have other options. I can go to another team. I can go to another league.' So in that transition stage it was a difficult time for Baun."

With the Maple Leafs, Frank Mahovlich worked under the same dictatorship alongside Bobby Baun, who, as coach of the Toros, revealed himself to be a product of that environment. While it was easier for Frank to let it slide, several of the young lions were ready to stand up to their detractor when his methods began to wear thin. As one of the younger Toros, Gavin Kirk had the perspective to relate how his teammate Jim Dorey struggled with Baun's approach: "One night Bobby Baun, 'Boomer' was his nickname, came into the dressing room to give us a little crap and stir things up. His motivational speech in those days consisted of yelling and screaming at people. He's in the middle of his speech and all of a sudden you hear this loud sound, and there was Jimmy Dorey in the bathroom blow-drying his hair between periods. He's got two hairdryers going and this interrupts Baun's speech which makes him even more furious and off he goes, leaves the dressing room and slams the door. Another night Boomer came in and challenged all of us. He said, 'You're a bunch of chickenshit guys—you wouldn't even fight me!' Dorey stood up and said, 'Should I leave my skates on, or take them off?'"

Needless to say, the extent of the antagonistic relationship between Baun and his players wasn't helping the Toros win games. Nevertheless, amid the turmoil that percolated through a lackluster season and resulted in the dismissal of Baun, Mahovlich, as always, took care of business. The Big M topped his previous season's totals with 34 goals and 55 assists while Vaclav Nedomansky led the team in goals with 56. Still, the defense was a weak link, and with that deficiency the Toros finished last in their division, out of the playoffs.

With their second season at Maple Leaf Gardens over, John Bassett was left to assess the two possible scenarios for the team's future. Remaining in Toronto meant paying exorbitant rent to Harold Ballard for the use of Maple Leaf Gardens—an arrangement that provided little hope for prosperity. Alternatively, Bassett was working out a deal to move his team down South. Aside from securing the financial backers, Bassett would have to gain the support of his marquee players to make a go of it.

Before the final decision was made, the Toros gave Toronto one last shot with a Bassett-inspired phone blitz. Faced with another move, Mahovlich was happy to participate in the effort to help the team stay put. "It was a funny thing. John asked me and some of the other players to get on the phone and see how many season's ticket holders we could get. If we could secure five thousand the team would stay in Toronto. So we went into the office and got on the phones with the lists of our ticket holders, and it was going well. We were at three thousand after a week and all we had to do was keep calling but John stopped us. He got a deal down in Birmingham, the rent was good, ten new investors, plus the ones he already had, so he wanted to move."

Chapter Eleven

Day 13—Afternoon

On the road to Chilliwack this afternoon we pulled over at a truck stop for lunch. The team piled out of the bus and instantly filled the greasy spoon restaurant to capacity. The faint sound of a country music station provided the entertainment while we patiently waited for the one server to take our thirty orders. There was ample time to mull over the menu choices and I, as most of the players did, ordered the spaghetti. Pasta before a game is always a safe bet—unless of course you're dining at an understaffed truck stop when everyone orders the same thing at once. When my plate arrived the spaghetti was so bloated from waiting its turn out of the pot it was like eating a water balloon. As we were leaving the establishment groans of disappointment came from every player that ordered the waterlogged pasta. Red Storey, who put the smart money on a sandwich, was standing next to me outside our bus when I muttered, "Not exactly fine Italian dining." Red replied, "I take one look at a place like that and say, 'Grilled cheese, please!'"

After checking into our hotel we had a couple of hours to kill. I found Maurice Richard relaxing in the hotel's courtyard where I stopped for a friendly visit. With just two days left on the tour, the Rocket had his mind on responsibilities that awaited him upon his return home. Being as well-loved as the Rocket is results in exhausting amounts of fan mail, which he faithfully answers every year. Maurice told me that to keep on top of it he has to write twenty-five letters a week. I don't think I've ever written that many letters in a year. I remember that when I was a kid Mom and Dad used to sit down with a bag of fan mail on Sunday afternoons. One lady used to send Dad a birthday cake every year on his birthday. I guess one can't complain about that kind of admiration.

A scheduled interview with Ken Linseman required that I leave Maurice to his cigar and I went to meet Ken in the coffee shop. Ken's experience with Dad on the Birmingham Bulls would bring my taped research on the tour to a close. I particularly wanted insights on Dad's reaction to the team that John Bassett assembled when the Toros moved down South. Our talk confirmed my appreciation for Ken. I'm also grateful for the chance to get to know him a little. I've heard several stories about Ken Linseman over the years and I believe that Dad is quite fond of him.

Prior to Ken Linseman Jr. commencing his professional hockey career in Birmingham, Alabama, Ken Linseman Sr. had called Frank Mahovlich to get his opinion on the offer John Bassett had put forth. "Kenny Linseman and his father came over to our house one day and his father asked me about Kenny going to play in the WHA. He told me what they were offering and I was amazed. I said, 'Yes, I think that's great for him.' Compared to the NHL rookie wages from twenty years prior, the starting salaries for WHA players was remarkable. With this in mind and the guaranteed ice time, Frank assured the Linsemans that the WHA was a great place for a promising young player.

But although Mahovlich felt it was a good opportunity for some, he wasn't certain that moving to Birmingham was best for him or his family. After moving from Windsor to Montreal and back to Toronto for hockey, Frank and Marie decided that it would be in their children's best interests to stay in Toronto rather than uproot them again. This meant that Marie would stay in Toronto to raise the kids while having to run their two travel agencies on her own.

As always, Marie's dedication to her family and husband was steadfast and she took care of all matters on the home front.

In the decision to play out the remainder of his contract, Frank showed his loyalty to the man who had earned it. "That was a judgment call I made because of John Bassett. He wanted me to go down there so I went. I didn't want to leave him out in the cold. I could have said 'No, I'm retiring,' and I still would have been paid because my contract stipulated that I didn't have to play if the team moved from Toronto. But John Bassett was great to me and Marie. He was very generous. I have no complaints about Johnny Bassett Jr., he was just great to us—in a way he was too nice a guy. I didn't understand some of the things he did as far as managing a hockey team went. He was more of a promoter. That's what John was."

Picking up the pieces from where the team left off in Toronto, Bassett began building up his franchise in Birmingham, Alabama. It's safe to say that Birmingham has never been considered a hockey hotbed; nevertheless, the city made a lasting impression on the Hendersons and Mahovlichs when Bassett flew them down in the summer of 1976 to sell them on the move. Paul Henderson expressed his initial concern after disembarking and exiting the airport. "My first impression when we got off the plane—they had the mayor there, and all the southern people are so nice and they talk with that drawl. Well, we walked out of that confounded airport and it had to be about 105 degrees. The humidity was just brutal. I took about fourteen steps and my shirt was absolutely soaked. I turned to my wife and said, 'There isn't a man or a beast that could live in this bloody climate.' I'd never been down there and I was ready to get back on the plane. I could hardly breath. It was just unbelievable and I thought, what have we done?"

While the team had to learn to live with the heat, the bigger concern for the organization was familiarizing Birmingham with the game of hockey. Needless to say, John Bassett had plenty of ideas that would surely win the southern folk over to the great sport of the North. Gavin Kirk recalled Bassett's plan and the reaction of the people. "When we moved to Birmingham I think Johnny

Bassett thought we could take the South by storm and do some different promotions. It was a strange crowd. They used to cheer when the puck hit the glass because it made a loud noise. Or they'd cheer when you'd change on the fly—they just loved that! So they didn't understand the game, but it was interesting educating these people. At all the press conferences and the meet-the-fans type of dinners and luncheons we'd have, the number-one question was, how do you guys know when to jump over the boards? Changing on the go—they were mystified by that."

When the first season down south got under way, the Toronto Toros became the Birmingham Bulls. Conscientious about their funds on every level, management recycled their old sweaters, keeping the same logo with newly-sewn-on name patches. Bassett also economized by making Gilles Leger the new coach. Leger had worn several hats for the Toros and Bulls in management and as a scout. On top of his other duties it became his turn behind the bench.

Recently Billy Harris was reminiscing about the Toros over brunch with Mahovlich when the subject of Leger came up. When Mahovlich brings up the character of Gilles Leger it is more than likely prefaced with a mention of the man's penchant for cigars. Across the table, Harris was no different as he recalled the fellow who perpetually chomped a stogie. "I remember Gilles tried to quit smoking cigars one Christmas when his boys told him that all they wanted from Santa was to have their dad quit smoking. Gilles tried for a couple of weeks but couldn't do it. It was like it was part of his personality." Further discussion led to the conclusion that it wasn't part of his personality, it was his personality—period.

With his mind on various responsibilities, Leger, like the four coaches in the two seasons before him, would be relieved of his coaching assignment before the season's end. Gavin Kirk described what it was like with Leger as head coach, chief scout, and whatever else he had on his plate. "Gilles started out the year in Birmingham as coach. I was the centerman, so I'd always check on the bench what the next line and defense would be. One night I asked just that, and Gilles said, 'Gavin, your line—and, [Pat] Stapleton, you go on defense.' Well, Stapleton wasn't on our team! They were looking to trade for him—so he kind of let the cat out of the bag."

As was the case in Toronto, Bassett continued experimenting with players in Birmingham. The result of this trend was that the team's protracted standing at the bottom of their division. While the lower-grade players continued to come and go, after just seventeen games, under different circumstances, Mahovlich too would be forced to leave the team. Marie was back in Toronto with the kids when the call came that broke the routine of Frank's phoning schedule. "It was Saturday night and I was aware of the time because I'd always be thinking of what Frank would be doing through the day. Nancy answered the phone and said, 'It's Daddy,' and I knew right away he was injured before I even got to the phone, because he shouldn't have been calling at that time."

Mahovlich has described it as the worst injury he received in his career. "Medial collateral and cruciate ligaments torn completely! I was going up center ice and I had to turn my back for a pass. As I turned I got hit. My skate was caught in a rut in the ice and that was it. I had terrible pain and when I got off the ice and went in to see the doctor he grabbed my leg and he moved it from my knee. There was nothing holding it. It was just like flesh moving this way and that way. He said, 'Tighten your knee,' and he just moved it in a direction that the knee doesn't go. I went to the operating room the next day."

Aside from the injury, Marie and the children were delighted to have Frank return home for the remainder of the season. It was the first time ever that the family got to spend an entire winter together, and although he was confined to a stovepipe cast, Frank made the most of the situation. In the backyard he made an outdoor rink. After dusk he would faithfully flood the ice with a garden hose after the kids and their friends had torn it up all day.

While the time spent in Toronto recovering from surgery was pleasant for Mahovlich, the team he left in Birmingham once again finished last in their division and missed the playoffs. But this was just scratching the surface of the problems the Bulls faced. Paul

Henderson recalled the economy of Birmingham in 1977 that affected the team's bottom line. "The first year we averaged about eleven thousand per game. The problem was that the next year was when the recession hit. Birmingham is a steel town and the steel industry and the whole country went into recession. We lost three thousand business season's tickets in one year."

John Bassett was in a desperate situation with his hockey franchise. Other than blasting Lynyrd Skynyrd's "Sweet Home Alabama" over the public address during the warm-ups, something had to be done to fill the seats with people who knew little, if anything, about the game of hockey. With Birmingham's sports fans deeply rooted in football, Bassett reasoned that a physical brand of hockey would be the key to saving the game in the South. Other teams in the WHA had earned a reputation with a tougher brand of hockey and the Bulls would do the same.

The veterans who left the NHL to join the WHA had never experienced the kind of players the WHA became known for in its dying years. Paul Henderson remembered one of the more alarming characters in the league. "The best had to be Goldie Goldthorpe. We were in San Diego—they billed themselves as the San Diego Mariners. We were standing there for the national anthem and I looked over and Goldthorpe was growling like a dog. He was almost frothing at the mouth and honest to God I actually started to laugh. I thought, is this WWF wrestling or what?"

Asked to comment on how the Big M dealt with this sort of individual, Gavin Kirk told of a scarcely seen Frank Mahovlich. "Goldthorpe was one of the goons of those years—blond hair, big curly afro. We were playing in San Diego, it was the first period and I was playing with Frank and Mark Napier. Frank had the puck and was skating up the ice when Goldthorpe started thinking he'd take a run at the big guy. Goldthorpe tried to hit him and Frank just sort of stood there, planted his feet, took the check and Goldthorpe went down. The play went on and Goldthorpe got really frustrated.

"Two shifts later he decided to take another run at Frank. Frank stuck his shoulder out and BANG, Goldthorpe went down again. So the third time he took a real cheap shot at Frank, cross-checked him and dropped the gloves. This was the first and only time I ever saw Frank get mad. He grabbed Goldthorpe by the throat of his jersey, drilled him and Goldthorpe hit the ice. Frank looked down, then he picked Goldthorpe up off the ice and he said, 'Don't do that again!' When Frank hit him and lifted him up it was the funniest thing I've ever seen in my life. Everyone was sort of looking around like, did you see that? Frank got mad. We knew his physical power. [Jim] Dorey would always kid him because Frank would be skating down the ice with three guys hanging off him and nobody could take the puck from him. He had the wide stance, the balance, the big long reach. It was just great to watch. People would take runs at him and fall over."

When Mahovlich returned from his knee injury during the 1977–78 season, the tougher-style team that Bassett wanted to assemble was there thanks to yet another new coach, Glen Sonmor. Mahovlich recalled Sonmor and the motley crew he brought to the party. "Glen Sonmor played his junior hockey in Guelph and ended up in the American Hockey League and somewhere along the line he had lost an eye. So one day we were behind the bench and I turned around and his false eye was gone. There was nothing in the socket. I said, 'Glen, your eye—you've lost it.' He looked around, checked on the floor and there it was on the darn floor behind the bench, a glass eyeball. This guy was something else.

"Anyway, Sonmor knew all these tough guys and we had about five of them on this team. We always had one or two tough guys on our team with the Toros, but when we got to Birmingham, they started to purchase players that were *really* tough. Oh boy, there was Frank 'Never Been Beaten' Beaton, Steve Durbano, Gilles 'Bad News' Bilodeau from up in the woods in northern Quebec. They brought him down. This guy had a neck that was 18½ inches. He was a big guy but he could hardly skate. You know, standing on his skates was a difficult time—but he was tough."

In no time the Bulls established themselves as a team that opposition players loathed to play. Paul Henderson, who resorted to being a peacemaker, commented on just how bad the Bulls were in relation to the NHL's closest match, the Broad Street Bullies of Philadelphia. "Oh, they were nothing. That team we had in Birmingham was the worst goon squad ever assembled. If I hadn't have been there I'm sure they would have killed somebody. I stopped at least a hundred fights. We had Frank Beaton, Gilles Bilodeau, Dave Hanson, Serge Beaudoin, Steve Durbano. It was just awful. I mean, players on the opposition would run into me and apologize. We played in Cincinnati one night—it was Thanksgiving Day. They dropped the puck and at the twenty-four-second mark it took fifty-five minutes to get things settled down."

Mahovlich's memories of the enforcers began with a story involving Frank Beaton prior to his arrival in Birmingham. "Beaton was playing for Edmonton and was driving down to Florida for a holiday. He had a brand-new Corvette and he pulled into a gas station in Cincinnati to fill up. The gas station attendant spilled some gasoline on the car. This upset Beaton and there was an altercation. Well, the fellow wrote the license plate number down, got the name. So what happened was, every time Edmonton was going to play Cincinnati, Beaton wouldn't go because he knew they would catch him. So Edmonton said, we can't have that, we've got to trade him.

"They traded him to Birmingham. When it came time for Birmingham to play Cincinnati, Beaton told John Bassett that he couldn't go to Cincinnati. Bassett said, 'Oh no, you have to go. You have to go or we don't pay you.' So Beaton made the trip and the first time nothing happened. The next time the gas station attendant had spotted Beaton's face in the newspaper and said, 'Ah-hah.' We got on the ice and after the warm-up there were five cops in the dressing room and they wanted to see our identification. I said to the cop, 'My name is on the back of my sweater. What do you mean I have to identify myself? It's there, Mahovlich.' He said, 'Get your identification out.' Well, the opposition's stick boy knew that the cops were there and he told Beaton. So Beaton hid in the stick room and the cops couldn't find him! After about fifteen minutes Beaton gave himself up and they took him away. Bassett got him out of jail and hired a lawyer. They settled out of court. But every day there was something like this."

To better illustrate just how outrageous a day in the life with the Bulls could be, Mahovlich recounted the aftermath of an infamous game in Winnipeg versus Bobby Hull's Jets. "Someone had ripped the hairpiece off of Bobby Hull. He had a toupee that was woven into his remaining hair and all this blood came down. The fans were really upset and there was a huge brawl.

"They said it was Hanson that did it, although it could have been Durbano, it could have been Beaton. We had a bunch of guys that could have done it. It could have been Bilodeau, I don't know. Anyway, after the game Linseman, Durbano, and I were walking through the arena on our way back to the hotel and this fellow who had his young boy with him started yelling at Durbano—he was a fan upset about Bobby Hull. Durbano turned around and tried to kick the guy in the groin. The guy jumped back and a fight broke out between them. Well, the guy was a tough guy. But you don't know that, if a guy is dressed in a shirt and tie, you don't know how tough he is. Well, he put Durbano on the floor and started giving him a beating.

"When the fight started Gilles Leger ran into our dressing room and shouted, 'They've got Durbano and they're kicking the hell out of him.' Then five of our guys in the nude came running out of the showers. There were about seventy-five people around, fans were trickling out of the arena, women and children and everything else and these guys came out of the showers buck naked. They ran right out and grabbed the guy and put him down in the hallway of the arena.

"At that time John Brophy, who later on coached the Toronto Maple Leafs, was our assistant coach. He was a buddy of Sonmor's from when they played together in the American Hockey League years ago. Sonmor and Brophy got this guy down who was beating on Durbano. Brophy had the guy pinned and they were kicking the daylights out of him trying to make him apologize. Well, the guy wouldn't say that he was sorry. This guy was tough as nails. Finally they let him up. The guy got to his feet, he straightened his tie and he said, 'Who's next?'" Mahovlich laughs. "He was ready to take on everybody! And his son was there and I was thinking, geez, this is the kind of guy I like. That was the WHA."

Although Mahovlich admired the constitution of the Winnipeg fan who stood up for Bobby Hull, the extent of the dispute was a little much. Consistent with to the incident's physical excessiveness was Sonmor's approach to the game, which clearly wasn't Mahovlich's style of hockey. Nevertheless, as Ken Linseman recalled, Mahovlich remained a positive force in a situation ill-suited to him. "Take Dave Hanson. Because a guy was a tough guy and his job was to be aggressive and fight and try to intimidate the other team, Frank didn't look at this guy in any different light than he would a talented hockey player. Frank looked at him as a person. He didn't have an attitude of, you know, I'm a big star and treat me with respect. He was more like, man to man. I am what I am, you are what you are, and we go from there kind of thing. He just had a good attitude."

For the 1977–78 season Mahovlich had rented an apartment that he shared with Vaclav Nedomansky. Over the three years they played together, they developed a strong friendship. Earlier in the season, as Glen Sonmor was putting together his tougher-than-a-nickel-steak dream team, Gilles Leger dropped by to see Nedomansky. Leger had taken on the role of general manager and was quite uneasy about the immediate task he faced. Aside from the fact that Nedomansky was one of the few talented hockey players the Bulls had, Mahovlich was incensed by Leger's visit for personal reasons. "They traded Nedomansky to the Detroit Red Wings and I was so mad. Ned was a close friend and I thought I'd finish my career off with him as my centerman but Sonmor wanted a certain type of team—a lot of tough guys."

Mahovlich played out the season, helping where he could in what was an unsettling time for the World Hockey Association. The upstart league, once characterized by energy, optimism, and investment, saw its vitality spent. The evidence of this became stronger with each passing season and the dwindling number of franchises. By the 1977–78 season, just eight teams remained and what was left of the WHA began talking of merging with the NHL.

As it turned out, that season was the last run for the Big M in professional hockey. In his 72 games played, Mahovlich scored 14 goals and helped with 24 assists. It was an arduous year in which Mahovlich tried to overcome bone chips in his right elbow as well as the blown-out knee. "I was running up and down the steps in our rink getting into shape. I remember that was a tough deal for me and I had to wear a brace which I wasn't used to. So I had this brace and I started to play and I had a very difficult time that year."

Paul Henderson witnessed Mahovlich battle the knee injury that in the end was the critical factor in Frank having to say goodbye to hockey. "It was sad in a way because Frank hurt his knee and it never came back. When he tried to come back the knee was not good. He probably came back too soon. It was really unfortunate the way that it ended. But for a lot of people it happens to them when they are very young. The injury really set him back."

The Birmingham Bulls stayed afloat one more season. In a last-gasp effort to reinvent themselves, the team abandoned the rough-stuff image and began to build a team of talented youngsters. Mahovlich spent that summer at his cottage with hockey as a constant in the back of his mind. Whether he knew it or not, it would not be long before Frank would have to ponder his future.

Chapter Twelve

Day 13—Evening

Dad had a great game today filling the net. After he scored his third goal, in recognition of the hat trick, Eddie Shack skated by and put his cowboy hat on Dad. Well, doesn't Dad stay on the ice and score a fourth goal while sporting the twenty-gallon lid! It was great, because while Dad broke in on net, he was laughing the whole way hoping that the hat wouldn't fly off. It's funny to see him ham it up a little. The crowd certainly enjoyed it. Tomorrow we're off to Vancouver for the final game of the tour.

Day 14—Afternoon

The team checked into the Westin Bayshore, a hotel that hockey teams have been staying at for years. This was evident in the greeting the doorman gave the players, that and the ensuing conversation as we waited for our room keys.

I have several friends from Toronto now residing in Vancouver whom I have arranged tickets for. Tonight should be fun. Mom, Nancy, and her family have also joined us from Seattle. We are now in our hotel room, which is quite luxurious. In a few minutes Dad and I are going to meet the film crew to do another piece for the promotional video they've been shooting. They want to capture Dad and me walking and talking as though I'm interviewing him for the book.

This sort of thing makes me feel a little uneasy, because I don't believe I belong in anyone's film. On the other hand, I'm grateful to be here, and if they'd like my participation I'm happy to help out. It's similar to the situation I'm in when the team is signing autographs in the dressing room. The promoters for the tour have a draw during the first period of each game. In the intermission the winners are walked through the Legends' dressing room to get their programs signed. At the beginning of the tour I used to explain to each winner that I was just a guest. What they should do is skip by me, and get the signature of the fellow in the next stall. But sitting in my equipment, the kids were often too young to recognize that I was not the genuine article. After my spiel I'd receive a blank look that said, I can't hear you in this noisy dressing room—and why aren't you signing my program? So I realized it would be easier to scribble my name, pass the program along, and live with the guilt.

Day 15—Morning

Last night was great. We played in a packed Pacific Coliseum for the farewell game of the tour. In the dressing room I sat beside Guy Lafleur and got to experience him slamming his stick one last time. Guy had to catch a flight that required him to leave part-way through the first period. Before the game I made sure I got a picture with him and he wished me well. Playing with Guy was a definite highlight of this trip.

By the second period of the game Dad was on another scoring tear. Once again Eddie Shack gave him the cowboy hat. Moments later, Dad (with Eddie's hat on) and I were in alone on goal. Dad elected to shoot but the goalie made a good save. When our line got back to the bench Kenny told Dad that he should have made the pass. Dad nodded in agreement. Then Kenny looked at me and I suggested that Dad went Hollywood because he scored in the last game with the hat on. We all had a good laugh. Dad ended up with five goals to my one.

Afterwards, all of my buddies who were at the game came to the hotel for the reception and we had a fine reunion-style evening. I'm now at my friend's place, where I stayed last night after catching up with my old gang. Tomorrow I'll get a bus up to Whistler to join Mom, Dad, Nancy, and company for a few days on the slopes.

Day 17—Evening

Two days have passed since we parted ways with all the folks on the tour. And though I've had an excellent time with my family in Whistler, I feel fairly depressed. I guess it's to be expected. The natural course of one's spirit after a two-week high is logically going to be a down cycle. Nevertheless, I didn't expect this much of a decline. At the end of our incredible day of skiing I asked Dad if he ever felt bad after leaving the team. In his reply I knew he understood exactly how I was feeling. With a smile he said, "We had a pretty good time, didn't we."

To say I had a pretty good time is an understatement of gigantic proportions. From my first game playing with Gilbert Perreault and Guy Lafleur to my last shift with Kenny and Dad, I've had the trip of a lifetime. From this fortnight, two things stand out as highlights above and beyond all the wonderful experiences I've been so fortunate to have. I will always remember them, and I feel they deserve special mention.

The first occurred during a warm-up, when Maurice Richard picked up one of the sticks off of our bench. The team was skating around, firing shots on goal from the slot; I was doing just that when a crisp pass hit me on the fly. I can't remember my shot, or where it went—but from across the ice I saw that it was Rocket Richard who gave me the perfect pass. I get chills when I think about it.

The other and most important highlight of the tour was every moment on the ice with Dad. No words can express the joy or sense of completeness I have after fulfilling this dream. I have played hockey, the game I love, with my father.

Further contemplating my sorrow over this adventure coming to an end, I think of my emotions in the context of this trip's purpose. An obvious question comes to mind: How did Dad to adjust to life when he reached the end? If I am emotionally drained after two days away from the game, I shudder to think what it must have been like to retire after twenty-one years of professional hockey.

The Big M never made a grand exit from the game of hockey. Despite his celebrated career, the end didn't pan out the way Mahovlich had envisioned. The possibility of leaving the game on a high note was understandably something that he would have wanted. When Frank came home for the summer after his last season with the Bulls, he had yet to determine if he was indeed retiring from the game.

With no indication from the Bulls that Birmingham was no longer an option, he ventured to explore that possibility. Regrettably, Marie met a dejected husband upon his return from the scheduled meeting. "Frank had finished his four-year contract. He had suffered his major knee injury and really didn't play much in his last year because he hadn't returned to form. But he hoped, as every hockey player does, that he still had another year in him. Gilles Leger said he would meet him at a restaurant and discuss the next year. Well, Gilles Leger never turned up and Frank came home feeling very down."

With the competitive fire still burning inside, Mahovlich worked with a professional trainer to regain what he had lost. The following year a call came expressing interest in the Big M. However, as Marie recalled in a damning tone, the effort to gain Mahovlich a shot in Detroit was stonewalled back in Montreal. "Ted Lindsay phoned and offered Frank an invitation to the Detroit Red Wings training camp. But Montreal Canadiens management blocked Frank from going. In the NHL Frank was still property of the Montreal Canadiens. I can remember friends of ours being shocked that at 42 years of age Frank would be prevented from having the opportunity to earn a living. He certainly wasn't going to be a big threat to the Montreal Canadiens, but perhaps because he left for the WHA they were punishing or blackballing him."

Frank confirmed his wife's account. "Marie is right about that. There was something going on. I remember Ted Lindsay had to make a phone call in order for me to go to training camp. The first year they stopped me but the next year they didn't oppose me going, and I went to training camp." Having been out of hockey for two years Mahovlich paid a brief visit to the Red Wings camp. The end result was peace of mind that allowed the Big M to retire from hockey for good. "After a trip the team made to Glens Falls I told Ted, 'This isn't for me.' I knew I didn't want a contract—not that they had offered me one. But my mind was clear that I was out of hockey, and I just came home."

Although Mahovlich was at ease with the thought of putting hockey behind him, the difficult part was still to come. From his own experience, Yvan Cournoyer explained his old teammate's predicament and the search that takes place when the blades are finally hanging in the basement. "It's very hard, and it takes a long time. Knowing Frank, he loves to play hockey and it's hard to find something that you like to do after you retire. So you've got to find something that you really enjoy because the nervous feeling that you used to get before the game and all the action is gone. It's very quiet after you retire."

The travel business that Frank and Marie had initially started as something for Frank to fall back on became his nine-to-five. Other than that, Frank concentrated on making up for the time he had spent away from home. Traveling is never optional for a hockey player, and inevitably it's the family that must give way to the career. "It's part of the job. It's like being in the army. You toughen yourself and think, I can't feel sorry about it, I have to go. You accept it, like you have to accept the traveling and the waiting. You grow immune to everything as an athlete and you get used to it, just like being in the army. And when the season is over, then you have time off and you spend it with your family."

Together, Frank and Marie began to enjoy a lifestyle completely new to their relationship. For the first time in over thirty years Frank was without a hockey schedule. No more practices to get up for, no teams to meet, and no more planes to catch. While the career transition wasn't easy on Frank, he fared well with the things that mattered. Just as Marie had cared for and supported their children on a daily basis, now Frank was skiing with Michael, driving to Nancy's basketball games, and helping Ted with his paper route on rainy mornings. "I enjoyed that part of my life too. But it was an effort, whereas hockey wasn't an effort—I was born to do it. When I finished playing hockey the change of pace was difficult, to slow down and get into the family routine. But I was fortunate in a lot of ways. I had Marie—she was great. She helped me quite a bit in the business we had, and guided me through that time. Like if I got upset at the coach watching Ted play hockey she'd say, 'Off you go—take a walk.'" Mahovlich laughs. "She helped me that way, and it was fun. We really enjoyed going to Ted's tournaments and meeting other families. It was a good time. So I managed and got through it."

The bright side of the 1980s saw Frank and Marie reap the benefits of their travel agency, as the couple vacationed every year in different destinations. Along with their love for travel the couple's longstanding attraction to art took them to the museums and galleries of every city they went to.

Their enjoyment of art took root back when Marie was at the Ontario College of Art. "When Frank and I were first married and had no children we decided to go to night school. This was back in the era of the Original Six, when they always had Monday nights off—you could count on that. Frank wanted to take art lessons, which he enrolled in, and all that was left for me was a choice between woodworking and millinery. So I chose millinery and I never had so many hats in my life. I kept churning out the hats while Frank was taking painting lessons.

"The CBC got wind of the fact, and they were always trying to have some kind of interesting segment between periods for television. So they invited Frank up to the McMichael Gallery. They filmed him walking through the gallery and that was when we met the McMichaels for the first time. After that they invited us up on a regular basis."

Like hockey, art was something that both Frank and Marie were naturally attracted to. "I can't explain why we took a liking to art. I've always liked paintings, so we started an art collection. I got that invitation to the McMichael Gallery and on subsequent visits we got to meet A. J. Casson, A. Y. Jackson—some great artists. Art is something the world focuses on. Picasso, and the works that some of these other people have created will stay with us as long as we can possibly hold on to them. They've captured the future and the past in some of these paintings."

Excluding the legion of great European Impressionists that the Mahovlichs have viewed around the world, Frank named his personal friend from the Group of Seven—A. J. Casson—as his favorite artist. In the first decade of his retirement Frank and Marie would have Casson and his wife as guests at their cottage on many occasions. Casson would do sketches for the kids and tell stories of his days camping and painting with the Group of Seven. Frank explained their preference for Casson's work. "We'd see him paint, so when we look at one of his paintings, we have a great understanding and appreciation of it. To get to know the man was a real honor."

Casson's knowledge and experience never ceased to amaze Mahovlich. Without fail, every day spent with his wise old friend spawned another story. "One day we were up in Rosseau with someone that wanted to build an art gallery there. The guy was talking about a honeycomb design. The shape was supposed to allow for a lot of paintings in one small room. Cass told him that he didn't think it would work because you wouldn't be able to view them properly.

"So we were up having lunch at this chap's place when a huge black bear came out of the woods. This bear marched across the road right behind Cass who was sitting on a chair. I said, 'Cass, look behind you.' He turned around, saw this bear, and said, 'Oh, it's his property,' just as if he'd seen a bear every day of his life." Mahovlich laughs. "So I guess when they were painting up north they saw a lot of wildlife and knew how to handle it. He didn't think anything of this bear walking by."

As an extension of art and wildlife, Frank and Cass found more common ground in the garden. "We had a mutual appreciation for gardening. He knew all the names of all the plants and when he started naming all the different types of lilies and wildflowers, I became very interested. So we were at the cottage and we had an area where we could build a rock garden. He helped me move rocks and told me what would grow where. I was very keen on gardening after that—so we've got a nice garden up at the cottage. I'm going to find that a great hobby over the years, it's a lifelong project. They've got a saying. If you want to be happy for a day, get a bottle of wine. If you want to be happy for a year, get married. But if you want to be happy for a lifetime, build a garden."

While Frank Mahovlich has kept busy with his varied interests, many accolades have been bestowed upon him since his retirement. The first honor of great significance was his 1981 induction into the Hockey Hall of Fame. For the ceremony, though most of Frank's immediate family was present at their table, sadly Peter Mahovlich Sr. was not. "I got inducted in 1981 and my dad was dying of cancer. I went to the hospital and whispered the news in his ear. Whether he heard me or not, I don't know. He was in and out of consciousness. Earlier in the week my mom had called me at one in the morning. He had fallen down on his way to the bathroom. He had an open wound where the cancer was coming out of his shoulder."

Three years earlier, Peter Mahovlich Sr. had been diagnosed with cancer. His doctor had told the family that chemotherapy treatments might buy him another three years—which is exactly what happened. In that precious time of grace Peter actively enjoyed his grandchildren and lived life to the fullest. When the cancer returned, rather than stay in a hospital he had Cecilia care for him at home up until the very end. Although his pain was great, Peter would not let his loved ones believe he was suffering. With his family gathered around his bed he raised his arms, now reduced to skin on bone, and clenched his fists to say don't worry about me, I'm still strong. Marie remembered when he finally had to be taken from his home. "Frank went in the ambulance with him and the last lucid thing he said to Frank was, 'I'm sorry to make so much trouble for every-body.'" Peter Mahovlich Sr. died the week of his son's induction into the Hall of Fame. He had lived an extraordinary life.

Knowing that all had been done that could be done for her mate, Cecilia Mahovlich continued to live a healthy and active life herself. In spending time with their family, Peter had found joy, and Cecilia continued to do the same. Two years after her husband's passing she went to California to spend the Christmas holidays with her grand-daughter and her family. She returned from her trip in high spirits, but shortly thereafter, an otherwise fit Cecilia suffered an aneurysm and passed away.

Family gatherings have never been the same without her coleslaw and apple strudel and his homemade wine, but what are truly missed are Peter and Cecilia themselves at either end of the table. In further reflections on his growing up, Frank expressed appreciation for his role models in family life: "I was so lucky to have them for parents. They were great people. They came from very little and gave so much to all of us. In raising our kids, I went back to how my mom and dad were. They treated their three children equally. They gave each of us the same amount of love and that's what I try to do. Help each of our kids, let them find their way, and encourage them in whatever they choose to do.

"We have three kids that got through university and there wasn't one of us that made it, so we're very proud of that. And now I'm looking to my grandsons, they're coming up, it's just great. What a great life—and I still have a lot that I'm looking forward to. I'm 61 years old. It's been pretty damn good."

In the last decade Frank Mahovlich has been recognized for his life accomplishments and good standing in society with a remark-able succession of honors. In 1990 he was inducted into the Canadian Sports Hall of Fame. In 1994 he received the Order of Canada. And most recently, to his great surprise, in 1998 Frank Mahovlich was appointed to the Senate of Canada. "My immediate reaction was that I was shocked. Other than keeping on top of it through reading the newspapers, knowing what's going on, I've never been involved with politics. To think I'd be in Ottawa—I had never thought about it."

Before Frank accepted this career move, he and Marie had to consider how the commitment would affect their already busy lives. Several years earlier, the couple had sold their travel business and moved north of Toronto as part of their retirement plan. But the move to Unionville wasn't the shrewd and convenient choice he figured it would be. "I used to play a lot of golf and there was a new development of homes up by my golf club. We bought this lovely piece of property overlooking the course but it turned out that I didn't play as much as I thought I would. Back when I quit playing hockey there wasn't that much of a demand for public appearances. Well, fifteen years later, all of a sudden I was in great demand when I thought I wouldn't be anymore." After learning of the Senate's duty requirements, Frank and Marie agreed to make it work around his schedule.

When the news broke, the reaction from the public and press was, for the most part, very positive. The exceptions were either detractors of the Senate or people with long political backgrounds—the latter preferring patronage appointments rather than those given to folks who haven't paid their dues in politics. But regardless of political opinions, Mahovlich was eager to take on the challenge. "The Prime Minister said to me, 'You know, Frank, I wanted to do something good for hockey.' I said, 'Well, I'm delighted and thrilled that you chose me.'"

There were congratulatory letters and calls from friends, including Serge Savard, who expressed support from his office in Montreal. Savard, who was known as "the Senator" long before the Big M received the title, says, "They call me the Senator here—one reporter started that and it stayed with me. I talked a lot about politics so I got that nickname. I don't think Frank was ever *involved* with politics, although we talked about politics a lot. But I never knew if he was a Liberal." Savard laughs. "He is now! I think it's a good nomination, the choice of Frank. These days it's tough to get good people in politics here. Usually it's a political nomination when you are appointed to the Senate. But to have different people in the Senate I think is a good thing. Sport has never been very well represented in Canadian politics—it is in the United States though."

Aside from the individual recognition, Mahovlich took pride in the fact that he represented all hockey players. Henri Richard was one of the first of his many close friends from the game whom he contacted to share the news. "I was at home when I read it in the newspaper and I said, I'm going to call Frank on Monday. It was Saturday afternoon, the phone rang and it was Frank. He said, 'Senator Mahovlich speaking.' I said, 'Jesus Christ, I was waiting for Monday to call you.' I thought the appointment was great for him—he deserves it."

Since Frank Mahovlich took his seat in the Senate, the appeals for his time have increased exponentially. His being a celebrity in a political world has brought people out of the woodwork wanting, needing, or demanding Senator Mahovlich for a mélange of causes. "It seems that there isn't a day that goes by in Parliament that some-body doesn't grab me in the hall and say, 'Will you come to my riding?' 'Will you help us raise money?' or 'A friend of mine is in the hospital, will you come to the hospital?' Every day somebody wants me here or there. I'm not complaining. It's nice to be wanted. It's just that a lot of times I have to say no—it's got to be a positive no."

While Mahovlich deflects the less legitimate requests, he remains focused on working in the areas in which he feels he can make a difference. "I'd like to make a contribution in agriculture and natural resources. Going and inspecting different forests and making sure they are properly looked after. What are the pulp and paper companies doing about the stripped forests? Knowing as much as I do about trees and plants I think I'd be a great asset to the boreal forests. There's not a space on that committee right now but I'm hoping one might come up."

In the field of sports Mahovlich has confidently expressed his opinions on one of the hot issues regarding the federal government and his former workplace. "Should professional hockey teams be subsidized? I've taken a stand on that. My stand is that every business must have a game plan that is both feasible and reasonable if it is to be successful. I don't see any problems that are going to be solved by dumping money into some of these smaller markets. For example, from what I have seen so far, nobody has shown me a plan that would solidify a team in Edmonton. If we gave them a million dollars, would it turn things around? Well, there is nothing there to indicate to me that they would be better off. They are going to have more problems down the road with the way the NHL is heading. So I take a stand on this problem and I get a few letters that disagree with me, but I get ten times that amount that do agree with me."

Some people have questioned why Frank Mahovlich was selected for the Senate. While it's true that he was a well-known athlete, the fact remains that being a hockey player is just as much a profession as any of the backgrounds of the other non-political senators. Mahovlich gives his thoughts on this with a sense of optimism for the institution that has recently come under fire: "I'm not an expert on the government's past, but from what I've seen, and what I know, I believe the Senate is a good thing. These people are very caring people. They're Canadians who give a lot of time and thought to the bills that come through to make sure they will serve the people properly.

"If these folks weren't appointed, you'd never get the diverse backgrounds of knowledge in Parliament otherwise. Take Senator Lois Wilson, who was a moderator for the United Church. She was appointed with me. Well, I don't think she'd have ever run for Parliament. Yes, there should be some people in the Senate that have been in politics all their lives. But diversity is a good thing and it's healthy for the country."

Knowingly, Dick Duff has described the path that Mahovlich has followed his entire life, and in doing so he revealed more than a few reasons why the Big M is where he is today: "He knew early on that he was a special player, but he handled it well. He was a humble man who always led an orderly life. There's no rough edge to him. Some of us had different ways of doing things, like we may have done things to extremes. But Frank got married, had a nice family, and personally he has always been a friend to me—he's always been considerate. He has a fuller life than some guys might have wanted, but he also sees the big picture. So he walks with the Prime Minister and is in Ottawa with the people that make the laws governing this country. And he'll have an effect. I think it's great. I would say they're lucky to have him."

Frank Mahovlich was once asked what he would like to have been if he could have been something other than a hockey player. He paused before giving this thoughtful reply: "If I had another gift, what would I choose? Well, if God made me an artist, and I could create a masterpiece with three strokes of the brush, that would be beautiful. And that's what some of these artists can do. But that's a gift that is God-given. God gave me the ability to be a hockey player. So when you ask me, what else would I like to have been, I don't think I ever wanted to be anything but a hockey player.

"I can remember being with the St. Michael's Junior A team, and they had me sitting on the bench. You know, as a young rookie they didn't want to give me the opportunity, they wanted to work me in slowly. But I knew even then, if I could get on that ice, I would do my three strokes."

Among his family and friends, Frank Mahovlich is loved for the wonderful qualities that have always defined the man—he is caring, dependable, generous, thankful, loving, and enthusiastic about life. But while those closest to him have enjoyed all these fine attributes, there is one gift for which he will forever be remembered. That gift was shared with every person who ever got to see the Big M paint his masterpiece.

Ken Dryden: "When you are playing hockey, the person who scores 50 goals, or 45 goals, or some very high total depending on the era, that person is a great player and seems like a real star. What you find out as time passes, and you likely find it out after you've stopped playing, is that there are lots of people who score that many goals. And there are lots of people who make the first team All-Stars. There are even lots of people who win scoring championships, and there are even lots who score 500 career goals. There aren't at any given moment, but over time there are lots. If your claim to fame is 50 goals or a couple of first team All-Star selections, or 500 career goals, there is no image that's left. Within ten years, or fifteen years, it's gone. You become part of the glut of people who also have that beside their name.

"The people who are *truly* great players, there is something of them left in the imagination that is beyond statistics. If you close your eyes you can see that person. There are a lot of people, quite amazingly, who have scored 500 goals, who have done a variety of these other things—you close your eyes and imagine them, and there's nothing there. You can't even see them anymore. There was nothing beyond their 50 goals or 500 goals over a career, nothing that lingers, nothing that stands out. If you close your eyes and think about Frank Mahovlich there is an image—it's there. That image for me, and I think for a lot of people, is Frank Mahovlich in full flight. That was a sight."

MAHOVLICH, FRANK   Frank "The Big M" Mahovlich   LW – L. 6', 205 lbs.   b. Timmins, Ont., 1/10/1938

			REGULAR SEASON				PLAYOFFS							
Season	Club	League	GP	G	A	Pts	GP	G	A	Pts	PIM	PP	SH	GW
1953–54	St. Michael's Majors	OHA	1	0	1	1	...	...	...	...	...	...	...	...
1954–55	St. Michael's Majors	OHA	25	12	11	23	...	...	...	...	...	...	...	...
1955–56	St. Michael's Majors	OHA	30	24	26	50	8	5	5	10	24	...	...	...
1956–57	St. Michael's Majors	OHA	49	52	36	88	4	2	7	9	14	...	...	...
	Toronto Maple Leafs	NHL	3	1	0	1	...	...	...	...	...	...	...	...
1957–58	Toronto Maple Leafs	NHL	67	20	16	36	...	...	...	...	...	...	...	...
1958–59	Toronto Maple Leafs	NHL	63	22	27	49	12	6	5	11	18	...	...	...
1959–60	Toronto Maple Leafs	NHL	70	18	21	39	10	3	1	4	27	...	...	...
1960–61	Toronto Maple Leafs	NHL	70	48	36	84	5	1	1	2	6	...	...	...
1961–62	Toronto Maple Leafs	NHL	70	33	38	71	12	6	6	12	29	...	...	...
1962–63	Toronto Maple Leafs	NHL	67	36	37	73	9	0	2	2	8	...	...	...
1963–64	Toronto Maple Leafs	NHL	70	26	29	55	14	4	11	15	20	...	...	...
1964–65	Toronto Maple Leafs	NHL	59	23	28	51	6	0	3	3	9	...	...	...
1965–66	Toronto Maple Leafs	NHL	68	32	24	56	4	1	0	1	10	...	...	...
1966–67	Toronto Maple Leafs	NHL	63	18	28	46	12	3	7	10	8	...	...	...
1967–68	Toronto Maple Leafs	NHL	50	19	17	36	...	...	...	...	...	...	...	...
	Detroit Red Wings	NHL	13	7	9	16	...	...	...	...	...	...	...	...
1968–69	Detroit Red Wings	NHL	76	49	29	78	...	...	...	...	...	...	...	...
1969–70	Detroit Red Wings	NHL	74	38	32	70	4	0	0	0	2	0	0	0
1970–71	Detroit Red Wings	NHL	35	14	18	32	...	...	...	...	...	...	...	...
	Montreal Canadiens	NHL	38	17	24	41	20	14	13	27	18	1	0	0
1971–72	Montreal Canadiens	NHL	76	43	53	96	6	3	2	5	2	0	0	1

			REGULAR SEASON				PLAYOFFS							
Season	Club	League	GP	G	A	Pts	GP	G	A	Pts	PIM	PP	SH	GW
1972–73	Canada	Summit	6	1	1	2	...	...	...	...	...	...	...	...
	Montreal Canadiens	NHL	78	38	55	93	17	9	14	23	6	1	0	0
1973–74	Montreal Canadiens	NHL	71	31	49	80	6	1	2	3	0	0	0	0
1974–75	Canada	Summit	6	1	1	2	...	...	...	...	...	...	...	...
	Toronto Toros	WHA	73	38	44	82	6	3	0	3	2	...	...	...
1975–76	Toronto Toros	WHA	75	34	55	89	...	...	...	...	...	...	...	...
1976–77	Birmingham Bulls	WHA	17	3	20	23	...	...	...	...	...	...	...	...
1977–78	Birmingham Bulls	WHA	72	14	24	38	3	1	1	2	0	...	...	...
NHL Totals			1181	533	570	1103	137	51	67	118	163	2	0	1
Other Major League Totals			237	89	143	232	9	4	1	5	2	...	...	...

Won Calder Memorial Trophy (1958) • NHL First All-Star Team (1961, 1963, 1973) • NHL Second All-Star Team (1962, 1964, 1965, 1966, 1969, 1970)

Played in NHL All-Star Game (1959, 1960, 1961, 1962, 1963, 1964, 1965, 1967, 1968, 1969, 1970, 1971, 1972, 1973, 1974)

Traded to Detroit by Toronto with Pete Stemkowski, Garry Unger and the rights to Carl Brewer for Norm Ullman, Paul Henderson and Floyd Smith, March 3, 1968. Traded to Montreal by Detroit for Guy Charron, Bill Collins and Mickey Redmond, January 13, 1971. Selected by Dayton-Houston (WHA) in 1972 WHA General Player Draft, February 12, 1972. WHA rights traded to Toronto (WHA) by Houston (WHA) for future considerations, June, 1974. Transferred to Birmingham (WHA) after Toronto (WHA) franchise relocated, June 30, 1976.

Acknowledgements

I would like to express my sincere gratitude to the following people for their generosity in contributing to the book: Don Awrey, Jean Beliveau, Carl Brewer, Brian Conacher, Yvan Cournoyer, Bob Davidson, Jim Dorey, Ken Dryden, Dick Duff, Gilles Gilbert, Paul Henderson, Pat Hickey, Gordie Howe, Bobby Hull, Red Kelly, Gavin Kirk, Guy Lafleur, Ken Linseman, Wilf Paiement, Henri Richard, Maurice Richard, Serge Savard, Eddie Shack, Red Storey, and all the folks with the Greatest Hockey Legends.

For their help and guidance I would like to thank: Scott Young, David Piper, Craig Campbell and the Hockey Hall of Fame, and Don Loney and the staff at HarperCollins.

I would also like to extend a special thank you to Red Fisher for the wonderful foreword.

For their support beyond the call of friendship, thanks to Ward Porritt, Ildiko Gyorgy and, most of all, Per Matthews.

To my family—Mom, Dad, Michael, Nancy, Auntie Anne, Uncle Peter, Billy Kyle and the rest of the tree—my thanks and love.

Index

A

Abel, Sid, 112, 120, 121–22, 123
Adams, Jack, 121, 122
All-Star game, 146–47
Amell, Jack, 78
Angotti, Lou, 141
Armstrong, George, 58, 93, 99, 102
Awrey, Don, 23, 131, 150, 157, 159

B

Ballard, Harold, 60–61, 76, 90, 105, 188, 203
    role in "Million Dollar Deal," 72, 78
    tricks to make Toronto Toros fail, 193–94
Baseball, 27, 30–31, 47, 50, 54
Bassett, John, 183–84, 198, 211
    move to Birmingham, Alabama, 206–7, 208, 209
    ownership inexperience, 193, 194, 196
    publicity stunts, 200, 203, 205
Bastien, Baz, 120
Bathgate, Andy, 83, 84
Baun, Bob, 58, 82, 84, 102, 116, 125, 139, 202–3
Beaton, Frank, 210, 211–12
Beaudoin, Serge, 211
Beliveau, Jean, 39, 127, 133, 136, 139, 140–41, 144, 145, 173, 175–76, 184
    on line with Frank, 131–32, 134–35, 142
Bergman, Gary, 160
Bilodeau, Gilles, 210, 211
Binkley, Les, 196, 200
Birmingham Bulls, 205–14
Blake, Toe, 101, 102, 173, 178
Bobrov, Vsevolod (Russian coach), 161
Boston Bruins, 1971 playoffs, 136–40
Bower, Johnny, 58, 80, 81, 97, 98, 101, 102
Bowman, Scotty, 145, 150, 173, 174–75, 176, 177, 182, 185
Brewer, Carl, 53, 58, 60, 89, 107
    Imlach's toughness with, 61, 80–81, 93–94, 174
    move to Detroit, 109, 119, 121, 124, 125
Brewer, Marilyn, 82
Bronfman brothers, honoring of Frank, 180–81

F

Fans:
    Canada/Russia series, 160, 162
    Detroit, 115
    mail to Maurice Richard and Frank, 204–5
    Montreal, 142–43, 145, 180
    Toronto, 88–89, 90
Ferguson, John, 139, 145, 199
Fisher, Red, iii–v
Flanagan, Father Ted, 19, 20, 28–29
Fleming, Reg, 171
Francis, Emile, 127

G

Gadsby, Bill, 55, 112, 116, 118, 119–20, 122
Gainey, Bob, 183
Gilbert, Gilles, 22–23, 129, 134–35
Goaltending, 196
    Bower and Sawchuk, 97–99, 100–1
    Dryden, 137–38, 140, 141, 142, 144
Goldthorpe, Bill "Goldie," 23–24, 209–10
Gorman, Tom, 33–34, 68
Gornji Ośtrc, 5, 10–11
Gratton, Gilles, 196, 198–99
Greatest Hockey Legends Tour (Ted's journal), 1–5, 22–24, 44–46, 63–65,
    85–88, 106–7, 129–31, 148–50, 167–69, 185–87, 204–5, 215–18
Gresko, Alexander, 162
Gretzky, Wayne, 113
Guevremont, Jocelyn, 158

H

Hadfield, Vic, 158
Haggert, Bobby, 110
Hall, Glenn, 40
Hannigan, Pat, 25, 86
Hanson, Dave, 211, 212, 213
Harkness, Ned, 124–25, 126–27
Harper, Terry, 175
Harris, Billy, 52, 56–57, 61, 68, 190, 191, 194, 202, 207
Harvey, Doug, 196
Henderson, Paul:
    Canada/Russia 1972 series, 159, 160, 163

S

T

U

V

W